WISDOM BEYOND WORDS

For forty years Sangharakshita has been playing an important part in the spread of Buddhism throughout the modern world. He is head of the Western Buddhist Order (Trailokya Bauddha Mahasangha), and is actively engaged in what is now an international Buddhist movement with centres in thirteen countries worldwide. When not visiting centres he is based at a community in Norfolk. His writings are available in eleven languages.

Also by Sangharakshita:
A Survey of Buddhism
Flame in Darkness
The Enchanted Heart
The Three Jewels
Crossing the Stream
The Essence of Zen
The Thousand-Petalled Lotus
Human Enlightenment
The Religion of Art
The Ten Pillars of Buddhism
The Eternal Legacy
Travel Letters
Alternative Traditions
Conquering New Worlds
Ambedkar and Buddhism
The History of My Going for Refuge
The Taste of Freedom
New Currents in Western Buddhism
A Guide to the Buddhist Path
Learning to Walk
Vision and Transformation
The Buddha's Victory
Facing Mount Kanchenjunga
The FWBO and 'Protestant Buddhism'
The Drama of Cosmic Enlightenment

The Meaning of Orthodoxy in Buddhism
Mind—Reactive and Creative
Aspects of Buddhist Morality
Buddhism and Blasphemy
Buddhism, World Peace, and Nuclear War
The Bodhisattva: Evolution and Self-Transcendence
The Glory of the Literary World
Going For Refuge
The Caves of Bhaja
My Relation to the Order
Hercules and the Birds and Other Poems
Buddhism and the West
Forty-Three Years Ago

SANGHARAKSHITA

WISDOM BEYOND WORDS

·

SENSE AND NON-SENSE

·

IN THE BUDDHIST

·

PRAJNAPARAMITA TRADITION

·

WINDHORSE PUBLICATIONS

Published by Windhorse Publications
3 Sanda Street
Glasgow G20 8PU

Printed by The Cromwell Press
Melksham, Wiltshire

Cover design Dhammarati
The cover shows Prajnaparamita
Detail from a book cover, Tibet, 13th century,
courtesy of the Trustees of the British Museum

The publishers gratefully acknowledge HarperCollins for permission to reproduce the text of
the Diamond Sutra and Heart Sutra from Edward Conze's *Buddhist Wisdom Books*, London
1988, and the Four Seasons Foundation for permission to quote the Ratnaguna-samcayagatha
from *The Perfection of Wisdom in Eight Thousand Lines and its Verse Summary*, San Francisco 1983.

British Library Cataloguing in Publication Data.
A catalogue record for this book is available from the British Library

ISBN 0 904766 61 6

CONTENTS

Editor's Preface

THERE ARE PLACES in the universe where natural laws go into reverse—and these 'black holes' have to be accepted as a very real challenge to the ultimate validity of those laws. Likewise, in the sphere of human communication, there are documents which invert the laws of logic holding it all together. These documents make up the *Prajñāpāramitā* or Perfection of Wisdom literature, dedicated to confounding our assumption that we can 'get our heads round' what Buddhism is ultimately about, that there is some ultimate basis in reality for the operations of the rational mind. According to the *Prajñāpāramitā*, while our reason has brought us instant access to seemingly limitless stores of information and learning, it represents at the same time the ultimate restriction to our knowledge.

One feels there must be some significance—for our mass-communication-dominated age—in the fact that the world's earliest extant printed book should in fact be a copy of the *Vajracchedikā-prajñāpāramitā*, the 'Sūtra on the Perfection of Wisdom that Cuts Like a Diamond-Thunderbolt', for the tradition this text comes from is still the most forceful attempt yet made to break the circuits of our cognitive processes in the face of ultimate reality. With this agenda, it provides—especially in the *Diamond Sūtra* and the *Heart Sūtra*—the core teachings of both Tibetan and Zen Buddhism.

Profound as these texts are, they are meaningless unless they are read—or rather, undertaken—as a device for the transformation of one's life. And it is this understanding of the true value of spiritual texts, even very 'difficult' ones like these, which informs all of Sangharakshita's work. Though he is known throughout the Buddhist world for the rigour and breadth of his scholarship, he is first and foremost a teacher. This is especially evident in the present work, which is edited from recorded lectures and seminars led by Sangharakshita and attended by members and friends of the Western Buddhist Order.

The provenance of this book makes it a new departure in terms of Sangharakshita's published work, because it very largely represents his *ad hoc* oral teaching. It must be admitted that were Sangharakshita to *write* a book on the Perfection of Wisdom, the style, the content, and the construction would all be markedly different. However, the fact is that he has specifically chosen, in a great number of cases, to explore important Buddhist texts either in lectures or in the company of small groups of people who are committed to deepening their commitment to the ideals of Buddhism—rather than to write books about those texts.

There are various consequences arising out of the conditions under which Sangharakshita discussed these texts for the commentaries that are now being produced. Firstly, though he is just as articulate in the informal context of a seminar as he is in his writings—which has made the task of editing remarkably easy—the informal and relaxed delivery preserved in this book will be unfamiliar to those who are used to his tightly organized and carefully crafted literary style. The fact that he is communicating with individuals he knows—the fact that he is, in many cases, their preceptor—brings a tone of person-to-person engagement and intimacy to what he says that one would not look for in his literary work.

Secondly, the content of these commentaries is to some extent determined by the dynamics of the seminars. That is, while the central themes and significant details of the texts are conscientiously covered, Sangharakshita is at the same time always ready to be stimulated by the flow of discussion to move away from a close explication of a text in order to deal with broader issues. The practical exigencies of Sangharakshita as a teacher needing to respond to the immediate spiritual situation of the individuals present on a seminar necessarily bring out points and implications that might not come into the purview of a purely scholarly commentary. For purposes of concision and clarity, however, and to get an uninterrupted view of Sangharakshita's argument, the questions and interjections of those participating in the seminars have been removed and the twists and turns of discussion to some extent ironed out.

Thirdly, the material collected together in this book originated at widely different periods in the development of the Friends of the Western Buddhist Order, founded by Sangharakshita in 1967. Particularly in its formative years Sangharakshita made use of lectures and seminars in order to provide spiritual direction to the movement as a whole. Thus his approach to the text under discussion, as well as his choice of text, would be strongly influenced by whatever aspect of the Dharma needed to be emphasized at the time.

The earliest material in this book, which appears as the short commentary on the *Heart Sūtra* and the introduction to the *Diamond Sūtra*, was originally delivered as lectures which were designed simply to plant the seeds of two very important Buddhist texts into the fresh soil of a very young Buddhist movement.

The seminar on the *Ratnaguṇa-saṁcayagāthā* took place in 1976 at Padmaloka, a country house near Norwich which is still an important retreat centre for men in the FWBO. According to Dharmacāri Subhūti, the effect of this seminar was a general spirit of expansive inspiration and a loosening of nose-to-the-grindstone Protestant values that wreaked havoc with work schedules and necessitated some radical re-thinking of the methods then being employed to push projects within the FWBO forward. All of a sudden it seemed that people could not even be persuaded to take the rubbish out without feeling personally inspired to do so.

As it turned out, the development of the movement did not grind to a standstill as a result of this re-assertion of the primacy of spiritual values over temporal objectives. By 1982 there were annual ordination retreats for men being held in an old convent in Tuscany, rented for three months in late summer, and it was here that the seminar on the *Diamond Sūtra* took place. With the ordinations completed, the new Order members divided into groups and alternated study with harvesting olives. The setting for this seminar needs to be imagined as one of faded Italianate grandeur—a room with a high ceiling, warm colour-washed walls, velvet curtains, deep red terracotta tiles, and a great log fire. However, these congenial surroundings were a stark contrast to the rarefied atmosphere into which Sangharakshita led the seminar. Indeed, there were times when he was being followed, if at all, by no more than one or two of those present, though as Subhūti again recalls, the insights Sangharakshita brought to the *Diamond Sūtra* were awe-inspiring for anyone who did manage to keep up.

There is one final seminar to be mentioned, substantial parts of which have been incorporated into this book, a seminar which was held in 1974 at Abhirati, a huge, crumbling rectory in the Norfolk village of Tittleshall. The subject was an early but very influential work by D.T. Suzuki,

Outlines of Mahāyāna Buddhism. As with other early seminars there was a definite agenda for the FWBO being laid out before the participants. On this occasion what Sangharakshita introduced was an awareness of the importance of clear and critical thinking and an apprehension of the ruinous effects of *micchā-diṭṭhis* or 'wrong views'. For those who were there the ten days of the seminar exploded a good deal of the spurious mystique surrounding the 'higher teachings' of Buddhism, and—in the words of one young Order member present, Nāgabodhi—the experience was at once exhilarating and upsetting. Sangharakshita's primary target was the muddle and confusion suffered by Buddhists in the West as a result, particularly, of the whole trend towards thinking in terms of 'cutting through spiritual materialism' (to quote the title of the most widely read book on Buddhism at the time). In doing so, he also, incidentally, provided a specifically Buddhist tool with which to cut through parallel areas of confusion and superficial thinking that vitiate much of Western cultural and intellectual life today.

If the result of bringing together these lectures and seminars, with their disparate angles on the Buddhist vision, is a clear and unified statement of essential Buddhist principles as illuminated through the *Prajñā-pāramitā*, this is because Sangharakshita's teaching is based on what now amounts to fifty years contemplation of those principles. However, as an Englishman with a rich and diverse experience of the practice of Buddhism in India and in the West, he is also able to leaven a formidable subject with anecdotes, both humorous and startling, and with strong doses of common sense. The result is a lively and vigorous appreciation of the real issues and difficulties experienced by Westerners living in the late twentieth century who want to make use of the wisdom and guidance of traditional Buddhist texts.

A number of individuals have contributed significantly to the preparation of this book. Sangharakshita himself has provided material help, encouragement, and co-operation at every stage of the project. Next, I must acknowledge the immense labours of all those who have helped to transcribe tape-recordings, particularly the director of the transcriptions unit, Śīlabhadra. I should also like to thank Karen Stout, Nāgabodhi, and Śāntavīra for their very considerable editorial assistance in cleaning up the typescript. Sthiramati, of Wolfson College, Oxford, went out of his way to furnish me with the latest academic work being done on the subject of this book, and Subhūti kindly and promptly delved into his memory of seminars long ago for the purposes of this Preface. The index was compiled by Helen Argent. Finally, I should like to express my gratitude to those individuals who provided the funds to get Sangharakshita's Spoken Word Project off the ground, namely, Kulamitra, Mahāratnapriya, Satyarāja, and Nāgabodhi, and to the Windhorse Trust, funded by Windhorse Trading, for their continuing financial support.

Jinananda
Spoken Word Project Editor
West London Buddhist Centre
March 1993

•

'WE USE WORDS TO GET FREE FROM WORDS

•

UNTIL WE REACH THE PURE WORDLESS ESSENCE'

•

AŚVAGHOSHA

•

Part One

GENERAL INTRODUCTION

THE PERFECTION OF WISDOM TRADITION

THE PRAJNAPARAMITA IS CONCERNED WITH SEEING REALITY EVERYWHERE, AT ALL TIMES, IN ALL PLACES, AND UNDER ALL CIRCUMSTANCES

The three texts that are brought together here, though divided in time by up to five hundred years, belong to the same group of Mahāyāna sūtras: the *Prajñāpāramitā*, or 'Perfection of Wisdom' sūtras. Before looking at them individually it may therefore be helpful to look at the links between them, and explain these terms we are using. What is the *Prajñāpāramitā*? What is a sūtra? What, indeed, is the Mahāyāna?

People only started to write down the Buddha's teachings some four hundred years after his death. By that time a number of different Buddhist schools had arisen, and the texts they started to produce reflected those differences. The large body of teachings preserved in Sri Lanka in the ancient Pāli language presented the Three Jewels—the Buddha, the Dharma (the Buddha's teaching), and the Sangha (the spiritual community)—very much in their historical context. These fundamentally important texts are upheld by the Theravāda School of Buddhism, which still survives today, as representing the literal word of the Buddha, and as exclusively constituting the canonical literature of Buddhism.

Despite this claim for the Pāli Canon's monopoly on the Buddha's teaching, other texts, produced by other schools, *did* begin to appear at around the same time, and these sought to give expression to the spirit of the Buddha's teaching rather than merely preserving its letter. They represented a movement that, while still recognizing the value of the forms of discipline and doctrine that had come down to them, focused on keeping a clear vision of the Dharma as a living spiritual force. The result was that the followers of this movement, who called it the Mahāyāna, or 'Greater Vehicle', as opposed to the Hīnayāna, or 'Lesser Vehicle', did not identify the Dharma with any particular set of hallowed words. Nor indeed can their canonical texts be thought of as having recorded a teaching delivered in a particular historical context. There were thus no limits set to the Mahāyāna Canon, and it was produced over a very much longer period than was the Pāli Canon.

It must not, of course, be forgotten that the Theravādins do not accept the label Hīnayāna at all. To be fair, it might be more accurate to call the Hīnayāna a purely literary phenomenon, because the likelihood of meeting an actual Hinayanist in the flesh is slight indeed. The term Hīnayāna is simply useful for the purpose of referring to the early schools, and even later schools like the Sarvāstivādin and Sautrāntika, from which the Mahāyāna schools evidently differed. Used in this way, it should not be understood in any pejorative sense whatsoever.

Buddhist canonical works come in a variety of forms of which the most important is the *sūtra*—the Sanskrit equivalent of the Pāli *sutta*. This is the literary record of a discourse delivered by the Buddha, or of a dialogue in which the Buddha takes a part, usually a leading part. It can be short—even just a few lines—or it can go on for volume after volume. There are hundreds of sūtras, some in the original Pāli or Sanskrit, others surviving only in Chinese or Tibetan translations. The thing they have in common is that they all represent the communication of the Buddha.

How this kind of communication is to be distinguished from any other religious text naturally depends on what a Buddha is. Briefly, a Buddha is one who is wise, awake—in a word, Enlightened. The term Buddha comes from a root meaning 'to know' or 'to understand', so it means 'one who knows'—one who sees reality face to face, one who experiences reality fully and integrally at every level of his being. A sūtra therefore represents the utterance of an Enlightened mind—the utterance, even, of *the* Enlightened mind. It is a communication from the heart of reality, the truth of existence speaking, or even appealing, to the truth in us. When we read a sūtra—at least if we read it receptively—we are in contact with a higher level of being, a higher level of consciousness.

The group of sūtras known as the *Prajñāpāramitā* constitutes certainly the largest and probably the most important group of Mahāyāna sūtras. The subject-matter of this voluminous literature is transcendental wisdom. But what kind of wisdom is this? In what way, if any, does it differ from the wisdom to be found in the wisdom literature of other ages and cultures? Come to that, what do we mean when we talk about 'wisdom literature'?

'Wisdom literature' can in fact mean quite a lot of different things. Firstly there are collections of proverbs and wise sayings in which someone has encapsulated their deep and mature reflections on life for the benefit of younger people and future generations. This is sometimes called gnomic literature, and it includes such works as the Elegies of Theognis (some of them at least), the Book of Proverbs, and the Hindu *Hitopadesa*—a collection of short stories and sayings. Among modern literatures the French tradition of maxims is particularly rich, but there is no shortage in other languages—one thinks of Dr Johnson, Emerson, the essays of Schopenhauer, and so on.

Wisdom in the sense of something that looks beyond the world, something that moves towards the transcendental, is represented in the *Apocrypha* by the Wisdom of Solomon (though this shades off into wisdom in the more ordinary sense) and in Neo-platonic and Gnostic literature. Some scholars would claim that the wisdom of these texts can be equated with the Perfection of Wisdom, on the grounds that wisdom is a universal phenomenon. For example, the foremost authority on the *Prajñāpāramitā*, Edward Conze, regarded the Gnostic concept of Sophia as in some way parallel to the Buddhist concept of *prajñā*. Certainly there is a tendency in the Perfection of Wisdom literature to extol the *Prajñā-pāramitā* as the Mother of all the Buddhas—a development encouraged perhaps by the fact that *prajñā* is grammatically feminine—but the point of this symbolism is simply that it is Perfect Wisdom that makes a Buddha a Buddha; wisdom 'gives birth to' Buddhas in that sense. Sophia, on the other hand, is as much a cosmological idea as one connected with wisdom in the strict sense.[1]

The word *prajñā* has a precise and quite distinctive meaning. It comes from a Sanskrit root *jñā* meaning 'to know' which is reinforced with an emphatic prefix *pra*. *Prajñā* is not just knowledge; it is supreme or even superlative knowledge, knowledge *par excellence*, knowledge with a capital K. But knowledge of what? What is the object of this supreme knowledge? The answer to this, throughout all Buddhist literature, throughout all Buddhist tradition and teaching, is quite unambiguous. *Prajñā* means knowledge of reality; it means knowledge of things as they really are, in their ultimate depth, their ultimate transcendental dimension.

To be rather more precise, according to Hīnayāna tradition knowledge of reality consists in seeing what we usually perceive as persons and things in the external world in terms of what are technically known as *dharmas*. The word *dharma* means 'teaching' or 'doctrine' in some contexts, but here it means something different. When you look at anyone or anything closely enough, when you analyse them (or it) down far enough, you end up with no more than a flow of impersonal, psychophysical processes. It is these ultimate psycho-physical elements or events that are called *dharmas*. The discoveries of atomic physics can perhaps help us to get to grips with this aspect of Buddhist teaching, but only up to a point, because Buddhism applies this analysis to the mind as well as to the material universe.

There are different lists of *dharmas* which have been set forth by different schools of Buddhism, but all schools—especially those of the Hīnayāna—agree that *prajñā* (*paññā* in Pāli), or wisdom, consists in reducing all the phenomena of existence to a flux of these *dharmas*. This the Hīnayāna scholastic tradition, the Abhidharma, did in great detail—and very literally indeed. It was the literal-mindedness of these scholars which gave rise to the Mahāyāna view of *prajñā*. The Abhidharmists, having analysed existence down to a flux of *dharmas*, proceeded, apparently, to take these *dharmas* quite literally as ultimate realities, thus turning the different factors into which the ego, for example, had been broken down into little bits of ego. These had to be broken down in their turn, and the Mahāyāna did this by resolving them into what is called *śūnyatā*, or 'voidness'.

The translation 'voidness' is misleading; *śūnyatā* is not to be thought of as something like empty space. *Dharmas* are *śūnyatā*, according to the Mahāyāna, in the sense that they are void of any independent, fixed existence. When we see the world in terms of objects or persons, this, for the Mahāyāna, is on account of our *gross* delusion, which is removed by learning to see these objects and persons in terms of *dharmas*. The Mahāyāna is not content with this, however, maintaining that seeing things in terms of *dharmas* still leaves *subtle* delusion in place, and is thus not to see the world in its ultimate reality. This subtle delusion is only removed by seeing—by *knowing*—that the *dharmas* themselves are void and insubstantial, *śūnya*.

The knowledge that all *dharmas* are *śūnya* is what is known as *Prajñā-pāramitā*, the 'Perfection of Wisdom'—although this is not the best translation of the term. *Pāramitā* means 'that which goes beyond', or 'the transcending'—that which crosses over to the further shore, to nirvāṇa.

Prajñāpāramitā is hence the wisdom that goes beyond all duality, the wisdom that transcends all mind-made distinctions and divisions. It is the wisdom of Enlightenment, or Buddhahood. All Buddhist scriptures of course have some bearing on the development of transcendental wisdom, but those which deal directly, almost exclusively, with the Perfection of Wisdom are known as *Prajñāpāramitā* sūtras. They are concerned above all with seeing all *dharmas* as *śūnya*, with penetrating not only beyond objects and persons, but even beyond the psycho-physical processes which make up those objects and persons. In other words, the *Prajñāpāramitā* is concerned with seeing reality everywhere, at all times, in all places, and under all circumstances.

THIS TEACHING DOES NOT SPRING FROM THE CONCEPTUAL LEVELS OF THE MIND;

IT IS NOT THE PRODUCT OF THE INTELLECT.

IT COMES FROM SOURCES INFINITELY DEEPER

There are altogether some thirty-five of these Perfection of Wisdom texts, and they are of widely varying lengths. The entire tradition was original-ly an oral one, of course, and it took about six hundred years to write it down, bit by bit. This period may be divided into three phases, each of about two hundred years, followed by a fourth, much longer phase of Tantric and commentarial development. The first phase saw the produc-tion of two fundamental texts: the *Aṣṭasāhasrikā-Prajñāpāramitā*, the 'Per-fection of Wisdom in 8,000 Lines'; and a summary of the same text in verse, which is known as the *Ratnaguṇa-saṁcayagāthā*, the 'Verses on the Accumulation of Precious Qualities'—the precious qualities being of course those of Enlightenment. The most ancient of all this material is found in the first two chapters of the *Ratnaguṇa-saṁcayagāthā*, of which the following thirty chapters are elaborations. These two chapters—which we are going to be looking at in detail—may well go back to 100BCE.[2]

In the second phase a number of works were produced which spun out the earlier texts to an ever greater length, culminating in the 'Perfection of Wisdom in 100,000 Lines'—that is, 100,000 *ślokas*.[3] Tradition has it that when the Buddha originally preached this sūtra it was found to be so profound and difficult that nobody could understand it, so he entrusted it to the submarine kingdom of the nāgas to be guarded until such time as someone arose who would not only understand it, but make its contents known. Eventually, of course, such a person did appear, the great Mahāyāna sage Nāgārjuna (born about 150CE) who was presented with the text of the sūtra by a nāga princess. This scene is a popular one with Tibetan artists: we see Nāgārjuna sitting on a raft which is floating on a great expanse of water, and a sort of mermaid emerging out of the water with a big, heavy book which she's handing over to him.

It is worth taking a look at the symbolism of this legend. *Nāga* means 'serpent', and as in almost all traditions this stands for wisdom. Indeed, the Buddha makes this quite explicit in a discourse from the *Majjhima-Nikāya* where in the course of explaining a riddle he says 'The serpent, brother, is a name for the brother who has destroyed the *āsavas*'[4]—in other words, for an Enlightened disciple. The symbolism of the ocean is also employed by the Buddha in two different contexts recorded in the Pāli Canon, in both of which he likens the doctrine and discipline—the Dharma-Vinaya—to the mighty ocean, and the Arhats to mighty creatures of the deep.[5]

Just as the dragons or serpents are not to be taken literally, in the same way we can accept the spirit of the tradition without necessarily having to believe that the nāgas were entrusted with an actual text. The tradition that Nāgārjuna received the *Prajñāpāramitā* from the nāga kings suggests perhaps that he was the disciple of a community of Arhats who had received and transmitted not a book, but a teaching or realization that transcended the formal and analytic approach to the Dharma prevailing at the time. The composition of the earliest of the Perfection of Wisdom sūtras is generally considered to pre-date Nāgārjuna.

The symbolism of this tradition tells us much more, and speaks to us much more deeply, however, than any kind of bare interpretation can do. The ocean, after all, as well as being a symbol for the profundity of the transcendental world in which Enlightened beings quite literally live and move and have their being, also represents, we may say, the unconscious, in the Jungian sense; and the nāgas, the dragons, are the forces of inspiration emerging from the depths of the unconscious. This teaching does not spring from the conceptual levels of the mind; it is not the product of the intellect. It comes from sources infinitely deeper—or, one could just as well say, from a dimension infinitely higher; from a different, transcendental dimension of consciousness.

In addition to the 'Perfection of Wisdom in 100,000 Lines' there are a number of other lengthy versions—in 10,000 lines, in 18,000 lines, and in 25,000 lines. All of these are available in English, having been translated very laboriously over some twenty years by Dr Edward Conze.

It may come as something of a relief to discover that the third phase in the production of this literature, from 300 to 500CE, was one of contraction. As we can imagine, it was getting to be scarcely possible even for full-time monks to study this increasingly unwieldy corpus. So now several very short Perfection of Wisdom sūtras were produced, presenting the teaching in a highly condensed and concentrated form. Of this phase the *Hṛidaya* or *Heart Sūtra* and the *Vajracchedikā* or *Diamond Sūtra* were the finest flowerings.

Indians like to go to extremes. Having expanded the Perfection of Wisdom to 100,000 lines, they now contracted it into *dhāraṇīs* (magical formulae), or into mantras, or even, in one case, into just one letter, which was entitled the 'Sūtra on the Perfection of Wisdom in One Letter'. The one letter which comprises the whole teaching of the *Prajñāpāramitā* is in fact the letter A, for the simple reason that in Sanskrit *a-* is the negative prefix, meaning 'no' or 'not'. (If you want to express the negative of a word you just put *a-* in front of it.) *Manas* means 'mind', so 'no-mind' is *amanas*; *vijñāna* means 'consciousness', so 'no-consciousness' is *avijñāna*, and so on. Hence, according to the 'Sūtra on the Perfection of Wisdom in One Letter', *śūnyatā* can be known simply by the negation of all concepts. Ultimate reality can be experienced by putting *a-*, 'not', in front of anything and everything you can conceive of—including all Buddhist concepts, all Buddhist philosophy, without exception. It is like the *neti, neti*, 'not this, not this', of the Upanishadic tradition.[6]

Eventually, in the fourth, Tantric phase which extended the literary tradition to about 1200CE, the Perfection of Wisdom appeared as a goddess to be worshipped in various ways, and with these ritual evocations or *sādhanas* the production of this stupendous literature came to an end.

THE POSSIBILITIES OF OUR SPIRITUAL LIFE AS BUDDHISTS ARE RICHER TODAY THAN AT ANY TIME SINCE THE DAYS OF THE GREAT MONASTERIES OF NALANDA

So how are we to go about understanding it all? It may help to begin by looking at the Perfection of Wisdom literature not as a series of discrete works but as a single stream, crystallizing here and there into smaller or larger deposits or structures, none of which exhaust the content of that tradition, but all of which express the same fundamental insight into *śūnyatā*. Once we have taken up one of these texts, tradition suggests that we consult a commentary on it. This is not necessarily, however, a straightforward undertaking.

In the West we tend to have an impatience—perhaps a healthy impatience—with the way critics and scholars insist on interposing themselves between reader and text. Commentaries on the sūtras sometimes start to lose sight of the point of the whole thing in fine points of detail, and do not really in the end get very deep. They are usually at least twice as long—and they can be quite ten times as long—as the original sūtras. And on top of these we can add the sub-commentaries—which are in general, mercifully, much shorter.

As well as commentaries on the sūtras, there are a number of *śāstras* which must be included within the Perfection of Wisdom literature. A *śāstra* is a work of exposition composed by a great Buddhist teacher or philosopher, and not purporting to represent the word of the Buddha as a sūtra does. For instance, the (*Mūla-*) *Mādhyamakakārikā* of Nāgārjuna is a *śāstra*, but can also be regarded as a commentary on the Perfection of Wisdom literature—not line by line, but firmly based on it. Amongst the *śāstras* are also counted versified summaries which attempt to put the topics dealt with in the Perfection of Wisdom into some kind of systematic arrangement. All these *śāstras* are of course supported by further commentaries. The originator of the text explains it to a disciple who embodies the explanation in a commentary, and then passes further reflections on to a disciple of his own who writes them up into a sub-commentary.

In the end, therefore, we find ourselves confronted by a literature of truly staggering dimensions. However, it cannot be ignored. Commentaries very usefully embody the deep reflections on the canonical texts of generations of teachers and disciples. The fact is that Indian holy texts are not to be read by the uninstructed person on their own—otherwise there cannot but be misunderstanding. To be frank, a Western Buddhist might be better off reading the classics of English literature than reading books on Buddhism without proper guidance.

Ramakrishna used to say that if you want to conquer an army you need thousands of weapons and tons of equipment, but if you want to commit suicide a single pin will do. In the same way, if you want to convert and teach others you need to know thousands of books, but if you just want to get on with your own spiritual practice one single mantra may be sufficient. Of course, this is rather extreme—in the West we probably don't go to extremes as much as they do in the East—and it would only work if you were a *saddhānusārin*, or devotional sort of person, rather than a *dhammānusārin*, or intellectual type.[7] *Dhammānusārins* need to understand and accept a lot of things intellectually before they can go for Refuge to the Three Jewels, but *saddhānusārins* can get started very quickly with minimal explanations. The great Chinese Sixth Patriarch Hui Neng just happened to hear the *Diamond Sūtra* being recited—he was illiterate—and at once attained a degree of Enlightenment. One might even say that it's best to read books only after you're Enlightened, or at least after you've got some higher spiritual experience under your belt, so to speak. I have known gurus who have taken this approach, only starting to read texts when they had no need for them personally, but just required them for the purpose of communicating with others.

If we *are* going to approach these sūtras, not only do we need the help and guidance of a commentator or teacher; we must also rely on all the donkey work carried out by scholars of Sanskrit, although we need to be careful not to swallow their scholarly conclusions wholesale. These texts were composed not in classical Pāṇinian Sanskrit (named after the great Sanskrit grammarian Pāṇini) but in what is known as Buddhist Hybrid Sanskrit. Scholars used to think that this was just bad Sanskrit, Sanskrit spoken by ill-educated people who didn't know their grammar. In fact it is just another, richer form of Sanskrit, closer to Prakrit, the vernacular language of the time (*prakrit* meaning 'natural' and *sanskrit* meaning 'cultivated' or 'polished'). It does not keep to the grammatical rules of Pāṇinian Sanskrit, being rather closer in fact to Vedic Sanskrit, the language of the Hindu Vedas. To disparage Buddhist Sanskrit, as the old Brahminical scholars used to, would be like Addison disparaging Shakespeare for his ungrammatical English. Shakespeare is not as neat and polished as Addison, certainly, but there is a great deal in Shakespeare—even purely in the way of linguistic expression—that is missing in Addison.

Even so, one might still think that the more polished classical Sanskrit would provide a more appropriate vehicle for the conveying of abstract ideas than would the Hybrid form. But a question lurks at the bottom of this sort of discussion, a question to which we shall be returning as we examine individual texts more closely. To what extent is the Perfection of Wisdom concerned with abstract ideas? Sanskrit, even Buddhist Sanskrit, is, as Conze observes, a highly rational language, and amenable to thorough grammatical analysis. In other words we can get at the meaning quite precisely via the grammar. But we must be careful not to start thinking that because the grammar can help to make the rational meaning of the text clearer, the meaning of the text is therefore a rational meaning.

There is another danger for scholars. It is certainly true that a good deal of meaning in Sanskrit is lost in translation because we lose sight of the roots of words. To take a simple example, if we translate *jñāna* as 'knowledge' and *prajñā* as 'wisdom' we conceal the fact that they are both derived from the root *jñā*. But the temptation is to suppose that the verbal roots from which basic words or clusters of words are derived represent some sort of primitive, even primeval, intuition of the nature of existence which then becomes reflected in words. Some scholars seem to suggest that words were originally used with a very profound meaning which was gradually lost to mankind, but that wise beings like the Buddha used words according to their original primeval meaning.

Plainly we cannot accept this kind of linguistic theosophy without looking into it much more carefully. We can probably say in a more straightforward way that people simply tend to abuse words. We can hardly assume that we will necessarily understand exactly what the Buddha meant by going back to the original Indo-European root of the words he used. This would suggest that the Buddha was aware of the meaning of the roots of the words he was using, which is unlikely.

It is also easy to get the impression from the carefully defined technical meanings of key Buddhist terms that the Buddha himself carefully defined his terms from the beginning. In fact, going back to the Pāli suttas, we find that quite a lot of terms are used in a non-technical sense, some of them having become clearly defined only in the course of hundreds of years. When it comes to translating these Buddhist technical terms we also need to be able to understand what they mean in their different contexts. No one single English translation will help very much. For example, 'law' may sometimes do for *dharma*, but only if we ignore a lot of the implications that the word 'law' has in English.

This principle even applies to *śūnyatā*, the central concept of the *Prajñāpāramitā*. There are two Pāli suttas called the 'Greater and Lesser Discourses on Emptiness'[8] which record the historical Buddha's teachings on *śūnyatā*, and in these the Buddha uses the term 'emptiness' to refer in general terms to the absence of 'self' (*ātman*) in various objects. It was the Mahāyāna scholars who then honed and developed this concept, first defining *śūnyatā* more acutely as the absence of *svabhāva*, 'self-substance' or 'own-being', rather than simply 'self', and then applying this absence of 'own-being' in a more thoroughgoing way to all possible objects, and especially to the *dharmas* which the Abhidharma had posited as the irreducible elements of phenomenal existence.

The development is entirely in keeping with the Buddha's original teaching. Indeed, there are passages in the Pāli Canon which would support a contention that the whole of the Perfection of Wisdom teaching was a continuation and development of the teaching of the historical Buddha. Scholars have identified teachings recorded in the *Sutta-nipāta*, one of the oldest texts in the Pāli Canon, which seem very close to the Perfection of Wisdom.[9]

It is in this sort of way that a religious tradition develops. The Buddha was very much an initiator rather than a founder who laid something down once and for all. All the teachings are there in the Pāli Canon, but a single lifetime—even a Buddha's lifetime—could never be enough to develop all their implications. It is not as though the initiator of certain general principles of thought could have worked out these principles conceptually if he had only lived long enough—say, for two or three hundred years. In fact, such principles cannot be developed theoretically at all, but can only be worked out by individuals in the course of their spiritual practice. As different individuals assimilate the living spiritual principle according to their different natures, qualities, and situations, they are able to bring out aspects and applications of that spiritual principle which the initiator could not have brought out simply because his situation was different.

Taking the average follower of the Buddha during the Buddha's own lifetime, his spiritual outlook would have been broad enough, but his intellectual horizons would have been quite narrow. He would have had relatively few intellectual doubts and questions, and those he had would have been relatively straightforward, so he could follow the spiritual path quite wholeheartedly. But as civilization advanced in India, as communications improved with foreign trade and the growth of empires, as social and economic life became more complex, people naturally started asking more sophisticated questions. The response Buddhism made to these historical developments was the Mahāyāna. As more and more people brought out different aspects of the original teaching, the whole spiritual tradition became richer and more multi-faceted.

So it is not as if the Mahāyāna arose because a group of people arbitrarily took it into their heads to start up a new Buddhist sect. Nor is it, on the other hand, that the Mahāyāna necessarily represents an essentially *spiritual* unfoldment: this is a separate question, although it is connected. The spiritual vision, together with the broad principles of its application, is all there in the teachings of the historical Buddha. The nuances, the subtleties, the richness of its implications, however, can only be brought out over the centuries and the millennia. In a way, we are very fortunate to be living two thousand years after the Buddha. Not only do we have the Buddha; we also have all the teachers who have followed him, and we are able to read all their teachings in our own language. The possibilities of our spiritual life as Buddhists are richer today than at any time since the days of the great monasteries of Nālandā. And of these riches none gleam with a more brilliant and penetrating radiance than the *Prajñāpāramitā*.

In a book like this we can touch only the fringes of a vast subject. If we fly too near the sun we shall be scorched, blinded, and eventually consumed; but if we keep a respectful distance we may see by its light and feel its warmth. So with the *Prajñāpāramitā*. If we keep a respectful distance from it we may feel the compassion of its teaching. We may even have an apprehension of the transcendental wisdom of which it speaks. And one day, perhaps, we shall be ready to plunge right into the heart of the sun, to become one with it. At that moment we shall die spiritually—and at the same time we shall be spiritually alive as never before.

Part Two

THE HEART SUTRA

The Sutra

Avalokita, the Holy Lord and Bodhisattva, was moving in the deep course of the Wisdom which has gone beyond. He looked down from on high, he beheld but five heaps, and he saw that in their own-being they were empty.

Here, O Śāriputra, form is emptiness and the very emptiness is form; emptiness does not differ from form, form does not differ from emptiness; whatever is form, that is emptiness, whatever is emptiness, that is form, the same is true of feelings, perceptions, impulses and consciousness.

Here, O Śāriputra, all dharmas are marked with emptiness; they are not produced or stopped, not defiled or immaculate, not deficient or complete.

Therefore, O Śāriputra, in emptiness there is no form, nor feeling, nor perception, nor impulse, nor consciousness; No eye, ear, nose, tongue, body, mind; No forms, sounds, smells, tastes, touchables or objects of mind; No sight-organ element, and so forth, until we come to: No mind-consciousness element; There is no ignorance, no extinction of ignorance, and so forth, until we come to: there is no decay and death, no extinction of decay and death. There is no suffering, no origination, no stopping, no path. There is no cognition, no attainment and no non-attainment.

Therefore, O Śāriputra, it is because of his indifference to any kind of personal attainment, and through his reliance on the Perfection of Wisdom, that a Bodhisattva dwells without thought-coverings. In the absence of thought-coverings he has not been made to tremble, he has overcome what can upset, and in the end he attains to Nirvāṇa.

All those who appear as Buddhas in the three periods of time fully awake to the utmost, right and perfect enlightenment because they have relied on the perfection of wisdom.

Therefore one should know the prajñāpāramitā as the great spell, the spell of great knowledge, the utmost spell, the unequalled spell, allayer of all suffering, in truth—for what could go wrong? By the prajñāpāramitā has this spell been delivered. It runs like this: Gone, gone, gone beyond, gone altogether beyond, O what an awakening, all-hail!—This completes the Heart of perfect wisdom.[10]

COMMENTARY

IF WE REALLY KNOW THE HEART SUTRA WE KNOW—IN A SENSE—EVERYTHING

The *Heart Sūtra* is so called because it constitutes the heart, or essence, of the *Prajñāpāramitā*, giving us in a highly condensed form the essential meaning of all the Perfection of Wisdom sūtras. It is no wonder that in the Mahāyāna Buddhist countries of the East it is recited and chanted so often. If we really know the *Heart Sūtra* we know—in a sense—everything.

There are two recensions of the *Hṛidaya* or *Heart Sūtra* in the original Sanskrit, the only difference between them being that the longer one provides, both at the beginning and at the end, an account of the circumstances in which it was delivered. We are using the shorter and more popular version, and I have chosen the translation by Dr Conze—with slight emendations of my own—because it is the most literal.

As regards the text itself I am going to make a suggestion that has not, so far as I know, been made before. I suggest that in the *Heart Sūtra* form and content—that is, the literary form and the spiritual content—are of equal importance. The form of the sūtra is in reality part of the content. We might even say that in the case of the *Heart Sūtra* 'the medium is the message'—the frame is really part of the picture.

This frame or medium takes the form of a drama. The sūtra is a sort of dialogue which takes place between Avalokiteśvara and Śāriputra. If we understand who these characters are, and what they represent, then we will understand a very great deal of the meaning of the sūtra.

Avalokiteśvara is one of the great Bodhisattvas. In the highest sense, a Bodhisattva is an embodiment of one special aspect of Buddhahood, and the aspect which Avalokiteśvara represents in this context is Perfect Wisdom. This might seem surprising; usually he embodies compassion while it is Mañjuśrī who represents wisdom. But any Bodhisattva can, as an Enlightened being, an emanation of the *dharmakāya*,[11] do anything. Perhaps this reversal of our expectations serves to remind us that a Bodhisattva is not limited to the expression of one particular quality. On the other hand, it may be that Avalokiteśvara was such a popular Bodhisattva that he played a prominent part even in those situations for which his association with compassion did not particularly qualify him.

Ultimately, of course, wisdom and compassion are inseparable. Through wisdom one knows reality; through compassion one makes it known to others. Wisdom is here emphasized in the content of the text, compassion in the symbolism of the figures involved in the dialogue. The name *Avalokiteśvara* means 'the Lord who looks down', and at the beginning of the sūtra, out of the depths of his Perfect Wisdom, he is looking down in compassion on the world, and especially on Śāriputra.

Historically, Śāriputra is one of the Buddha's two chief disciples, the other being Mahā-Maudgalyāyana. While Mahā-Maudgalyāyana was famous for his psychic powers, Śāriputra was famous for his wisdom. But as, according to tradition, Śāriputra was the founder of the Abhi-dharma, in the context of the *Heart Sūtra* he stands for wisdom in a limited, Hīnayāna sense.

So at once we have a clue to the meaning of the whole work. It is a dialogue between wisdom on the one hand and Perfect Wisdom on the other. But it is not just a dialogue—it is a tension, even a clash. But how is it that there should be a tension or clash between what might seem to be simply more or less of the same quality? We can begin to understand this if we approach it on a lower level, taking the tension as being between the spiritual insight represented by Avalokiteśvara and the more intellectual type of understanding represented by Śāriputra (even though we cannot, as we shall see, lean on this interpretation too heavily).

There is, moreover, something quite unusual and significant about this dialogue or confrontation, at least in the shorter version of the *Heart Sūtra*. This is that Śāriputra doesn't say a word. In other words, in the context of the *Heart Sūtra*, the intellect doesn't answer back as it usually does. It has reached the point where it is able to transcend itself. There is a saying from the Christian mystical tradition: 'Reason dies in giving birth to ecstasy.' We can say here that wisdom dies in giving birth to Perfect Wisdom.

Here, represented in the *Heart Sūtra*, is—in a way—the central situation of the spiritual life: wisdom in the process of becoming Perfect Wisdom; the *dharmas* in the process of being dissolved into *śūnyatā*; intellectual understanding in the process of being transformed into spiritual insight. When we read the Sūtra, when we recite it, when we reflect upon it, we are addressing a dramatic situation that is not taking place outside us at all. Śāriputra is inside us; Avalokiteśvara too is inside us. The Śāriputra in us must learn to listen to the Avalokiteśvara in us.

In this way the form of the sūtra says dramatically what its content says didactically. The literary form speaks in terms of images, and is directed at the unconscious. The content, on the other hand, uses concepts, and addresses the conscious mind. This conceptual content consists mainly in six great statements made by Avalokiteśvara, six thunderclaps which progressively shatter all of Śāriputra's prejudices, destroying the lower wisdom and revealing the higher wisdom.

> *Avalokita, the Holy Lord and Bodhisattva, was moving in the deep course of the Wisdom which has gone beyond. He looked down from on high, he beheld but five heaps, and he saw that in their own-being they were empty.*

> *Here, O Śāriputra, form is emptiness and the very emptiness is form; emptiness does not differ from form, form does not differ from emptiness; whatever is form, that is emptiness, whatever is emptiness, that is form, the same is true of feelings, perceptions, impulses and consciousness.*

The first statement made by Avalokiteśvara is that the five *skandhas* are empty. This statement represents common ground between himself and Śāriputra; both Hīnayāna and Mahāyāna start from this point. According to this fundamental Buddhist teaching, the entire range of existent phenomena can be reduced to five groups or aggregates: material form, feelings (pleasant, painful, and neutral), perceptions, impulses, and consciousness. Whether one is dealing with things or persons, one can discuss them completely, exhaustively, in terms of these five categories. It isn't necessary to bring in any such separate, independent category as a self or a soul. What we call 'the self' is not anything independent of the *skandhas*; it is not something separate from form, feeling, perceptions, impulses, and consciousness. The 'self' is only a label for the *skandhas* in their collective aspect. This first great statement is that the five *skandhas* exhaust the whole of existence, and that there is nothing beyond them. At the same time, they are empty of any self or soul.

Here, O Śāriputra, all dharmas are marked with emptiness; they are not produced or stopped, not defiled or immaculate, not deficient or complete.

Avalokiteśvara's second great statement goes a bit further. All *dharmas*, he now says, are empty. Here we begin to get into deep water. The early Buddhist classification of the whole of existence under the headings of the five *skandhas* was rejected by the Abhidharma tradition of which Śāriputra was said to be the founder. It was not—you might say—quite scientific enough for the Abhidharma. So they replaced the original five *skandha* classification with a fourfold one—into form, thought, mental concomitants, and miscellaneous, each of which was sub-divided again and again. The ultimate sub-divisions of these four categories, the irreducible elements beyond which analysis cannot go, they called the *dharmas*.

The Sarvāstivāda, perhaps the most important school of the Hīnayāna, made out that there were seventy-two of these *dharmas*, the ultimate irreducible elements into which the whole of phenomenal, conditioned existence can be reduced. These are known as the 'conditioned *dharmas*', to distinguish them from a much shorter list of just three 'Unconditioned *dharmas*', consisting of space and the two kinds of nirvāṇa. (These Unconditioned *dharmas* were seen as eternal, and as not arising by way of cause and effect as did the conditioned *dharmas*.) Altogether these make up the famous seventy-five *dharmas* of the Sarvāstivāda. The philosophy is a form of pluralistic realism.

The early Abhidharma philosophers had a great deal of fun classifying and cataloguing their *dharmas* in all sorts of different ways. They sorted out conditioned *dharmas* from Unconditioned ones. They distinguished *dharmas* that were 'defiled' by greed, hatred, and delusion from 'undefiled *dharmas*'; and *dharmas* which were limited or incomplete from those which were infinite or complete. They noted how every conditioned *dharma* was produced and then stopped, whereas Unconditioned *dharmas* were characterized solely by *nirodha*, stopping. Scores upon scores of different types of relationship between *dharmas* were worked out, giving tens of thousands of permutations, and forming an enormously elaborate structure. It is hard to conceive just how elaborate this structure was, but the results fill volume after volume after volume of analysis and co-ordination of *dharmas*.

Avalokiteśvara asserts that all these *dharmas* are empty. They are not ultimately real. With this statement he dismisses the whole scholastic apparatus of the Abhidharma. The entire edifice is empty. It's all right as far as it goes—it takes us beyond the gross delusion that things are things and persons are persons—but as a system of analysis and classification it is a product of the subtle activity of the mind, and as such it represents a subtle delusion which must ultimately be transcended.

Perfect Wisdom, represented by Avalokiteśvara, destroys not only the Abhidharma, but *all* attempts, both philosophical and scientific, to give a systematic intellectual account of reality. The only way you can get to reality is by destroying your *ideas* about reality, however subtle, however sophisticated, however convincing they may be. Their validity can only ever be provisional. So all *dharmas* are empty.

Therefore, O Śāriputra, in emptiness there is no form, nor feeling, nor perception, nor impulse, nor consciousness; No eye, ear, nose, tongue, body, mind; No forms, sounds, smells, tastes, touchables or objects of mind; No sight-organ element, and so forth, until we come to: No mind-consciousness element;

Third statement: in *śūnyatā* no *dharmas* exist. This is the corollary—the more positive counterpart, if you like—of the previous statement. It suggests that reality is quite bare, quite pure, devoid of all our intellectual constructions, all our philosophies, all our concepts. These ideas are ours. They do not belong to reality, for reality knows nothing about them. Reality rejects—to anthropomorphize a little—all our thoughts. In *śūnyatā* there is no distinguishing whatsoever between conditioned *dharmas* and Unconditioned *dharmas*, or defiled *dharmas* and pure *dharmas*. All such dualisms are transcended. It is like—to use a favourite image of the Mahāyāna—the unclouded sky. Clouds may be very beautiful, but they obscure the naked brilliance of the sky itself. Reality in its true state, above and beyond all our systems of thought about it, is like the clear, cloudless sky. In *śūnyatā* no *dharmas* exist.

There is no ignorance, no extinction of ignorance, and so forth, until we come to: there is no decay and death, no extinction of decay and death. There is no suffering, no origination, no stopping, no path. There is no cognition, no attainment and no non-attainment.

Philosophy, even Buddhist philosophy, has been disposed of. Do we imagine, then, that religion—even Buddhism itself—is going to escape? Avalokiteśvara's fourth great statement is to the effect that there is no such thing as Buddhism. I'm paraphrasing a little—and this fourth statement is really a broader or more universal version of the third one—but this is what it comes to. He eliminates religion considered as an end in itself. There is nothing absolute or ultimate about religion. So in this part of the sūtra various well-known categories of Buddhist thought are enumerated: the five *skandhas*, the six sense organs, the eighteen elements, the twelve links of the chain of dependent origination, the Four Noble Truths, knowledge itself, attainment, and even non-attainment. The last two items, *prāpti* and *aprāpti*, differ from the rest in that they are terms that do not occur in the Pāli Canon. They were introduced by the Sarvāstivādins as a category of the *saṁskāras*, and as such they represent an extreme example of abstract concepts being reified.

Avalokiteśvara declares all these philosophical and even practical religious categories, all the operative bases of our religious life, including the idea of Conditioned Co-production and even the idea of Enlightenment itself, to be *śūnya*, void, without ultimate validity. He is saying that if you want to develop—if your goal is Perfect Wisdom—well, you have to go beyond Buddhism. In reality, you have to realize, there is no such thing as Buddhism. Buddhism is only a raft to take you to the other shore; then it must be abandoned. It is only a finger pointing to the moon.

At this point the Zen connection with the *Heart Sūtra*—or rather, the way the *Heart Sūtra* works itself out practically in terms of Zen—is unmistakable. The Zen Master who replied to the question 'Suppose I met the Buddha on the road, what should I do?' with the terse instruction 'Kill him' was telling his pupil that he had to leave Buddhism behind. If you are really set on Enlightenment, don't let the concept of the Buddha get in the way. There is nothing that hinders you in your search for reality so much as that which is there to help you, namely religion. What should be a means to an end is so easily taken for an end in itself.

Buddhism is probably unique in seeing this so lucidly. It sweeps the path to Enlightenment clear even of Buddhism itself. No doubt you need Buddhism for a long time. You need your mantras and your meditations, your chanting and your scriptures, your lectures and retreats and seminars, and you need to use Buddhist terms and ideas. But in the end you have to go beyond the limits of their guidance, sweeping it all aside to encounter reality alone.

Therefore, O Śāriputra, it is because of his indifference to any kind of
personal attainment, and through his reliance on the Perfection of Wisdom,
that a Bodhisattva dwells without thought-coverings. In the absence of
thought-coverings he has not been made to tremble, he has overcome what
can upset, and in the end he attains to Nirvāṇa.

Fifth great statement: the Bodhisattva gains Enlightenment and becomes
a Buddha only by relying on Perfect Wisdom. There is no other way. You
cannot become Enlightened unless you develop Perfect Wisdom. You
may be a great scholar; you may be deeply versed in the techniques of
concentration and meditation; you may be very devoted, pious, and full
of faith; you may be forever doing good works, even to the extent of
giving your own life for the sake of others; but none of these worthwhile
attainments are ultimately any help. Only Perfect Wisdom, in the sense
of direct, face to face knowledge of ultimate reality, beyond Buddhism
itself, will confer Enlightenment.

All those who appear as Buddhas in the three periods of time fully awake to
the utmost, right and perfect enlightenment because they have relied on the
perfection of wisdom.

The sixth and last statement is that all Buddhas of the past, present, and
future gain Enlightenment through the development of Perfect Wisdom.
There are no exceptions. If there are any Enlightened persons of the past,
of the present, or of the future, they have become—or will become—
Enlightened only by the development of Perfect Wisdom. Here the *Heart*
Sūtra is absolutely, ruthlessly unambiguous.

These six statements represent the main content of the *Heart Sūtra*.
There's just one more thing. The sūtra concludes with the mantra of
Perfect Wisdom. And just as the sūtra condenses the *Prajñāpāramitā*
literature, so the mantra condenses the sūtra itself. Conze translates
mantra as 'spell', but that is completely misleading. A mantra is a sort of
sacred utterance—one can't really offer any more explanation of it than
that.

The mantra of Perfect Wisdom is *gate gate pāragate pārasaṁgate bodhi*
svāhā. Mantras are not really translatable, but according to Conze's
translation one can render this one as 'Gone, Gone, Gone beyond, Gone
altogether beyond, O what an awakening, All hail!' The bare meaning of
the words doesn't help us very much, however. The first *gate* means gone
from the conditioned, gone from the phenomenal world, from the world

as we know it. The second *gate* means gone even from the Unconditioned, even from nirvāṇa—that is, gone from the concept of nirvāṇa or Enlightenment as something distinct from this world and this state. It isn't enough to go beyond the conditioned; you have to go beyond the Unconditioned. It isn't enough, we may say, to overcome Satan; you have to overcome God too. Then, *pāragate* means 'gone beyond': gone beyond the distinction of conditioned and Unconditioned, saṁsāra and nirvāṇa, this world and that, defiled and undefiled; gone beyond all dualistic distinctions whatsoever. *Pārasaṁgate*—gone altogether beyond—means that one goes beyond the conception even of *śūnyatā*. When one leaves behind the conception of reality itself, then one has gone altogether beyond.

The next word, *bodhi*, is not a statement of any kind. It means Enlightenment, Buddhahood, knowledge of the ultimate, but the mantra is not saying 'Oh, and then you realize *bodhi*.' It is not even really saying 'O what an awakening!' This is not bad, but it misses the force of the single word *bodhi*, 'awakening'. Finally, *svāhā* is untranslatable, but its general meaning in Indian literature is 'all is well', 'auspiciousness', 'blessing'. When you have awoken, when you are a Buddha, well, everything is completely auspicious, all is well.

This, then, is the heart or essence of the *Heart Sūtra*, which is itself a distillation of the meaning of the entire Perfection of Wisdom scriptures. 'Gone, gone, gone beyond, gone altogether beyond. Awakening. All is well.' Constantly reciting the mantra, constantly meditating on it, eventually one assimilates its deep meaning.

In the case of the Prajñāpāramitā *sādhana*, or visualization practice, the mantra is different. In this context it is *oṁ āḥ dhih hūṁ svāhā*, which invokes the Bodhisattva Prajñāpāramitā. But *gate gate pāragate pārasaṁgate bodhi svāhā* is the mantra of wisdom itself—it is a sort of impersonal mantra, as it were. If you didn't want to meditate on a particular Bodhisattva form, you could take this mantra, or indeed any verses or passages from the Perfection of Wisdom literature—the similes at the end of the *Diamond Sūtra* would do very well—and reflect on their meaning. In doing that, you would be calling to mind verses or mantras which embody the Perfection of Wisdom *aurally*, instead of invoking a *visual* or *formal* embodiment of it.

PERHAPS IT IS TIME WE HAD A NEW SUTRA, ONE IN WHICH THE PLACE OF SARIPUTRA IS
TAKEN BY AVALOKITESVARA—AN AVALOKITESVARA WHO HAS TAKEN THE CATEGORIES
OF THE MAHAYANA LITERALLY AND NEEDS TO HAVE THE REAL MEANING OF SUNYATA
REVEALED TO HIM BY A HIGHER BEING

The *Heart Sūtra* as a whole is quite compact enough for regular recitation
and reflection. In the way I have demonstrated it, the sūtra represents a
path of regular steps, but it would not be a bad idea to break down these
six stages into a number of smaller stages. For instance, you don't need
to plunge into the five *skandhas* cold. You could start, perhaps, with the
division of the 'person' into *nāma* and *rūpa*. Then you could break *nāma*
and *rūpa* down into its four constituent parts, so to speak, to arrive at the
five *skandhas* (*rūpa* being the fifth). From there you could go on to deal
with the twelve *āyatanas* (the six senses and their objects) and the eighteen
dhātus (the twelve *āyatanas* plus the respective consciousness that arises
in dependence on the contact of each sense with its object). There is no
need to start speculating as to the whys and wherefores of these various
classifications. Originally they were intended not as any kind of statement of epistemological doctrine, but simply as a framework for meditation. The idea is that on the basis of a deeply concentrated and positive
meditative state you simply turn your attention to your own being, and
by analysing it in this way start trying to see yourself as a complex process
instead of as a self.

Going further, you can approach the *dharmas* more systematically by
distinguishing between *saṁskṛita dharmas* and *asaṁskṛita dharmas* (compounded and uncompounded *dharmas*), and then proceed to the Abhi-
dharma-type classification of *cittas* (consciousnesses) and *caitasikas*
(mental concomitants). Finally you can relate each successive *gate* in the
mantra to a different level of *śūnyatā* in the way I have outlined.

In a way, one has to recapitulate Śāriputra's progress. One has got to *be*
Śāriputra fully before one can start listening to Avalokiteśvara.
Avalokiteśvara's statements represent not the exploding of an error or
the removal of a wrong understanding, but the deepening of a limited
understanding. If that limited understanding were not there to begin
with, it could not be deepened. Some exceptional individuals might make
the leap into the Perfection of Wisdom from nowhere, but they are very
rare, and one cannot assume that one belongs to that class oneself.

Avalokiteśvara is addressing someone who has reached a definite level
of understanding. But what level are we really talking about? We need to

be clear, to begin with, that we are dealing with the Śāriputra of Mahayanistic myth, not with the historical Śāriputra. And to be fair to the myth, it does not suggest that Śāriputra represents a merely intellectual understanding of the Dharma—because, after all, the Abhidharma itself distinguishes between *śruta-mayī-prajñā*, wisdom based on book-learning, and *bhāvanā-mayī-prajñā*, wisdom based on direct meditative experience.[12] If we are going to take up the *Heart Sūtra* at all, however, we have to accept on some level the Mahāyāna distinction between the limited insight of an Arhat and the deeper insight of the *Prajñāpāramitā*, even if in the end the distinction does not bear very close scrutiny.

It is probably best to regard Śāriputra as representing that aspect of the mind which tends to take things literally, and Avalokiteśvara as the aspect which goes to the heart of things. For the purposes of communication, of course, you need both the letter of the teaching and the spirit. This is as true for the Perfection of Wisdom teachings as it is for the Abhidharma. The Mahāyāna warns us not to take *śūnyatā* as a thing but as an operational concept, since otherwise we would find in it yet another home for the ego. Even the 'ultimate' psycho-physical elements of the Abhidharma were operational concepts originally, however. It is not the depth of our analysis that matters so much as the spirit in which we take its results. After all, although there is an explicit awareness of the limitations of conceptual formulations in the Mahāyāna Buddhist world, this is no absolute insurance against a spiritual hardening of the arteries and a decline into literalism.

No copy of the Sanskrit text of the *Heart Sūtra* has ever been found in India, but at the end of the nineteenth century an original Indian palm-leaf manuscript of the Sanskrit text was unearthed in a Japanese temple. It was not in fact a Zen temple, but this is no great surprise, for the *Heart Sūtra* is recited and meditated upon in many different schools of Japanese Buddhism. They generally chant it in Japanese, quite fast and rhythmically, just as in Tibet it is chanted in Tibetan, and in England and the USA it is spoken in English (and sometimes also chanted in the original Sanskrit).

The Perfection of Wisdom tradition has had a strong influence on both Tibetan Buddhism and Zen. The Tibetan approach to it is more dialectical—Tibetan Buddhists tend to be rather intellectual—and the Zen approach is more intuitive, more poetic, but in both schools the *Heart Sūtra*, along with the *Diamond Sūtra*, is highly esteemed. One of the greatest of Zen—or, more strictly, Ch'an—masters, Han Shan, wrote particularly beautiful commentaries on both these texts, which have now been published in English in a very illuminating translation by Charles Luk.[13]

We may go so far as to say that the *Heart Sūtra*, together with the *Diamond Sūtra*, constitutes the spiritual backbone of the Buddhism of China, Japan, Mongolia, Tibet, Korea, and Vietnam. The health of the backbone does not in itself, of course, guarantee the spiritual health of the whole body of the Far Eastern Buddhist tradition. Zen and Tibetan practitioners are just as likely to be narrow-minded, dogmatic, bigoted, and literalistic as any Theravādin. There is a tendency towards literalism in all schools of Buddhism because it is a tendency in the human mind itself.

Perhaps it is time we had a new sūtra, one in which the place of Śāriputra is taken by Avalokiteśvara—an Avalokiteśvara who has taken the categories of the Mahāyāna literally and needs to have the real meaning of *śūnyatā* revealed to him by a higher being. In the meantime, we can continue this tradition in the West not by merely looking at words on a page, but by learning to listen to the voice of Avalokiteśvara in our own hearts, and waiting for the flower of Perfect Wisdom to bloom there.

Part Three

THE DIAMOND SUTRA

Introduction

IT IS A TERRIBLE, FEARFUL THING TO FALL INTO THE HANDS OF THE DIAMOND SUTRA—

BECAUSE ONCE YOU ARE CAUGHT, WELL, YOU ARE CAUGHT.

WRIGGLE AS MUCH AS YOU LIKE, YOU WILL NOT GET FREE

It was through no kind of serendipity that I came across the *Diamond Sutra* in the summer of 1942. I was about seventeen then, still living in London, though shortly to be conscripted into the Signals Corps and shipped off to India, and I was reading all the oriental teachings and translations, particularly Buddhist ones, that I could lay my hands on. It was thus inevitable that sooner or later the *Diamond Sutra* should fall into my hands—or rather, perhaps, that I should fall into the hands of the *Diamond Sutra*. When I encountered it, this sutra—together with the *Platform Sutra* (which in our ignorance we then called the *Sutra of Wei Lang*)—made an impression on me that can truly be described as tremendous. I call it an impression, but it was more like an impact. Just reading these two texts for the first time was an overwhelming spiritual experience which changed the whole course of my life—or perhaps I should say that it made me realize for the first time what the course of my life really was. It made me realize that I was a Buddhist—whatever that may mean.

The *Diamond Sutra* does not, of course, need my—or anyone else's—personal recommendation in order to call upon the attention of anyone with a vital interest in Buddhism. It is one of the most spiritually valuable of all Buddhist texts, and also one of the best known. In China, Tibet, Japan, Mongolia, Korea, and Vietnam, the *Diamond Sutra* is recited daily, commented upon, explained, and expounded. It is an essential current in the mainstream of Mahāyāna Buddhism. In short, until we have at least some acquaintance with this great work, there will be a gaping hole in our knowledge of Buddhism.

Buddhists in the West have, no doubt, quite a lot to grumble about. Our employers are not usually sympathetic enough to our need for retreats to give us three months' paid leave when we want to go and meditate. We have no great monasteries full of monks, nor enthusiastic Buddhist processions through the streets of London, nor public holidays on full-moon days, nor cremation grounds to visit in the moonlight.... But there is one thing at least that we cannot grumble about. We cannot grumble about a lack of translations of the *Diamond Sūtra*.

The first European translations, going back to about 1830, were from the Chinese or the Tibetan versions of the text, which were in turn taken from the Sanskrit. Rather than rely on these twice-translated versions it is obviously best to keep to translations from the original Sanskrit text, copies of which were discovered in Japan around the turn of the century. Of the English translations from the Sanskrit the best is Edward Conze's quite literal version published in Rome in 1957. The seminar on which this commentary is based will work with the more readily available and idiomatic London version of Conze's translation, which was published in paperback in 1980 by George Allen and Unwin. Although this translation lacks the scholarly apparatus of the Rome edition, it is armed with a commentary that gives the general reader reliable access to the text. Conze's commentary is based in turn upon commentaries by Asaṅga, Vasubandhu and Kamalaśīla; and, in places, upon commentaries on the large *Prajñāpāramitā* sūtras by Nāgārjuna and Haribhadra.

The full title of the work is *Vajracchedikā-prajñāpāramitā Sūtra*. *Chedikā* means 'that which cuts', or simply 'a cutter'. *Vajra* means both 'diamond' and 'thunderbolt': something of impervious strength and irresistible potency which is capable of smashing, shattering, pulverizing everything that stands in its way. The vajra occupies an important place in Buddhist symbolism, even giving its name to a whole phase in the development of Buddhism: the *Vajrayāna*—the Diamond Path, or the Way of the Thunderbolt.

So *Vajracchedikā-prajñāpāramitā Sūtra* means: the discourse on the transcendental wisdom that cuts like the diamond-thunderbolt. And as you might expect, this title gives us a clue to the meaning and significance of the whole sūtra. As a sūtra it is by definition *Buddhavacana*—the word or utterance of the Buddha—so it is an expression of the

Enlightened Mind. It does not come from the brain, nor from the subconscious; it is not the product of any manner of mundane, conditioned consciousness. The *Diamond Sūtra* is the expression of the Enlightened mind, the mind which is one with reality, which sees reality face to face.

By reading the *Diamond Sūtra*, reflecting upon it, meditating upon it, bearing it in mind, we make contact with reality itself. The light of reality shines through the thick veil of our ignorance, so that transcendental wisdom can begin to glimmer in the inert darkness of our hearts and minds. At the same time, transcendental wisdom is also like a diamond, like a thunderbolt. It cuts through all our thoughts, all our ideas, all our concepts about reality, all our metaphysical assumptions. It shatters all our negative emotions—our fear, our anxiety, our anger, our jealousy, our possessiveness, our clinging, our craving. It cuts through all our psychological conditionings, all our prejudices, all the conditionings which arise out of belonging to this nationality rather than that one, originating from this race rather than that one, coming from this particular social background, speaking this language, living in this environment....

The diamond-thunderbolt of transcendental wisdom pulverizes all conditionings that stop you from seeing the truth face to face. Above all it smashes *you*—as you at present know yourself to be. When you contact that transcendental wisdom, you feel its impact like a thunderbolt, crushing and destroying you—and this is a very terrible thing. It is a terrible thing to be caught in the grip of reality—and it is a terrible, fearful thing to fall into the hands of the *Diamond Sūtra*, because once you are caught, well, you are caught. Wriggle as much as you like, you will not get free.

Are we ready for this? If not, we would be better to leave the *Diamond Sūtra* on the shelf collecting dust. And even if we do decide to let it take hold of us, we need to proceed very slowly and cautiously, for 'human kind cannot bear very much reality'. We can bear very little of it, in fact, if any at all, which is why we are working our way into the *Diamond Sūtra* so very circumspectly. Indeed, there can be no question of giving a complete, systematic exposition of the teaching of the *Diamond Sūtra* in all its depth and breadth, even if such an exposition were possible, because we simply could not bear it. If some Buddha or Bodhisattva were to come along and start really telling us what the *Diamond Sūtra* was all about—well, we should probably need to have the St John's Ambulance Brigade standing by.

If the *content* of the *Diamond Sūtra* calls for a health warning, it should also be said that trying to make sense of its *form* can give us quite a headache. While the original Sanskrit version of the sūtra—which, for all its formidable reputation, is quite short—runs continuously without a break, the Chinese versions are divided into thirty-two very short chapters, organized in two parts. The first part runs along quite nicely and comes to a neat enough conclusion at the opening of chapter 13. Part Two, though, is a different matter. It starts up for no apparent reason, and seems to repeat itself pointlessly, with little apparent order or sequence, and little sense of one topic leading smoothly on to the next.

THIS SUTRA IS GOING TO BE CONFUSING, IRRITATING, ANNOYING, UNSATISFYING ...

We have to entertain the possibility that the text itself may have been meddled with and shuffled out of any coherence it might once have possessed. I would even tentatively suggest that Part Two may represent an alternative version of Part One. If the whole thing is a work of compilation, perhaps the second part is the result of an earlier, less felicitous effort, which came to be tacked onto the later, more successful one. This is, in a sense, an almost profane suggestion, and quite untraditional, but not on that account to be ruled out of court.

The *Diamond Sūtra* has come down to us in a form to a great extent determined by the accidents of transmission, which means that, as with other Buddhist scriptures, we cannot take it too literally. Now compare this predicament with the comfortable situation in which adherents of other faiths find themselves. Christians have a Bible which is accepted by all denominations. After a few centuries of contention, of putting in and taking out, they all settled down with the canon of books that make up the standard Bible, and they have stuck with it, undisturbed even by the 'higher criticism' which revealed its all too human provenance and development. The Hindus have the four Vedas, which are clearly regarded as *śrutis*, or revealed works, together with the *Brahmasūtras* and the *Bhagavadgītā*. As for Muslims, they are, we may say, sitting pretty. They have one book, the Koran, the text of which is in a fair state of reliability, despite a few discussions and disputes, so they have a compact little volume, no bigger than the New Testament, which represents the Word of God in its entirety. They have all sorts of commentaries, and also the sayings of the Prophet—thousands of them—but these are all absolutely distinct from the Koran, which is the final authority.

As Buddhists we have no such authority to guide us. We have a whole library of books, without any clear line to draw under what might be called 'scriptures'. We have the Pāli Canon, and the Mahāyāna sūtras and tantras—but what sort of status do we give to the *Songs of Milarepa*, for example? It's all a bit confusing. Nichiren Shoshu Buddhists have tried to make things easier for us by isolating one particular text, the *Saddharma-Puṇḍarīka Sūtra*, as a sort of Bible—although they have not been able to avoid affording some sort of position to at least some of the other Mahāyāna sūtras—but the project has not caught on with the rest of the Buddhist world. And while the Theravādins do manage to adopt a rigid delimitation of Buddhist scriptures, this still leaves them with a good few shelves to sift through.

This means that it should be quite impossible for Buddhists to indulge in bibliolatry. We cannot hold up a book and say 'The Truth has been written down—it has found expression in a precise form of words—and here it is, all you need for your salvation: it's all *here*.' Piecing together many sources, comparing this with that, we have to work out the truth for ourselves. Besides being a good intellectual exercise this also helps us to maintain a sense of spiritual proportion, and guards against fanaticism and dogmatism. You may have your own favourite text—whole schools may grow up around particular texts—but that is quite another matter. Buddhism has no creeds. (Christmas Humphreys did essay a sort of creed with his 'Twelve Principles', but without much success, especially as one or two of his principles are slightly questionable. The item about 'all life being one' is certainly regarded as highly dubious by practically all Buddhists.)

So there is no reason why we should not examine the text of the *Diamond Sūtra* quite critically. To do this, however, we must be sure that we understand what we are dealing with, and it may be wiser to remain open to the possibility that we are not yet clear about this. It may be that the connection of the various themes and arguments, and the relation between the two parts, still eludes all the scholars of the sūtra. In the second part the tempo certainly accelerates. Whereas in Part One there is some thread of linear development to hang on to, Part Two is rather more uncompromising, with even more derangement of construction, and the complete abandonment of any attempt at sequential connections. But can we conclude from this that the sages and editors of old were so dense that they could not see what is as clear as day to us, which is that Part Two is in a mess? So we must ask *is* it in a mess, or is it *we* who are in a mess?

If we are going to accept the 'argument' as deliberately inconsequential, why should we expect consecutiveness in the arrangement of the paragraphs? In conventional terms a book is linear, the pages laid side by side or in one long strip or scroll so that one page is followed by the next. But if we imagine pages arranged like the letters on a typewriter's 'golf ball', so that each page could be read as being continuous with any of the pages surrounding it, we might get a more comprehensive view of the Perfection of Wisdom. Perhaps the *Vajracchedikā* only seems confusing because we are locked into linguistic and typographic conventions which require a text to offer itself in one specific sequence. We can hardly expect reality to conform to this convention any more than to the conventions of logic.

One way of making the whole sūtra appear more connected and intelligible is to follow the suggestion of Han Shan, who was an Enlightened master of the Ming dynasty in China. According to him, the Buddha's pronouncements in the sūtra are meant to resolve the unspoken doubts of the monk, Subhūti, whom he is addressing—hence the apparent lack of connection and continuity. In his commentary, Han Shan makes explicit thirty-five doubts: seventeen coarse doubts, which are dealt with in Part One of the sūtra, and eighteen subtle doubts, which are disposed of in Part Two. As Han Shan interprets the sūtra, when all your doubts—including your most subtle unconscious resistances—are cut off by the thunderbolt of transcendental wisdom, then your absolute mind, the mind of supreme Enlightenment, is made manifest. This is really the only reading of the text that seems to work.

In the end, however, if we insist that the requirements of the logical mind be satisfied, we are missing the point. What the *Diamond Sūtra* is actually delivering is not a systematic treatise, but a series of sledgehammer blows, attacking from this side and that, to try and break through our fundamental delusion. It is not going to make things easy for the logical mind by putting things in a logical form. This sūtra is going to be confusing, irritating, annoying, and unsatisfying—and perhaps we cannot ask for it to be otherwise. If it were all set forth neatly and clearly, leaving no loose ends, we might be in danger of thinking we had grasped the Perfection of Wisdom.

The Sutra

Homage to the Perfection of Wisdom, the Lovely, the Holy!

Introduction

1. Thus have I heard at one time. The Lord dwelt at Śrāvastī, in the Jeta Grove, in the garden of Anāthapiṇḍika, together with a large gathering of monks, consisting of 1,250 monks, and with many Bodhisattvas, great beings. Early in the morning the Lord dressed, put on his cloak, took his bowl, and entered the great city of Śrāvastī to collect alms. When he had eaten and returned from his round, the Lord put away his bowl and cloak, washed his feet, and sat down on the seat arranged for him, crossing his legs, holding his body upright, and mindfully fixing his attention in front of him. Then many monks approached to where the Lord was, saluted his feet with their heads, thrice walked round him to the right, and sat down on one side.

2. At that time the Venerable Subhūti came to that assembly, and sat down. Then he rose from his seat, put his upper robe over one shoulder, placed his right knee on the ground, bent forth his folded hands towards the Lord, and said to the Lord: 'It is wonderful O Lord, it is exceedingly wonderful, O Well-Gone, how much the Bodhisattvas, the great beings, have been helped with the greatest help by the Tathāgata, the Arhat, the Fully Enlightened One. It is wonderful, O Lord, how much the Bodhisattvas, the great beings, have been favoured with the highest favour by the Tathāgata, the Arhat, the Fully Enlightened One. How then, O Lord, should a son or daughter of good

family, who have set out in the Bodhisattva-vehicle, stand, how progress, how control their thoughts?'

After these words the Lord said to the Venerable Subhūti: 'Well said, well said, Subhūti! So it is, Subhūti, so it is, as you say! The Tathāgata, Subhūti, has helped the Bodhisattvas, the great beings with the greatest help, and he has favoured them with the highest favour. Therefore, Subhūti, listen well, and attentively! I will teach you how those who have set out in the Bodhisattva-vehicle should stand, how progress, how control their thoughts.' 'So be it, O Lord', replied the Venerable Subhūti and listened.

THE BODHISATTVA'S CAREER

3. The Lord said: Here, Subhūti, someone who has set out in the vehicle of a Bodhisattva should produce a thought in this manner: 'As many beings as there are in the universe of beings, comprehended under the term "beings"—egg-born, born from a womb, moisture-born, or miraculously born; with or without form; with perception, without perception, and with neither perception nor non-perception,—as far as any conceivable form of beings is conceived: all these I must lead to Nirvāṇa, into that Realm of Nirvāṇa which leaves nothing behind. And yet, although innumerable beings have thus been led to Nirvāṇa, no being at all has been led to Nirvāṇa.' And why? If in a Bodhisattva the notion of a 'being' should take place, he could not be called a 'Bodhi-being'. 'And why? He is not to be called a Bodhi-being, in whom the notion of a self or of a being should take place, or the notion of a living soul or of a person.'

4. Moreover, Subhūti, a Bodhisattva who gives a gift should not be supported by a thing, nor should he be supported anywhere. When he gives gifts he should not be supported by sight-objects, nor by sounds, smells, tastes, touchables, or mind-objects. For, Subhūti, the Bodhisattva, the great being, should give gifts in such a way that he is not supported by the notion of a sign. And why? Because the heap of merit of that Bodhi-being, who unsupported gives a gift, is not easy to measure. What do you think, Subhūti, is the extent of space in the East easy to measure?—Subhūti replied: No indeed, O Lord.—The Lord asked: In like manner, is it easy to measure the extent of space in the South, West or North, downwards, upwards, in the intermediate directions, in all the ten directions all round?—Subhūti replied: No indeed, O Lord.—The Lord said: Even so the heap of merit of that

Bodhi-being who unsupported gives a gift is not easy to measure. That is why, Subhūti, those who have set out in the Bodhisattva-vehicle, should give gifts without being supported by the notion of a sign.

5. The Lord continued: 'What do you think, Subhūti, can the Tathāgata be seen by the possession of his marks?'—Subhūti replied: 'No indeed, O Lord. And why? What has been taught by the Tathāgata as the possession of marks, that is truly a no-possession of no-marks.' The Lord said: 'Wherever there is possession of marks, there is fraud, wherever there is no-possession of no-marks there is no fraud. Hence the Tathāgata is to be seen from no-marks as marks.'

6. Subhūti asked: Will there be any beings in the future period, in the last time, in the last epoch, in the last 500 years, at the time of the collapse of the good doctrine who, when these words of the Sūtra are being taught, will understand their truth?—The Lord replied: Do not speak thus, Subhūti! Yes, even then there will such beings. For even at that time, Subhūti, there will be Bodhisattvas who are gifted with good conduct, gifted with virtuous qualities, gifted with wisdom, and who, when these words of the Sūtra are being taught, will understand their truth. And these Bodhisattvas, Subhūti, will not be such as have honoured only one single Buddha, nor such as have planted their roots of merit under one single Buddha only. On the contrary, Subhūti, those Bodhisattvas who, when these words of the Sūtra are being taught, will find even one single thought of serene faith, they will be such as have honoured many hundreds of thousands of Buddhas, such as have planted their roots of merit under many hundreds of thousands of Buddhas. Known they are, Subhūti, to the Tathāgata through his Buddha-cognition, seen they are, Subhūti, by the Tathāgata with his Buddha-eye, fully known they are, Subhūti, to the Tathāgata. And they all, Subhūti, will beget and acquire an immeasurable and incalculable heap of merit.

And why? Because, Subhūti, in these Bodhisattvas (1) no perception of a self takes place, (2) no perception of a being, (3) no perception of a soul, (4) no perception of a person. Nor do these Bodhisattvas have (5) a perception of a dharma, or (6) a perception of a no-dharma. (7) No perception or (8) non-perception takes place in them.

And why? If, Subhūti, these Bodhisattvas should have a perception of either a dharma, or a no-dharma, they would thereby seize on a self, a being, a soul, or a person. And why? Because a Bodhisattva should not seize on either a dharma or a no-dharma. Therefore this saying has been taught by the Tathāgata with a hidden meaning: 'Those who know the discourse on dharma as like unto a raft, should forsake dharmas, still more so no-dharmas.'

7. The Lord asked: What do you think, Subhūti, is there any dharma which the Tathāgata has fully known as 'the utmost, right and perfect enlightenment', or is there any dharma which the Tathāgata has demonstrated?—Subhūti replied: No, not as I understand what the Lord has said. And why? This dharma which the Tathāgata has fully known or demonstrated—it cannot be grasped, it cannot be talked about, it is neither a dharma nor a no-dharma. And why? Because an Absolute exalts the Holy Persons.

8. The Lord then asked: What do you think, Subhūti, if a son or daughter of good family had filled this world system of 1,000 million worlds with the seven precious things, and then gave it as a gift to the Tathāgatas, Arhats, Fully Enlightened Ones, would they on the strength of that beget a great heap of merit?—Subhūti replied: Great, O Lord, great, O Well-Gone, would that heap of merit be! And why? Because the Tathāgata spoke of the 'heap of merit' as a non-heap. That is how the Tathāgata speaks of 'heap of merit'.—The Lord said: But if someone else were to take from this discourse on dharma but one stanza of four lines, and would demonstrate and illuminate it in full detail to others, then he would on the strength of that beget a still greater heap of merit, immeasurable and incalculable. And why? Because from it has issued the utmost, right and perfect enlightenment of the Tathāgatas, Arhats, Fully Enlightened Ones, and from it have issued the Buddhas, the Lords. And why? For the Tathāgata has taught that the dharmas special to the Buddhas are just not a Buddha's special dharmas. That is why they are called 'the dharmas special to the Buddhas'.

THE RANGE OF THE SPIRITUAL LIFE

9. The Lord asked: What do you think, Subhūti, does it occur to the Stream-winner, 'by me has the fruit of a Stream-winner been attained'? Subhūti replied: No indeed, O Lord. And why? Because, O Lord, he has not won any dharma. Therefore is he called a Stream-winner. No sight-object has been won, no sounds, smells, tastes, touchables, or objects of mind. That is why he is called a 'Stream-winner'. If, O Lord, it would occur to a Stream-winner, 'by me has a Stream-winner's fruit been attained', then that would be in him a seizing on a self, seizing on a being, seizing on a soul, seizing on a

person. The Lord asked: What do you think, Subhūti, does it then occur to the Once-Returner, 'by me has the fruit of a Once-Returner been attained'?—Subhūti replied: No indeed, O Lord. And why? Because there is not any dharma that has won Once-Returnership. That is why he is called a 'Once-Returner'. The Lord asked: What do you think, Subhūti, does it then occur to the Never-Returner 'by me has the fruit of a Never-Returner been attained'?—Subhūti replied: No indeed, O Lord. And why? Because there is not any dharma that has won Never-Returnership. Therefore he is called a 'Never-Returner' The Lord asked: What do you think, Subhūti, does it then occur to the Arhat, 'by me has Arhatship been attained'?—Subhūti: No indeed, O Lord. And why? Because no dharma is called 'Arhat'. That is why he is called an Arhat. If, O Lord, it would occur to an Arhat, 'by me has Arhatship been attained', then that would be in him a seizing on a self, seizing on a being, seizing on a soul, seizing on a person. And why? I am, O Lord, the one whom the Tathāgata, the Arhat, the Fully Enlightened One has pointed out as the foremost of those who dwell in Peace. I am, O Lord, an Arhat free from greed. And yet, O Lord, it does not occur to me, 'an Arhat am I and free from greed'. If, O Lord, it could occur to me that I have attained Arhatship, then the Tathāgata would not have declared of me that 'Subhūti, this son of good family, who is the foremost of those who dwell in Peace, does not dwell anywhere; that is why he is called "a dweller in Peace, a dweller in Peace"'.

10. The Lord asked: What do you think, Subhūti, is there any dharma which the Tathāgata has learned from Dīpankara, the Tathāgata, the Arhat, the fully Enlightened One? Subhūti replied: Not so, O Lord, there is not.

The Lord said: If any Bodhisattva would say, 'I will create harmonious Buddhafields', he would speak falsely. And why? 'The harmonies of Buddhafields, the harmonies of Buddhafields', Subhūti, as no-harmonies have they been taught by the Tathāgata. Therefore he spoke of 'harmonious Buddhafields'.

Therefore then, Subhūti, the Bodhisattva, the great being, should produce an unsupported thought, i.e. a thought which is nowhere supported, a thought unsupported by sights, sounds, smells, tastes, touchables or mind-objects.

Suppose, Subhūti, there were a man endowed with a body, a huge body, so that he had a personal existence like Sumeru, king of mountains. Would that, Subhūti, be a huge personal existence?

Subhūti replied: Yes, huge, O Lord, huge, O Well-Gone, would his personal existence be. And why so? 'Personal existence, personal existence', as no-existence has that been taught by the Tathāgata; for not, O Lord, is that existence or non-existence. Therefore is it called 'personal existence'.

11. The Lord asked: What do you think, Subhūti, if there were as many Ganges rivers as there are grains of sand in the large river Ganges, would the grains of sand in them be many?—Subhūti replied: Those Ganges rivers would indeed be many, much more so the grains of sand in them.—The Lord said: This is what I announce to you, Subhūti, this is what I make known to you,—if some woman or man had filled with the seven precious things as many world systems as there are grains of sand in those Ganges rivers, and would give them as a gift to the Tathāgatas, Arhats, fully Enlightened Ones—what do you think, Subhūti, would that woman or man on the strength of that beget a great heap of merit?—Subhūti replied: Great, O Lord, great O Well-Gone, would that heap of merit be, immeasurable and incalculable.—The Lord said: But if a son or daughter of good family had taken from this discourse on dharma but one stanza of four lines, and were to demonstrate and illuminate it to others, then they would on the strength of that beget a still greater heap of merit, immeasurable and incalculable.

12. Moreover, Subhūti, that spot of earth where one has taken from this discourse on dharma but one stanza of four lines, taught or illumined it, that spot of earth will be a veritable shrine for the whole world with its gods, men and Āsuras. What then should we say of those who will bear in mind this discourse on dharma in its entirety, who will recite, study, and illuminate it in full detail for others! Most wonderfully blest, Subhūti, they will be! And on that spot of earth, Subhūti, either the Teacher dwells, or a sage representing him.

THE FIRST ENDING

13. Subhūti asked: What then, O Lord, is this discourse on dharma, and how should I bear it in mind?—The Lord replied: This discourse on dharma, Subhūti, is called 'Wisdom which has gone beyond', and as such should you bear it in mind!

TRANSCENDENTALITY

And why? Just that which the Tathāgata has taught as the wisdom
which has gone beyond, just that He has taught as not gone beyond.
Therefore is it called 'Wisdom which has gone beyond'. What do you
think, Subhūti, is there any dharma which the Tathāgata has taught?
—Subhūti replied: No indeed, O Lord, there is not. The Lord said:
When, Subhūti, you consider the number of particles of dust in this
world-system of 1,000 million worlds—would they be many?—
Subhūti replied: Yes, O Lord. Because what was taught as particles of
dust by the Tathāgata, as no-particles that was taught by the Tathāgata.
Therefore are they called 'particles of dust'. And this world-system the
Tathāgata has taught as no-system. Therefore is it called a 'world
system'. The Lord asked: What do you think, Subhūti, can the
Tathāgata be seen by means of the thirty-two marks of the superman?
—Subhūti replied: No indeed, O Lord. And why? Because those thirty-
two marks of the superman which were taught by the Tathāgata, they
are really no-marks. Therefore are they called the 'thirty-two marks of
the superman'.

The Lord said: And again, Subhūti, suppose a woman or a man were
to renounce all their belongings as many times as there are grains of
sand in the river Ganges; and suppose that someone else, after taking
from this discourse on Dharma but one stanza of four lines, would
demonstrate it to others. Then this latter on the strength of that would
beget a greater heap of merit, immeasurable and incalculable.

14. Thereupon the impact of Dharma moved the Venerable Subhūti
to tears. Having wiped away his tears, he thus spoke to the Lord: It is
wonderful, O Lord, it is exceedingly wonderful, O Well-Gone, how
well the Tathāgata has taught this discourse on Dharma. Through it
cognition has been produced in me. Not have I ever before heard such
a discourse on Dharma. Most wonderfully blest will be those who,
when this Sūtra is being taught, will produce a true perception. And
that which is true perception, that is indeed no perception. Therefore
the Tathāgata teaches, 'true perception, true perception'. It is not
difficult for me to accept and believe this discourse on Dharma when it
is being taught. But those beings who will be in a future period, in the
last time, in the last epoch, in the last 500 years, at the time of the
collapse of the good doctrine, and who, O Lord, will take up this
discourse on Dharma, bear it in mind, recite it, study it, and illuminate
it in full detail for others, these will be most wonderfully blest. In

them, however, no perception of a self will take place, or of a being, a soul, or a person. And why? That, O Lord, which is perception of self, that is indeed no perception. That which is perception of a being, a soul or a person, that is indeed no perception. And why? Because the Buddhas, the Lords have left all perceptions behind.

The Lord said: So it is, Subhūti. Most wonderfully blest will be those beings who, on hearing this Sūtra, will not tremble, nor be frightened, or terrified. And why? The Tathāgata has taught this as the highest perfection. And what the Tathāgata teaches as the highest perfection, that also the innumerable Blessed Buddhas do teach. Therefore is it called the 'highest perfection'.

Moreover, Subhūti, the Tathāgata's perfection of patience is really no perfection. And why? Because, Subhūti, when the king of Kalinga cut my flesh from every limb, at that time I had no perception of a self, of a being, of a soul, or a person. And why? If, Subhūti, at that time I had had a perception of self, I would also have had a perception of ill-will at that time. And so, if I had had a perception of a being, of a soul, or of a person. With my superknowledge I recall that in the past I have for five hundred births led the life of a sage devoted to patience. Then also have I had no perception of a self, a being, a soul, or a person.

Therefore then, Subhūti, the Bodhi-being, the great being, after he has got rid of all perceptions, should raise his thought to the utmost, right and perfect enlightenment. He should produce a thought which is unsupported by forms, sounds, smells, tastes, touchables, or mind-objects, unsupported by dharma, unsupported by no-dharma, unsupported by anything. And why? All supports have actually no support. It is for this reason that the Tathāgata teaches: By an unsupported Bodhisattva should a gift be given, not by one who is supported by forms, sounds, smells, tastes, touchables, or mind-objects.

And further, Subhūti, it is for the weal of all beings that a Bodhisattva should give gifts in this manner. And why? This perception of a being, Subhūti, that is just a non-perception. Those all-beings of whom the Tathāgata has spoken, they are indeed no-beings. And why? Because the Tathāgata speaks in accordance with reality, speaks the truth, speaks of what is, not otherwise. A Tathāgata does not speak falsely.

But nevertheless, Subhūti, with regard to that dharma which the Tathāgata has fully known and demonstrated, on account of that there is neither truth nor fraud.

In darkness a man could not see anything. Just so should be viewed a Bodhisattva who has fallen among things, and who, fallen among things, renounces a gift. A man with eyes would, when the night becomes light and the sun has arisen, see manifold forms. Just so should be viewed a Bodhisattva who has not fallen among things, and who, without having fallen among things, renounces a gift.

Furthermore, Subhūti, those sons and daughters of good family who will take up this discourse on Dharma, will bear it in mind, recite, study, and illuminate it in full detail for others, they have been known, Subhūti, by the Tathāgata with his Buddha-cognition, they have been seen, Subhūti, by the Tathāgata with his Buddha-eye, they have been fully known by the Tathāgata. All these beings, Subhūti, will beget and acquire an immeasurable and incalculable heap of merit. 15. And if, Subhūti, a woman or man should renounce in the morning all their belongings as many times as there are grains of sand in the river Ganges, and if they should do likewise at noon and in the evening, and if in this way they should renounce all their belongings for many hundreds of thousands of millions of milliards of aeons; and someone else, on hearing this discourse on Dharma, would not reject it; then the latter would on the strength of that beget a greater heap of merit, immeasurable and incalculable. What then should we say of him who, after writing it, would learn it, bear it in mind, recite, study and illuminate it in full detail for others?

Moreover, Subhūti, (1) unthinkable and (2) incomparable is this discourse on Dharma. (3) The Tathāgata has taught it for the weal of beings who have set out in the best, in the most excellent vehicle. Those who will take up this discourse on Dharma, bear it in mind, recite, study and illuminate it in full detail for others, the Tathāgata has known them with his Buddha-cognition, the Tathāgata has seen them with his Buddha-eye, the Tathāgata has fully known them. All these beings, Subhūti, will be blest with an immeasurable heap of merit, they will be blest with a heap of merit unthinkable, incomparable, measureless and illimitable. All these beings, Subhūti, will carry along an equal share of enlightenment. And why? (4) Because it is not possible, Subhūti, that this discourse on Dharma could be heard by beings of inferior resolve, nor by such as have a self in view, a being, a soul, or a person. Nor can beings who have not taken the pledge of

Bodhi-beings either hear this discourse on Dharma, or take it up, bear it in mind, recite or study it. That cannot be.

(1) Moreover, Subhūti, the spot of earth where this Sūtra will be revealed, that spot of earth will be worthy of worship by the whole world with its Gods, men and Āsuras, worthy of being saluted respectfully, worthy of being honoured by circumambulation,—like a shrine will be that spot of earth. 16. And yet Subhūti, those sons and daughters of good family, who will take up these very Sūtras, and will bear them in mind, recite and study them, they will be humbled,— well humbled they will be! And why? The impure deeds which these beings have done in their former lives, and which are liable to lead them into the states of woe,—in this very life they will, by means of that humiliation, (2) annul those impure deeds of their former lives, and (3) they will reach the enlightenment of a Buddha. With my superknowledge, Subhūti, I recall that in the past period, long before Dīpaṅkara, the Tathāgata, Arhat, fully Enlightened One, during incalculable, quite incalculable aeons, I gave satisfaction by loyal service to 84,000 million milliards of Buddhas, without ever becoming again estranged from them. But the heap of merit, Subhūti, from the satisfaction I gave to those Buddhas and Lords without again becoming estranged from them—compared with the heap of merit of those who in the last time, the last epoch, the last five hundred years, at the time of the collapse of the good doctrine, will take up these very Sūtras, bear them in mind, recite and study them, and will illuminate them in full detail for others, it does not approach one hundredth part, not one thousandth part, nor a one hundred thousandth part, not a ten millionth part, nor a one hundred millionth part, nor a 100,000 millionth part. It does not bear number, nor fraction, nor counting, nor similarity, nor comparison, nor resemblance. (4) If moreover, Subhūti, I were to teach the heap of merit of those sons and daughters of good family, and how great a heap of merit they will at that time beget and acquire, beings would become frantic and confused. Since, however, Subhūti, the Tathāgata has taught this discourse on Dharma as unthinkable, so just an unthinkable karma-result should be expected from it.

THE BODHISATTVAS

17. (Subhūti asked: How, O Lord, should one set out in the Bodhisattva-vehicle stand, how progress, how control his

thoughts?—The Lord replied: Here, Subhūti, someone who has set out in the Bodhisattva-vehicle should produce a thought in this manner: 'all beings I must lead to Nirvāṇa, into that Realm of Nirvāṇa which leaves nothing behind; and yet, after beings have thus been led to Nirvāṇa, no being at all has been led to Nirvāṇa'. And why? If in a Bodhisattva the notion of a 'being' should take place, he could not be called a 'Bodhi-being'. And likewise if the notion of a soul, or a person should take place in him.) And why? He who has set out in the Bodhisattva-vehicle—he is not one of the dharmas.

What do you think Subhūti, is there any dharma by which the Tathāgata, when he was with Dīpaṅkara the Tathāgata, has fully known the utmost, right and perfect enlightenment?—Subhūti replied: There is not any dharma by which the Tathāgata, when he was with the Tathāgata Dīpaṅkara, has fully known the utmost, right and perfect enlightenment.—The Lord said: It is for this reason that the Tathāgata Dīpaṅkara then predicted of me: 'You, young Brahmin, will be in a future period a Tathāgata, Arhat, fully Enlightened, by the name of Śākyamuni!'

And why? 'Tathāgata', Subhūti, is synonymous with true Suchness (*tathatā*). And whosoever, Subhūti, were to say, 'The Tathāgata has fully known the utmost, right and perfect enlightenment', he would speak falsely. And why? (There is not any dharma by which the Tathāgata has fully known the utmost, right and perfect enlightenment. And that dharma which the Tathāgata has fully known and demonstrated, on account of that there is neither truth nor fraud.) Therefore the Tathāgata teaches, 'all dharmas are the Buddha's own and special dharmas'. And why? 'All-dharmas', Subhūti, have as no-dharmas been taught by the Tathāgata. Therefore all dharmas are called the Buddha's own and special dharmas. (Just as a man, Subhūti, might be endowed with a body, a huge body.)—Subhūti said: That man of whom the Tathāgata spoke as 'endowed with a body, a huge body', as a no-body he has been taught by the Tathāgata. Therefore is he called, 'endowed with a body, a huge body'.

The Lord said: So it is, Subhūti. The Bodhisattva who would say, 'I will lead beings to Nirvāṇa', he should not be called a 'Bodhi-being'. And why? Is there, Subhūti, any dharma named 'Bodhi-being'?— Subhūti replied: No indeed, O Lord.—The Lord said: Because of that the Tathāgata teaches, 'selfless are all dharmas, they have not the character of living beings, they are without a living soul, without personality'. (If any Bodhisattva should say, 'I will create harmonious

Buddha-fields'), he likewise should not be called a Bodhi-being. (And why? 'The harmonies of Buddhafields, the harmonies of Buddhafields', Subhūti, as no-harmonies have they been taught by the Tathāgata. Therefore he spoke of 'harmonious Buddhafields'.) The Bodhisattva, however, Subhūti, who is intent on 'without self are the dharmas, without self are the dharmas', him the Tathāgata, the Arhat, the fully Enlightened One, has declared to be a Bodhi-being, a great being.

The Buddhas

18. What do you think, Subhūti, does the fleshly eye of the Tathāgata exist?—Subhūti replied: So it is, O Lord, the fleshly eye of the Tathāgata does exist.—The Lord asked: What do you think, Subhūti, does the Tathāgata's heavenly eye exist, his wisdom eye, his Dharma-eye, his Buddha eye?—Subhūti replied: So it is, O Lord, the heavenly eye of the Tathāgata does exist, and so does his wisdom eye, his Dharma-eye and his Buddha-eye.

The Lord said: What do you think, Subhūti, has the Tathāgata used the phrase, 'as many grains of sand as there are in the great river Ganges?—Subhūti replied: So it is, O Lord, so it is, O Well-Gone! The Lord asked: What do you think, Subhūti, if there were as many Ganges rivers as there are grains of sand in the great river Ganges, and if there were as many world systems as there are grains of sand in them, would those world systems be many?—Subhūti replied: So it is, O Lord, so it is, O Well-Gone, these world systems would be many.— The Lord said: As many beings as there are in these world systems, of them I know, in my wisdom, the manifold trends of thought. And why? 'Trends of thought, trends of thought', Subhūti, as no-trends have they been taught by the Tathāgata. Therefore are they called 'trends of thought'. And why? Past thought is not got at; future thought is not got at; present thought is not got at.

19. What do you think, Subhūti, if a son or daughter of good family had filled this world system of 1,000 million worlds with the seven precious things, and then gave it as a gift to the Tathāgatas, the Arhats, the fully Enlightened Ones, would they, on the strength of that beget a great heap of merit?—Subhūti replied: they would, O Lord, they would, O Well-Gone!—The Lord said: So it is, Subhūti, so it is. On the strength of that this son or daughter of good family would beget a great heap of merit, immeasurable and incalculable. But if, on

the other hand, there were such a thing as a heap of merit, the Tathāgata would not have spoken of a 'heap of merit'.

20. What do you think, Subhūti, is the Tathāgata to be seen by means of the accomplishment of his form-body? Subhūti replied: No indeed, O Lord, the Tathāgata is not to be seen by means of the accomplishment of his form-body. And why? 'Accomplishment of his form-body, accomplishment of his form-body', this, O Lord, has been taught by the Tathāgata as no-accomplishment. Therefore is it called 'accomplishment of his form-body'. The Lord asked: What do you think, Subhūti, is the Tathāgata to be seen through his possession of marks?—Subhūti replied: No indeed, O Lord. And why? This possession of marks, O Lord, which has been taught by the Tathāgata, as a no-possession of no-marks this has been taught by the Tathāgata. Therefore is it called 'possession of marks'.

21. The Lord asked: What do you think, Subhūti, does it occur to the Tathāgata, 'by me has Dharma been demonstrated'? Whosoever, Subhūti, would say, 'the Tathāgata has demonstrated Dharma', he would speak falsely, he would misrepresent me by seizing on what is not there. And why? 'Demonstration of dharma, demonstration of dharma', Subhūti, there is not any dharma which could be got at as a demonstration of dharma.

Subhūti asked: Are there, O Lord, any beings in the future, in the last time, in the last epoch, in the last 500 years, at the time of the collapse of the good doctrine who, on hearing such dharmas, will truly believe? —The Lord replied: They, Subhūti, are neither beings nor no-beings. And why? 'Beings, beings', Subhūti, the Tathāgata has taught that they are all no-beings. Therefore has he spoken of 'all beings'.

22. What do you think, Subhūti, is there any dharma by which the Tathāgata has fully known the utmost, right and perfect enlightenment?—Subhūti replied: No indeed, O Lord, there is not any dharma by which the Tathāgata has fully known the utmost, right and perfect enlightenment.—The Lord said: So it is, Subhūti, so it is. Not even the least dharma is there found or got at. Therefore is it called 'utmost, right and perfect enlightenment'. 23. Furthermore, Subhūti, self-identical is that dharma, and nothing is therein at variance. Therefore is it called 'utmost, right and perfect enlightenment'. Self-identical through the absence of a self, a being, a soul, or a person, the utmost, right and perfect enlightenment is fully known as the totality of all the wholesome dharmas. 'Wholesome dharmas, wholesome dharmas', Subhūti—yet as no-dharmas have they been

taught by the Tathāgata. Therefore are they called 'wholesome dharmas'.

24. And again, Subhūti, if a woman or man had piled up the seven precious things until their bulk equalled that of all the Sumerus, kings of mountains, in the world system of 1,000 million worlds, and would give them as a gift; and if, on the other hand, a son or daughter of good family would take up from this Prajñāpāramitā, this discourse on Dharma, but one stanza of four lines, and demonstrate it to others, compared with his heap of merit the former heap of merit does not approach one hundredth part, etc., until we come to, it will not bear any comparison.

25. What do you think, Subhūti, does it occur to a Tathāgata, 'by me have beings been set free'? Not thus should you see it, Subhūti! And why? There is not any being whom the Tathāgata has set free. Again, if there had been any being whom the Tathāgata had set free, then surely there would have been on the part of the Tathāgata a seizing of a self, of a being, of a soul, of a person. 'Seizing of a self', as a no-seizing, Subhūti, has that been taught by the Tathāgata. And yet the foolish common people have seized upon it. 'Foolish common people', Subhūti, as really no people have they been taught by the Tathāgata. Therefore are they called 'foolish common people'.

26. What do you think, Subhūti, is the Tathāgata to be seen by means of his possession of marks?—Subhūti replied: No indeed, O Lord.—The Lord said: If, Subhūti, the Tathāgata could be recognized by his possession of marks, then also the universal monarch would be a Tathāgata. Therefore the Tathāgata is not to be seen by means of his possession of marks.—Subhūti then said: As I, O Lord, understand the Lord's teaching, the Tathāgata is not to be seen through his possession of marks.

Further the Lord taught on that occasion the following stanzas:

Those who by my form did see me,
And those who followed me by voice
Wrong the efforts they engaged in,
Me those people will not see.

From the Dharma should one see the Buddhas,
From the Dharmabodies comes their guidance.
Yet Dharma's true nature cannot be discerned,
And no one can be conscious of it as an object.

27. What do you think, Subhūti, has the Tathāgata fully known the utmost, right and perfect enlightenment through his possession of marks? Not so should you see it, Subhūti. And why? Because the Tathāgata could surely not have fully known the utmost, right and perfect enlightenment through his possession of marks.

Nor should anyone, Subhūti, say to you, 'those who have set out in the Bodhisattva-vehicle have conceived the destruction of a dharma, or its annihilation'. Not so should you see it, Subhūti! For those who have set out in the Bodhisattva-vehicle have not conceived the destruction of a dharma, or its annihilation.

28. And again, Subhūti, if a son or daughter of good family had filled with the seven precious things as many world systems as there are grains of sand in the river Ganges, and gave them as a gift to the Tathāgatas, Arhats, fully Enlightened Ones,—and if on the other hand a Bodhisattva would gain the patient acquiescence in dharmas which are nothing of themselves and which fail to be produced, then this latter would on the strength of that beget a greater heap of merit, immeasurable and incalculable.

Moreover, Subhūti, the Bodhisattva should not acquire a heap of merit.—Subhūti said: 'Surely, O Lord, the Bodhisattva should acquire a heap of merit?—The Lord said: 'Should acquire', Subhūti, not 'should seize upon'. Therefore it is said 'should acquire'.

29. Whosoever says that the Tathāgata goes or comes, stands, sits or lies down, he does not understand the meaning of my teaching. And why? 'Tathāgata' is called one who has not gone anywhere, nor come from anywhere. Therefore is he called 'the Tathāgata, the Arhat, the fully Enlightened One'.

ADVICE TO THE IMPERFECT

30. And again, Subhūti, if a son or daughter of good family were to grind as many world systems as there are particles of dust in this great world system of 1,000 million worlds, as finely as they can be ground with incalculable vigour, and in fact reduce them to something like a collection of atomic quantities, what do you think, Subhūti, would that be an enormous collection of atomic quantities?—Subhūti replied: So it is, O Lord, so it is, O Well-Gone, enormous would that collection of atomic quantities be! And why? If, O Lord, there had been an enormous collection of atomic quantities, the Lord would not have called it an 'enormous collection of atomic quantities'. And why? What

was taught by the Tathāgata as a 'collection of atomic quantities', as a no-collection that was taught by the Tathāgata. Therefore is it called a 'collection of atomic quantities'.

And what the Tathāgata taught as 'the world system of 1,000 million worlds', that he has taught as a no-system. Therefore is it called 'the world system of 1,000 worlds'. And why? If, O Lord, there had been a world system, that would have been a case of seizing on a material object, and what was taught as 'seizing on a material object' by the Tathāgata, just as a no-seizing was that taught by the Tathāgata. Therefore is it called 'seizing on a material object'.—The Lord added: And also, Subhūti, that 'seizing on a material object' is a matter of linguistic convention, a verbal expression without factual content. It is not a dharma nor a no-dharma. And yet the foolish common people have seized upon it.

31. And why? Because whosoever would say that the view of a self has been taught by the Tathāgata, the view of a being, the view of a living soul, the view of a person, would he, Subhūti, be speaking right?—Subhūti replied: No indeed, O Lord, no indeed, O Well-Gone, he would not be speaking right. And why? That which has been taught by the Tathāgata as 'view of self', as a no-view has that been taught by the Tathāgata. Therefore is it called 'view of self'. The Lord said: It is thus, Subhūti, that someone who has set out in the Bodhisattva-vehicle should know all dharmas, view them, be intent on them. And he should know, view and be intent on them in such a way that he does not set up the perception of a dharma. And why? 'Perception of dharma, perception of dharma,' Subhūti, as no-perception has this been taught by the Tathāgata. Therefore is it called 'perception of dharma'.

32. And finally, Subhūti, if a Bodhisattva, a great being had filled world systems immeasurable and incalculable with the seven precious things, and gave them as a gift to the Tathāgatas, the Arhats, the fully Enlightened Ones,—and if, on the other hand, a son or daughter of good family had taken from this Prajñāpāramitā, this discourse on Dharma, but one stanza of four lines, and were to bear it in mind, demonstrate, recite and study it, and illuminate it in full detail for others, on the strength of that this latter would beget a greater heap of merit, immeasurable and incalculable. And how would he illuminate it? So as not to reveal. Therefore is it said, 'he would illuminate'.

As stars, a fault of vision, as a lamp,
A mock show, dew drops, or a bubble,
A dream, a lightning flash, or cloud,
So should one view what is conditioned.

THE SECOND CONCLUSION

Thus spoke the Lord. Enraptured, the Elder Subhūti, the monks and
nuns, the pious laymen and laywomen, and the Bodhisattvas, and the
whole world with its Gods, men, Āsuras and Gandharvas rejoiced in
the Lord's teaching.[14]

Chapter One

A Strangely Ordinary Beginning

**OUR EVERYDAY LIFE MAY BE PLEASURABLE OR PAINFUL; WILDLY ECSTATIC OR
UNBEARABLY AGONIZING; OR JUST PLAIN DULL AND BORING MUCH OF THE TIME.
BUT IT IS HERE, IN THE MIDST OF ALL THESE EXPERIENCES, GOOD, BAD, AND
INDIFFERENT—AND NOWHERE ELSE—THAT ENLIGHTENMENT IS TO BE ATTAINED**

*Thus have I heard at one time. The Lord dwelt at Śrāvastī, in the Jeta Grove,
in the garden of Anāthapiṇḍika, together with a large gathering of monks,
consisting of 1,250 monks, and with many Bodhisattvas, great beings. Early
in the morning the Lord dressed, put on his cloak, took his bowl, and entered
the great city of Śrāvastī to collect alms. When he had eaten and returned
from his round, the Lord put away his bowl and cloak, washed his feet, and
sat down on the seat arranged for him, crossing his legs, holding his body
upright, and mindfully fixing his attention in front of him.*

This may seem straightforward enough, but it is actually quite an unusual start to a Mahāyāna sūtra. A more standard opening would be an
extravagant description of how the Buddha is sitting in some heavenly
world on a great elaborate lotus throne surrounded not only by monks
and nuns, but by millions upon millions of non-human beings in their
various orders. Even before the Buddha opens his mouth we should
expect all sorts of marvels to occur—like thousands of great golden
flowers called *mandāravas*, as big as cartwheels, floating down from the
sky. And then of course Buddhas and Bodhisattvas are likely to start

arriving from other universes, having heard on some sort of intergalactic Bodhisattva radio that Gautama the Buddha is going to give a discourse.

But here in the *Diamond Sūtra* there is nothing of that, absolutely nothing—no signs, no wonders, no miracles, no lights appearing in the sky, nothing. Everything is simple, natural, ordinary—even prosaic. All we see is a group of huts in somebody's estate a few miles out of the city, and yellow-robed monks, some of them occupying the huts, and some no doubt just camping out under the trees. The Buddha leaves his hut early in the morning and walks into the city, there to move quietly from door to door with his begging-bowl, just receiving whatever is given—a few handfuls of rice, a little curry—and then retiring to the shade of a grove of trees to eat, before slowly and mindfully walking back to his hut. After he has rested for a while we see him going outside again to meditate, and in the cool of the evening the disciples gathering around, just waiting and listening.

It is a very subdued setting, of almost Doric simplicity, for the astounding discourse that follows. So do we skip over this uninspiring bit at the beginning and get to grips with the meat of the sūtra straightaway? By no means. If we do, we miss half the significance of the whole thing. Every word in a sūtra means something (as was the case with the *Heart Sūtra*). What seems to be the frame is part of the picture. So what is the compiler of this teaching about the Perfection of Wisdom, about *śūnyatā*, about Bodhisattvas, trying to tell us here? Why does he appear to want to have us believe that we are settling down to a meticulous account of another unsensational day in the life of Gautama the Buddha, as recalled by his attendant Ānanda?

Some light is shed on this question, and on the immense difference in character among the sūtras of the Buddhist tradition, by a certain Zen saying: 'At the beginning of your spiritual practice mountains are mountains and trees are trees. As you progress further on the Path mountains are no longer mountains and trees are no longer trees. But at the conclusion of your Buddhist career, on becoming Enlightened, mountains are once more mountains, trees again simply trees.'

In the suttas of the Pāli Canon, everything is down-to-earth. Mountains are mountains, trees are trees, and the Buddha appears as an ordinary human teacher, tidily putting away his bowl and cloak, and surrounded by quite nondescript disciples. Nothing very wonderful happens. They go for alms. They mend their robes. But no doubt the teaching is profound and important enough.

Then come the classic Mahāyāna sūtras—the *Vimalakīrti-nirdeśa*, the *White Lotus Sūtra*, the *Sūtra of Golden Light*—where, if we are on this Earth at all, it is an Earth transfigured almost beyond recognition, an Earth where all sorts of wonderful things happen. Mountains are no longer mountains and trees are no longer trees.

But with a third type of sūtra we are back with mountains that are mountains and trees that are trees. Everything is very ordinary again because the *un*ordinariness of things doesn't need underlining: 'How wonderful, how extraordinary,'—as another Zen saying goes—'I draw water and I carry fuel.'

This is surely what all the prosaic comings and goings in the garden of Anāthapiṇḍika are about. In the light of the teaching to come, they are surely intimating that ordinary life *is* Enlightenment; Enlightenment *is* ordinary life. Reality is to be experienced in the midst of ordinary life, because there is nowhere else to experience it. If you are to experience reality anywhere it can only be here; if you are to experience reality at any time it can only be now. Don't let your attention be diverted to higher heavenly realms—yes, the symbolism is very beautiful, it is very mean-ingful, but don't misunderstand it. It is *here* that we have to realize; it is *now* that we have to see. The ordinary is wonderful as it is; to add wonders and supernormal happenings would just be gilding the lily. It would be as if, to draw attention to the fact that you have a nose and that it is a wonderful organ, you were to paint it bright red. To someone who really understands what a wonderful organ the nose is, this sort of decoration is in no way necessary.

You don't have to get away from the conditioned in order to realize the Unconditioned. In its depth, the conditioned 'is' the Unconditioned. 'Form is emptiness and emptiness is form', as the *Heart Sūtra* says. Our everyday life may be pleasurable or painful; wildly ecstatic or unbearably agonizing; or just plain dull and boring much of the time. But it is here, in the midst of all these experiences, good, bad, and indifferent—and nowhere else—that Enlightenment is to be attained. This is what the introduction to the sūtra is trying to tell us. And in a sense it is the message of the whole sūtra.

So in this sūtra we are not in some heavenly realm or remote Buddha-field; we are firmly on this Earth, on the historical plane, in the workaday world. Other Perfection of Wisdom sūtras may be expounded by mythological or archetypal Bodhisattvas who cannot be said to have existed, historically speaking; in the case of the *Heart Sūtra* it is Avalokiteśvara, and in other Perfection of Wisdom sūtras you get

Mañjuśrī. But the *Diamond Sūtra* features a dialogue between two definitely historical characters: Gautama the Buddha and Subhūti, one of his disciples.

As for the audience, although Mahāyāna convention (and, Conze suggests, a later scribe) brings a lot of extras on at the end—'the whole world with its gods, men, asuras, and gandharvas'—to rejoice in the teaching, the *Diamond Sūtra* opens to a very select gathering of highly developed beings: 1,250 monks who, with the possible exception of Ānanda, can be assumed to be Arhats, and 'many Bodhisattvas'. Admittedly the Bodhisattvas add a touch of the Mahāyāna, but they are not named or described—we are not to be treated to visions of jewelled head-dresses and lotus-thrones.

This emphasis on the unspectacular continues with the description of the Buddha himself. In the larger Perfection of Wisdom sūtras we find him fixing his attention on the breath and entering 'the king of all *samādhis*', which he miraculously sustains throughout his discourse— the implication being that the Buddha's teaching proceeds from a higher state of consciousness, indeed from Enlightened consciousness. But the *Diamond Sūtra* eschews any suggestion of this sort. The Buddha is seen just 'mindfully fixing his attention in front of him'. Being undistracted either by what was around him or by wandering thoughts or doziness, his mind would perhaps naturally have gathered around the breathing process and his concentration would have deepened, but the compiler of the sūtra says nothing about 'the king of all *samādhis*'. He deliberately sets aside the precedent he has been set by earlier works in order to stress, we must once more assume, that nothing extraordinary is going on here.

As this brief introduction evidently represents the historical circumstances under which the Buddha taught, there is another point to be made. Obviously enough, the Buddha did not hire a hall when he wanted to give a talk. He delivered his discourses in the open air. In fact, he and his disciples lived outside most of the time. For nine months of the year they wandered about on foot from place to place, through forests, across rivers, and over mountains, taking their time, resting and meditating under trees, and calling at villages to teach and beg for food. Only in the rainy season did they stay indoors. And 'indoors' meant not a house, or even a monastery, but a cave or some kind of hut. There they would stay with their three robes and a bowl and perhaps a needle and a water strainer—no mortgage or telephone, no television, no refrigerator, no car, no newspaper, no books, no *Diamond Sūtra*.

Life was simpler than it is perhaps possible for us even to imagine—and thinking was simpler too. Great truths were surely more easily apprehended by such uncluttered, undistracted minds. We need not feel discouraged by this, or persuade ourselves that it was easy to develop transcendental wisdom then, and impossible now. We just have to realize how many factors have arisen between us and Enlightenment since the Buddha's day, factors which are not elements of normal human existence, but rather of a highly artificial way of life.

The opening of the sūtra raises the question of authenticity. It clearly purports to be the word of the Buddha as heard by Ānanda, to the extent of reproducing the formulaic expression 'Thus have I heard at one time,' the seal of authenticity for suttas throughout the Pāli Canon. All other evidence, however, suggests that the sūtra is a relatively late production of the *Prajñāpāramitā* tradition. If it were to be composed today we would call it a forgery, but as it is, it joins a distinguished company under the heading of pseudonymous works—works attributed to certain famous people that could not possibly have written them. The *Apocrypha* of the Bible are obviously pseudonymous but so also are the four Gospels, which were written not by Matthew, Mark, Luke, and John but by their respective disciples, who recorded the traditions that had come down to them as best they could, and therefore in good faith attributed their own writings to the original apostles.

The idea of literary property is rather modern. Marxist historians do not claim that their own books and articles are actually the work of Marx himself. Freudian psychologists put their own names to their writings even though Freud might be the *fons et origo* of their work. When Nietzsche entitled one of his books *Thus Spake Zarathustra*, he was not suggesting that the ancient Iranian sage of the title was actually responsible in any way for the content. The work is what we would call a literary fiction. In ancient times, however, teaching which belonged to a particular tradition was quite naturally ascribed to the originator of that tradition rather than to the person we would call the author. Many ancient writers seem to have genuinely believed that they were mere scribes or amanuenses.

This, indeed, must have been the attitude of the original compiler of the *Diamond Sūtra*. He must have been a man deeply imbued with the Perfection of Wisdom teachings, and no doubt he believed that they were originally taught by the Buddha. Perhaps he felt guided to write his own version of them by the inspiration of the Buddha, or maybe his spiritual teacher suggested to him that the existing records of the teachings were so detailed that there was a need for a simpler version stressing the main points. The compiler would have seen his task as simply to put the teachings of the sūtras in another form. The idea that he had compiled an original work and then deliberately passed it off as the word of the Buddha would never have occurred to him.

It is perhaps difficult for us to enter into this state of mind because we attach so much importance to originality, but things like copyright agreements were quite foreign to the thinking of people in ancient times. Wisdom wasn't anybody's property. If it could be said to belong to anybody, it belonged to the original teacher, which meant a book might well be signed with the name of the originator of the whole tradition even though it had been written by someone else on the basis of their personal understanding of that tradition. Of course, we cannot rule out an element of wishful thinking in this convention, and even, as time went on, a certain awareness that something was being passed off as the teaching of an ancient sage that was not really his and was possibly even at variance with his original teaching. Nonetheless it is clear from this convention that self-effacement was considered a virtue, and originality—that is, as a deliberate policy rather than as a by-product of being truly yourself—was not.

After implying that it is a record of Ānanda's memory of the Buddha's teaching in the standard way, the sūtra goes on to tell us that 'early in the morning the Lord dressed, put on his cloak, took his bowl, and entered the great city of Śrāvastī to collect alms.' According to the Vinaya there are three ways in which a monk can obtain food: by going on his alms round, by accepting invitations to the houses of the laity, and by allowing the laity to bring food to the vihara. We are told that on the occasion of the first turning of the wheel of the Dharma, while the Buddha was teaching two of the first five disciples, the other three went off to collect alms for the whole party, which shows that there were times when other monks went and begged on the Buddha's behalf, but the Buddha's usual practice, as on this occasion, seems to have been to go himself.

WHY DOES A BUDDHA MEDITATE?

Having eaten, we are told, the Buddha sits down to meditate. But why, if he has already attained Enlightenment, does a Buddha meditate? A Hīnayāna answer would be that he wanted to set a good example. If we go back to that archaic text the *Udāna*, however, we do find an occasion on which the Buddha just ups and goes off into the forest for several months without telling anybody, to get away from all the hustle and bustle of being the Buddha.[15] What this perhaps emphasizes is that although when one is Enlightened there is no 'need' to practise, what we think of as practice is in fact the natural activity of being Enlightened. Nirvāṇa can in no way be a static 'condition'. It is simply the last perceivable point on an infinite spiral towards absolutely unimaginable dimensions beyond. You never go beyond training.

This point may be explicated in specifically Mahāyāna terms. The Mahāyāna pointed out that affirmation is unthinkable without negation. Nirvāṇa therefore exists only in relation to saṃsāra: thus it is dependent, thus conditioned, and thus empty. All things, conditioned or Unconditioned, are empty, and therefore not different from one another. In this way the Mahāyāna asserts not only the emptiness of all *dharmas* but also the sameness of all *dharmas*: *sarvadharmasamatā*. Since it is ultimately impossible to discriminate between saṃsāra and nirvāṇa it follows that there can be neither abandonment of saṃsāra nor attainment of nirvāṇa. If on the attainment of Enlightenment one ceased to practise, that would imply that one was distinguishing between attainment and non-attainment, in which case one could hardly be Enlightened. The Buddha did not have the kind of dualistic attitude which would lead him to think 'Well, now I'm there—no more spiritual practice for me.' He was there, and he practised. The crucial corollary of this as far as we are concerned is that we are, from the very beginning, Enlightened. If it is to avoid being dualistic and thus self-contradictory, this knowledge carries with it the imperative to practise.

Then many monks approached to where the Lord was, saluted his feet with their heads, thrice walked round him to the right, and sat down on one side.

It was generally understood in India that out of respect for the teacher you didn't sit directly in front of him—this would have been considered perhaps a little presumptuous, a little lacking in modesty. In Theravāda countries today it is still considered more polite and decent, especially in the case of women, to adopt a sideways kneeling posture rather than directly facing an image of the Buddha. Significantly, the Vajrayāna flouted this convention. In the context of initiation you are supposed to sit directly in front of the teacher, even to look at the teacher—even to look the teacher in the face—quite immodest behaviour from the Hīnayāna and even the Mahāyāna point of view. There is a more intensely personal link or communication between teacher and disciple in the Vajrayāna. It is less, you might almost say, institutionalized.[16]

IF THE TEACHING HERE IS PURELY TRANSCENDENTAL HOW CAN IT BE MERITED BY ANY AMOUNT OF SKILFUL BEHAVIOUR? IT COMES AS AN ABSOLUTE FAVOUR, A FREE GIFT

At that time the Venerable Subhūti came to that assembly, and sat down. Then he rose from his seat, put his upper robe over one shoulder, placed his right knee on the ground, bent forth his folded hands towards the Lord, and said to the Lord: 'It is wonderful O Lord, it is exceedingly wonderful, O Well-Gone, how much the Bodhisattvas, the great beings, have been helped with the greatest help by the Tathāgata, the Arhat, the Fully Enlightened One. It is wonderful, O Lord, how much the Bodhisattvas, the great beings, have been favoured with the highest favour by the Tathāgata, the Arhat, the Fully Enlightened One.

When Subhūti arrives both his shoulders are in fact covered, so it is not so much that he puts his robe over one shoulder as that he uncovers one shoulder before making his salutation. Even now the custom not only in Theravādin countries but also in Tibet is that monks take the upper robe or cloak off the right shoulder and bring it round under the arm and over the opposite shoulder before they make their salutation to the Buddha or to their teacher. (The right shoulder may still be covered, especially in Tibet, but not with that particular robe.)

With this gesture of the most profound respect Subhūti demonstrates, even before he speaks, the primary qualification he needs for his role in the sūtra. He shows that he is receptive. Receptivity is the first requisite of the disciple, and indeed of anyone who wants to learn anything. We can be anything else we like: we can be wicked, we can be stupid, we can be full of faults, we can backslide.... In a sense, it doesn't matter. But we must be spiritually receptive; we have to be willing and ready to learn. When we know that we do not know, everything is possible.

Subhūti then has the grace to begin by thanking the Buddha, paying tribute to what he has done in the past, and rejoicing in what he has already given, before asking for further teaching. This kind of gratitude is the second great quality we need in approaching the Dharma. Subhūti does not launch straight into asking his first question; his opening words to the Buddha are words of praise and appreciation. He appreciates the help that the Buddha has given his disciples, specifically the great Bodhisattvas, and he realizes that the disciples have been 'favoured'.

We can probably be justified in taking Conze's translation literally here and interpreting the word favour to mean something essentially *un*-deserved or *un*earned. If the teaching is purely transcendental, how can it be merited by any amount of skilful behaviour? It comes as an absolute favour, a free gift. It is nothing which can actually be deserved under the law of karma because it belongs to another order, another dimension. Nothing conditioned can deserve the Unconditioned. The Buddha's compassion simply overflows without any consideration of merit. At a much lower level, the best way to act as a spiritual friend to someone is often to help them with their difficulties, but help in this sense is not always the most appropriate response to the situation. Sometimes a person may not need any help—they may be quite healthy and happy— but they might benefit from being 'favoured', being offered a glimpse of something beyond the problem-orientated mode, something altogether beyond their present level.

Subhūti shows us how to approach the *Diamond Sūtra*. We have to preserve a sense of wonder at the *gift* of the Dharma. Without this sense of wonder it is easy for familiarity to breed, if not contempt, at least indifference or carelessness. We may begin by reading Buddhist texts with great interest and enthusiasm, but if we are not careful, after a while the wonder wears off, the enthusiasm dies down. We need to watch out for this natural tendency to devalue what we have, and resolve never to lose sight of how valuable an opportunity we have been given.

Subhūti addresses the Buddha as the 'Well-Gone'. The Sanskrit is *sugata*—happily gone, gone to the happy state of nirvāṇa. In medieval India, Hindus often called Buddhists not only followers of the Buddha, but also *saugatas*, followers of the *Sugata*. It is something of a historical accident, in fact, that Jains, the followers of the *Jina*, 'the Conqueror', are not called Buddhists, and Buddhists not called Jinists. Their *Jina* is also called Buddha, just as our Buddha is also called *Jina*. So it is quite by chance that the title *Sugata* did not finally stick. If it had, we would be known now as Sugatists—or even 'Happies'!

The 'great beings'—*mahāsattvas*—who Subhūti says have been helped and favoured are generally understood to be Bodhisattvas who have attained the eighth *bhūmi*,[17] although this is perhaps a more precise later usage. Having attained the eighth *bhūmi*, they are 'irreversible'—that is, they are no longer liable to fall back from that level. At this stage of the path the Bodhisattva renounces the prospect of individual nirvāṇa, which is now within reach, in favour of full Enlightenment for the sake of all sentient beings. He represents the spiritual ideal on an unlimited or cosmic scale—it really becomes difficult to think of the Bodhisattva as an individual in the ordinary sense at this level.

'Those who have set out on the Bodhisattva-vehicle' presumably means those who fall short of irreversibility, either those who are simply Bodhisattvas of the Path or perhaps those who have not yet attained even the first of the *bhūmis*.

How then, O Lord, should a son or daughter of good family, who have set out in the Bodhisattva-vehicle, stand, how progress, how control their thoughts?'

After these words the Lord said to the Venerable Subhūti: 'Well said, well said, Subhūti! So it is, Subhūti, so it is, as you say! The Tathāgata, Subhūti, has helped the Bodhisattvas, the great beings with the greatest help, and he has favoured them with the highest favour. Therefore, Subhūti, listen well, and attentively! I will teach you how those who have set out in the Bodhisattva-vehicle should stand, how progress, how control their thoughts.' 'So be it, O Lord', replied the Venerable Subhūti and listened.

Subhūti asks how the son or daughter of good family 'stands'. How do we become firmly established in our basic aspirations, and remain faithful to our original goal? And how do we progress in our specific spiritual practices? But there is also a question we might be tempted to ask of Subhūti. Are only those people with the right background—sons and daughters of good family—eligible to travel in the 'Bodhisattva-vehicle'? Obviously not. The Buddha allowed no caste distinctions to operate within the Sangha, and refused to observe them in any way whatsoever.

On the other hand, although *kulaputra* can also mean someone of 'a good spiritual endowment' (Conze), traditional Buddhism seems to have regarded it as being advantageous to have a good social position even from a spiritual—or at least religious—standpoint. A good education may help to secure a reasonable intellectual understanding of Buddhism, which can be particularly useful in the early stages of one's spiritual career. It definitely makes communicating the Dharma easier too. Above all, it gives self-confidence, which is helpful psychologically and even spiritually. Ex-Untouchable Buddhists in India are noticeably lacking in social confidence simply because of their lowly social origins. They have difficulty in dealing with government officials even though some of them are now government officials themselves. In this country too there are those who are quite at ease with people like bank-managers, while others are nervous and hesitant. The other side of the coin, the 'near-enemy' of confidence, particularly perhaps for high-caste Hindus, is arrogance, a great spiritual handicap.

Chapter Two

THE ESSENTIAL REVOLUTION

IN REALITY THINGS CAN BE PERCEIVED NEITHER AS CHOPPED UP INTO MUTUALLY EXCLUSIVE BITS, NOR AS ABSORBED INTO A UNITY

The Lord said: Here, Subhūti, someone who has set out in the vehicle of a Bodhisattva should produce a thought in this manner: 'As many beings as there are in the universe of beings, comprehended under the term "beings" —egg-born, born from a womb, moisture-born, or miraculously born; with or without form; with perception, without perception, and with neither perception nor non-perception,—as far as any conceivable form of beings is conceived: all these I must lead to Nirvāṇa, into that Realm of Nirvāṇa which leaves nothing behind.'

Talking about 'producing a thought' makes the Bodhisattva sound a bit like a conjuror producing something out of a hat, which gives a false impression of how the thought in question—the thought of Enlightenment, the *bodhicitta*—does in fact arise. 'Should make arise a thought' might be a better way of putting it.

The text proceeds to exhaust the content of the term 'beings' by recourse to a traditional and not exclusively Buddhist enumeration of all the different possible classes of beings, even up to beings that dwell in the realm of neither perception nor non-perception, which in terms of meditative states corresponds to the fourth formless *dhyāna*.

The expression 'miraculously born' can be misleading. People in the West usually think of a miracle as representing the direct intervention of

God into mundane affairs, suspending the operation of natural conditions, but this is not at all the sense in which this kind of birth is 'miraculous'. As Conze rightly notes, miraculous or apparitional birth (that of gods, demons, beings of the *antarābhāva*,[18] and Never-Returners) is said to be much more common than the other modes of birth. Bearing in mind that 'moisture-born' refers to all the kinds of small-scale life-forms that are not subsumed under the other two categories, the 'miraculously-born' make up a class far too numerous to be labelled miraculous under any sensible interpretation of the word.

Conze offers 'apparitional birth' as an alternative, but this suggests something insubstantial or ghost-like, which is clearly not the case here, except perhaps with actual ghosts or *pretas*. The word *aupapattika* literally means 'just appearing' or, better, 'spontaneous'—though not in the sense of being causeless. It really means that these beings appear at a more advanced stage of development than is normal in the case of those born from a womb or an egg. They just appear fully-formed, without going through conception, gestation, infancy, and childhood—but also without being called into existence by some divine miracle. For example, in the *antarābhāva* beings are supposed to appear spontaneously with a fully formed subtle physical body and fully developed subtle sense organs.

'Beings … without perception' is Conze's translation of *asaṁjñā sattva*, the class of devas sometimes known as the unconscious gods who appear in the Pāli scriptures. Presumably these gods are 'unconscious' because they occupy a particular realm but do not direct their attention towards the realm itself as an objectively existing thing, rather in the same way that beings in this world who are absorbed in meditation might not be conscious of the world which they, in a sense, inhabit. The term *asaṁjñā* literally means 'non-perceiving'; it is questionable whether 'unconscious' means quite the same thing. Maybe these beings are just gods who do not take much notice of things.

The Buddha speaks of the Bodhisattva leading all these classes of beings to 'that Realm of Nirvāṇa which leaves nothing behind'. This, the 'nirvāṇa without substratum', is attained by a Buddha upon his *parinirvāṇa*, when his physical body dies. Conze notes, without comment, Candrakīrti's image for this sublime condition: 'A city which, after all the criminal gangs in it have been executed, has now itself been razed to the ground.' This suggests that nirvāṇa is something like Hiroshima after the atom bomb. This represents a kind of brutal nihilism that needs to be questioned even when it comes from the pen of so distinguished a commentator as Candrakīrti. In speaking of the Tathāgata the Buddha said 'It is not to be said of him that he exists after death, does not exist after death, or both, or neither.' So Candrakīrti's simile is quite misleading, although it might be much more apposite if the criminal gangs were all to be converted and the whole city was to become a Pure Land. After all, when we are trying to halt the wheel of conditioned existence, we are also engaged in ascending the spiral of the Unconditioned. That Candrakīrti felt able to use this kind of image at all says a lot for the innate positivity of the Indian people.

> 'And yet, although innumerable beings have thus been led to Nirvāṇa, no being at all has been led to Nirvāṇa.' And why? If in a Bodhisattva the notion of a 'being' should take place, he could not be called a 'Bodhi-being'. 'And why? He is not to be called a Bodhi-being, in whom the notion of a self or of a being should take place, or the notion of a living soul or of a person.'

Self is *ātman*, being is *sattva*, living soul is *jīva*, and person is *pudgala*; all these terms could refer to human beings. As a result of one's encounters with so-called beings, one forms the notion—the concept—of an objectively existing, unchanging, identifiable, separate self or being or living soul or person. The notion is a wrong one inasmuch as it does not correspond to the facts of the situation, whether in the Hīnayāna terms of *dharmas* or the Mahāyāna terms of *śūnyatā*. It is not that the facts of one's experience are in question. 'The notion of a being' is simply one's wrong interpretation of the facts of one's experience.

This is the fundamental insight of the *Diamond Sūtra*: that beings do not exist; *we* do not exist. This is easy enough to say, of course, but a staggering idea actually to take on board. We are being told that our present mode of perception, of consciousness, even of being, which tells us 'I am I', is false. We may be able to take in the idea that beings do not exist, that even we do not exist, on an intellectual level, but can we take it seriously enough? Are we prepared for this blotting out—as it would appear to be—of our present existence? Are we prepared for what is sometimes called spiritual death? If we are not, if there is no spiritual death, then there can be no spiritual rebirth.

If we *are* prepared to expose ourselves to this radical insight, we will find that it is worked out in the sūtra through various fields of application. According to Dr Conze, the Buddha establishes the realization of emptiness according to three perspectives: ontological, psychological, and logical.

Ontologically, the doctrine of emptiness means that no such thing as a separate entity exists. There is nothing which is really and truly and absolutely separate and itself. We are in the habit of chopping reality into bits, distinguishing one thing from another. This is this; that is that. Then we start preferring this to that; we choose this rather than that; we stick to this and reject that—which is where we go wrong (and this is not just the *Diamond Sūtra*, but the whole of the Buddhist tradition speaking). It is not that we are meant to see things as 'one' exactly, reducing all difference to unity, or somehow blotting out the difference. It is rather a question of seeing things as being in some way interfused.

For an illustration of this idea we may turn to the *Gaṇḍavyuha Sūtra*, in which the reality of things is compared to the intersecting of beams of light. If you have rays of light of all different colours, flashing in all directions, crossing and criss-crossing, what you find, obviously, is that one beam of light does not obstruct any of the others. They all shine through one another. They are not lost or merged in one great light—they all maintain what you might call their separate individualities—but they offer no obstruction to penetration by other individualities. They are all mutually interpenetrating. In reality things can be perceived neither as being chopped up into mutually exclusive bits, nor as being absorbed into a unity. When we see into reality we see all things as interfusing and interpenetrating one another. There is both individuality and unity—neither obstructing the other—at the same time.

Even the traditional categories of Buddhist thought cannot be excluded from this way of perceiving the world. Buddhist terms like 'the Buddha', the 'Bodhisattva', 'merit', 'wisdom', and so on, do not refer to any fixed or absolute or final entities. They are just devices, *upayas*, to help us on our way; their value is provisional, not ultimate or absolute. This, in the end, is how the ontological application of the doctrine of emptiness of self, *śūnyatā*, works out.

Psychologically, the doctrine of *śūnyatā* means not being attached anywhere, not standing or settling down anywhere, not depending or leaning on anything, or taking anything as a support. After all, if entities do not exist, there is nothing to lean on anyway. The problem is that it is very hard to realize this, because it is not what we actually want. We want to depend on something; we want to settle down somewhere, anywhere, particularly as we get older. This desire is not just material, but psychological, even spiritual. We want to find some cosy corner where we can be all warm and secure, like a little bird in its nest high up in a big tree, and say 'Well, here I am, fixed up; I've settled down; nothing can shake me.' But of course it can't be quite like that. It just isn't possible. Sooner or later, however safe and secure everything seems to be, our supports are going to be rudely pulled out from under us.

There is only one way out of the suffering that is built into the system in this way, according to the *Diamond Sūtra*, and that is to develop an attitude which does not settle down, which does not try to establish itself anywhere, which is free and flowing and spontaneous. This does not mean being impulsive or irresponsible; it is the spontaneity that arises freely and creatively out of a realization of the truth of emptiness.

Finally, from the standpoint of logic, the doctrine of *śūnyatā* shows rational thought being transcended. The basis of traditional logic, both in the East and in the West, is the Law of Contradiction, which says that a thing cannot be A *and* not A at the same time—that is, it can't be, say, both black and not black. The *Diamond Sūtra*, however, says 'Oh yes it can. A thing is itself because it is not itself; it is what it is because it is not what it is. It is A because it is not A. It is black because it is not black.' Logic is abrogated; reason breaks down, unable to cope with ultimate reality. Reason is very useful indeed in the affairs of everyday life, but it is of no use at all where ultimate reality is concerned. If we want to soar through the void, we must leave reason and logic far behind—not easy to accept, perhaps, but all too easy to misunderstand. There is no question of submerging into irrationality. Transcendental wisdom develops through the transcending of logic, through rising above reason, not through sinking below it.

The central and crucial paradox of the *Prajñāpāramitā* is here at the very start of the *Diamond Sūtra*. The Buddha says that the Bodhisattva should firstly resolve to guide all beings to nirvāṇa, and secondly realize that in reality no being exists. There is clearly a contradiction here—and it is clearly *meant* to be a contradiction—and it is meant to express the very essence of the Bodhisattva Ideal.

WE MAY START ON THE BODHISATTVA PATH NOT BY THINKING 'I SHALL LEAD ALL THESE BEINGS TO NIRVANA', BUT BY RESOLVING 'I SHALL TRY TO SEE THESE BEINGS AS THEY ARE IN THEMSELVES, AND SEE WHAT THEIR NEEDS ARE; RATHER THAN CONSTANTLY LOOKING TO SEE HOW THEY CAN FULFIL MY OWN NEEDS.' THIS IS THE ESSENTIAL REVOLUTION CALLED FOR BY THE BODHISATTVA VOW

Usually we think of compassion as being directed towards individuals, or perhaps groups of individuals. We see particular people suffering, and then our compassion, or at least our pity, arises. But the Bodhisattva does not perceive individuals. The Bodhisattva perceives the truth of selfless-ness, the truth of non-individuality, the truth of *śūnyatā*, or emptiness. It is out of this perception, this realization, that the compassion of the Bodhisattva arises—a compassion which we perceive, or interpret, as compassion for individuals.

But how does a Bodhisattva, without any notion of beings, actually go about leading them to nirvāṇa? The simple answer is that he or she doesn't—or rather that he or she only appears to do so. For example, on a much more ordinary level, you might see somebody helping others, being generally useful, thoughtful, and considerate, and conclude that this person has a definite idea of being kind and decent towards other people. But they might have no such notion at all. It might just be their nature to behave in this way. In the same way, on another level entirely, Bodhisattvas help people freely and spontaneously, without having any definite notion of helping people—without indeed having *any notion of people at all*.

Bodhisattvas are essentially free of self-consciousness in the less posi-tive sense of the term. The Bodhisattva Vow has permeated through to the very depths of their being, and fulfilling it is simply what they like to do. From their point of view there is nothing special about it. Indeed, in the sense in which people who have not taken it understand the Vow, there is no need for it. It is the arising of the bodhicitta—the Will to Enlightenment—which defines a Bodhisattva. Then the bodhicitta finds expression in the taking of the Vow and in the practice of the Six *Pāramitās*.[19] The Vow i̱s a starting point, but it isn't something the Bodhisattva leaves behind in the way that a literal starting point is left behind. It's a thread that runs through the whole of the Bodhisattva's career. A non-Bodhisattva may have to think quite consciously and deliberately about taking the Vow, but this is just preparing the ground for the actual taking of the Vow, which happens quite spontaneously.

Not only is the Vow in no way a vow in the ordinary sense of the word. It is also difficult to think of it as the act of an individual as such. A vow to lead all beings to nirvāṇa—and in a matter as solemn as a vow we cannot but take the words used absolutely literally—does seem a large responsibility for one individual to take upon him- or herself. Beings of the past, the present, and the future, beings of all kinds, on all levels, of all degrees—that's an awful lot of beings to lead to nirvāṇa. Can this tremendous responsibility really rest on the shoulders of one individual? And if again we are to understand the Vow, as we must, literally, then we have to imagine our Bodhisattva undertaking a task that innumerable other Bodhisattvas have already entered upon—yet the Vow is not 'I shall collaborate with all Bodhisattvas in leading all beings to Enlightenment.' How can it be possible for any one individual Bodhisattva to fulfil his or her vow to lead all beings to nirvāṇa unless all the other Bodhisattvas stand aside, unless they stop being Bodhisattvas?

We can begin to solve this, perhaps, by trying not to take too literally the idea of the Bodhisattva as an individual taking personal responsibility for the task. It is rather that the Bodhisattva perceives that the highest need of all beings is Enlightenment. This is his or her motivation. The Bodhisattva sees the mess people are in and perceives that the only real remedy for their plight is a spiritual remedy, and that the only person really qualified to help them is a Bodhisattva. The Bodhisattva identifies with this need of beings so clearly and completely that all his or her energies become devoted to its fulfilment; there is no energy left over to consider 'I am doing this.' It is as if you were present at some terrible accident and seeing a lot of people badly injured you were simply to throw yourself wholeheartedly into the practical business of helping them.

Furthermore, it is not really possible to think of the Bodhisattva's Vow as an event separate from the arising of the bodhicitta. It might be said that the bodhicitta can be 'subdivided' into two aspects: on the one hand the Vow—the Bodhisattva's consciousness of the goal and his or her determination to realize it—and on the other hand the actual steps to be taken for its realization—which means the practice of the Six *Pāramitās*. The Vow is an expression of the partially arisen bodhicitta functioning within a particular framework, or taking a particular direction according to the needs of sentient beings. At the same time—in a sense analogously—it has a disciplinary function, at least at first, when the bodhicitta is still relatively weak and embryonic. So it is at once expressive of the bodhicitta in a particular manner and supportive of the further development of the bodhicitta.

The implication of this is that the Bodhisattva Vow can be broken—the Bodhisattva giving up being a Bodhisattva—at any point up to the eighth *bhūmi*, when the bodhicitta becomes irreversible. There are various references in the Perfection of Wisdom sūtras to this possibility of losing one's vision, of getting fed up with beings—after all there are an awful lot of them, and they can be very tiresome. There you are trying to save them and lead them to nirvāṇa, and they are simply not interested. They feel more at home wallowing in the miseries of saṁsāra. So it can be quite frustrating being a Bodhisattva. Indeed, according to the scriptures this frustration might get the better of you one day, and lead you to think 'Oh, away with all these beings.' Then—in an instant—the bodhicitta would collapse, and you would sink to the level of the Arhat.

In saying that, of course, we have to remember that by Arhat we mean not the kind of person who would have been called an Arhat in the early days of Buddhism, but the classical Mahayanist conception of the Arhat: one who has seen through the notion of a self to the extent of perceiving that the so-called self consists only of *dharmas*, but has not seen that these *dharmas* are empty. From the Mahāyāna point of view, this subtle sense of self, of being—whether with respect to oneself or to others—only disappears completely at the point of full Enlightenment. Until then there is always going to be some notion of self, howsoever subtle, even for an irreversible Bodhisattva—otherwise there would be no distinction between a Bodhisattva, however advanced, and a *samyak-sambuddha*, a fully Enlightened One.

It is not always easy to step back a little from a text as profound as this and take what it is saying as a practical proposition. In the case of the Bodhisattva Vow we may simply interpret it as being a matter of seeing the needs of beings very clearly and forming a whole-hearted wish to devote ourselves to the fulfilment of those needs. It is a matter of beginning to overcome, or at least becoming more aware of, our almost instinctive, unconscious tendency to see people not in terms of what they need, but in terms of what we need from them—either practically, materially, or psychologically.

A Bodhisattva is galvanized to meet the very highest needs of beings, but we may start on the Bodhisattva path not by thinking 'I shall lead all these beings to nirvāṇa', but by resolving 'I shall try to see these beings as they are in themselves, and see what their needs are, rather than constantly looking to see how they can fulfil my own needs.' This is the essential revolution called for by the Bodhisattva Vow. On top of that it is just a matter of clarifying our vision until we really do perceive that what beings truly need is Enlightenment. But here and now, in our practice of the mettā bhāvanā—the cultivation of universal loving-kindness—we can work at developing goodwill to people irrespective of whether or not they are going to fall in with our own needs, wishes, or values. This is never going to be easy because we naturally feel our own needs much more strongly than we do those of other people. But we can practise thinking about other people's needs—how we can meet them, or if we cannot meet them ourselves, how we can help people to meet their own needs—even when we are also concerned with immediate, objective, legitimate needs of our own.

It is not often that we see people just as themselves rather than as instruments of our own needs, and very rare indeed for us to put ourselves out for other people in a completely disinterested way. We might do it for our own mother or father, friend, lover, or child, but mostly we look after number one. For monks or nuns there is a particular danger in this regard, inasmuch as they have left behind the natural and biological attachments that will draw the ordinary lay-person out of complete selfishness. The danger of the monastic life is well illustrated in the *Mahāvagga* section of the Vinaya, which recounts how the Buddha finds a monk suffering from dysentery and who is neglected by the other monks.[20] When the Buddha asks why the poor fellow is not being looked after, the monks reply 'Lord, he is not useful to us': a dreadful admission. They are duly reprimanded, and even though in the Pāli Canon there is no sort of mention of the Bodhisattva Ideal as such, something like it, or the seeds of it, are clearly implied. 'You have no father and mother to look after you', the Buddha says. As a member of a spiritual community you do not belong to any natural group to the members of which you may look for help simply on account of the ties of blood. The help you give one another can only be motivated by a purely spiritual impulse, a feeling of common membership of a purely spiritual body.

Caring for others on the basis of a spiritual motivation is much more difficult than caring for them out of a sexual or family interest. If your son needs a new pair of shoes, you may well be willing to put off getting yourself a new shirt—and this sort of thing has a maturing effect. So the danger of falling into selfishness and self-preoccupation is much greater for the spiritual community than it is for lay people with all their kith and kin to care for. The advantage of being a monk or nun is of course that you are able to avoid the often unconscious mutual exploitation that so often disguises itself as the caring and meaningful sexual relationship.

There is in fact only one need of one's own that has to be fulfilled before one can preoccupy oneself effectively with the needs of others, and it is not a physical or material need, but simply a matter of emotional positivity and security. We need to appreciate our own worth and feel that it is appreciated by others, to love ourselves and feel that we are loved by others. On this basis we can begin to develop the sensitivity and awareness to appreciate the real needs of others—not only their material needs, or even their educational needs, but their need for an ideal to which they can devote themselves, a spiritual path they can follow. At the same time, the group of others to whom our concern extends can grow to include not only our own family and friends, but people beyond our own kind, race, gender, and even views. It can even include quite different classes of beings.

If we are to make sense of what the *Diamond Sūtra* is saying, having established a preliminary intellectual understanding, we need to keep coming right down to earth. Once we understand that it is desirable that we should devote ourselves to working for the spiritual progress of all beings, and that in order to do this we have got to think in terms of the needs of others rather than our own needs, we still have to go one step further back and realize that we need to get ourselves into a positive enough state to be able to start thinking about the needs of others quite naturally and easily. This is, as it were, the bottom line; and it is a bottom line that many people, and particularly those in the caring professions, might well examine.

We have quite enough on our plate just at this level; the whole question of 'not having a notion of a being' is one that we can probably leave in full faith to the future. In the meantime we may consider that insofar as we have some feeling for others and their needs, we are no longer seeing them as being entirely separate from ourselves, and to that extent we are no longer seeing them—having a notion of them—as beings in the sense of *separate* beings. Such a construction is fair enough to begin with, so long as we are clear that it is a long way—if we are going to take the idea literally—from not having the notion of a being at all.

Chapter Three

THE NATURE OF GIVING

GIVING A GIFT 'UNSUPPORTED' MEANS GIVING WHATEVER IS APPROPRIATE
TO THE SITUATION, EVEN TO THE EXTENT OF SACRIFICING LIFE AND LIMB,
WITH NO MORE SELF-CONSCIOUSNESS THAN THAT OF SOMEONE
PASSING THE SALT ACROSS THE DINNER-TABLE

Moreover, Subhūti, a Bodhisattva who gives a gift should not be supported by a thing, nor should he be supported anywhere. When he gives gifts he should not be supported by sight-objects, nor by sounds, smells, tastes, touchables, or mind-objects.

According to Vasubandhu, who produced an early and authoritative commentary on the *Diamond Sūtra*, giving here is meant to stand for, or embody, all the Six Perfections: giving, morality, patience, vigour, meditation, and wisdom. How might this be so? We may say firstly that by practising morality and patience you give protection and security to other living beings—or at least to a limited number of them—by virtue of the fact that you are not actually assaulting them, or robbing them, or running off with their wives and daughters, or deceiving them, and by virtue of being forbearing with respect to their weaknesses. We may also say that you give protection to others by imparting confidence and inspiration through your own personal practice of morality and patience.

Secondly, you can give the gift of the Dharma only on the basis of practising vigour, meditation, and wisdom (rather than by just handing out uplifting little tracts, say). To give the gift of the Dharma constantly or on an extensive scale does require tremendous energy, and to give it at all is just not possible without some degree of mental clarity, not to speak of insight. So a fair case can be made for presenting giving (*dāna*) as the embodiment of all the Perfections, at least from a certain point of view.

This said, we may usefully remind ourselves of what giving means in its straightforward sense. The Mahāyāna was quite concerned at one stage with the question of wealth in this regard, inasmuch as it was thought hardly possible to practise *dāna pāramitā* if you had no material wealth to distribute. To people who do not have very much to give on the material front it may seem like rather a splendid idea to start giving in more refined ways—giving encouragement, giving one's time, even giving the Dharma—but that level of giving is simply beyond the capability of many people to carry out to any very helpful degree. To be able to give on the ordinary common sense level we do generally need a little spare cash. If we can manage to earn enough from the work we do to give away part of our earnings—without martyring ourselves, of course—this is very often the best way to practise *dāna*.

A Bodhisattva, the Buddha tells Subhūti, should not be supported anywhere. At one level this obviously means that one should practise giving, or indeed any of the Perfections, without thinking of the merit accruing from one's actions. There is a little more to it than that, however. It is not just that Bodhisattvas perform virtuous actions without the slightest impure motive; the point is that they see those actions—and their own merit—as *empty*.

But how do we approach this idea in practice? To be supported means that you are resting on something—either something you can touch, hear, smell, or taste, or an idea, a concept, a mind-object. You are placing your whole weight on it, relying on it, taking it literally, taking it at its face value, placing your whole confidence on it—almost going for refuge to it.[21]

The way to avoid 'being supported' in this way is not to allow our thinking to be totally determined by the immediate subject matter of our perception. We are not being expected to do without concepts of things altogether, but we should not treat those concepts as anything more than provisional. We should *use* concepts but not settle down in them. If we are going to develop this Bodhisattva-like attitude to concepts, we need to make sure that we do not allow our thinking to be ruled by the apparent objects of our perception.

When you are asked a question, you can choose either to reply in terms of the question or to go beyond the terms of the question in answering it; your answer can be limited by the question or not limited by it. The Bodhisattva would not allow the terms of the question to lay down the terms of the reply. In the same way, sense data may be putting questions, saying things, but the Bodhisattva does not allow his or her response to be determined by the sensory input. The Bodhisattva goes 'beyond' it because he or she is bigger than sense data or mind-objects. More simply, suppose you were idly to take a snapshot of a landscape which a great artist had also taken for a subject. The print you got back from the chemist would reproduce that landscape in as precise a way as the chemical process would allow, but the end result would be limited by that process. The artist, on the other hand, would bring himself or herself into the equation, refusing to be limited by appearances, and might well see and portray something more than was 'given'.

Generally speaking the artist needs expertise in representing the appearance of things in order to create an image that transcends appearances. Similarly, the Bodhisattva does not evade rational thought and the questions it raises, but is at the same time prepared to go beyond those questions. We find the same principle at work in the meditation on the six elements,[22] in which, far from denying our involvement with the material world, we in fact minutely examine the various components of our material existence. Our aim in doing this, however, is to realize that we are greater than these components, that our being transcends them (or at least the first *five* elements), and to reassert, so to speak, our original being.

The practice of *dāna pāramitā* is to give as an expression of one's innermost nature. Giving a gift 'unsupported' means giving whatever is appropriate to the situation, even to the extent of sacrificing life and limb, with no more self-consciousness than that of someone passing the salt across the dinner-table. It might almost surprise you if someone were to thank you for giving everything you have, because you are doing nothing special (from your point of view) when you are just (so to speak) being yourself. It would be as though someone were to come up to you after dinner and say 'Thank you for passing the salt.' So we can practise being less deliberately, less self-consciously, less 'heavily' virtuous—not letting our left hand know what our right hand is doing, as Jesus put it. And of course this applies to all the *pāramitās*. We need to understand that the practice of giving, ethics, patience, vigour, meditation, and wisdom is the expression of our own deepest need.

One of the many criticisms that the ancient Egyptians used to have of the ancient Greeks—and in those days the ancient Greeks were decidedly modern, not to say brash—was that they had developed *gymnasia* basically because they were not getting enough exercise in the course of their everyday life. From the Egyptian point of view this amounted to an admission on the part of the Greeks that they were living in an artificial, unhealthy, unbalanced way. The same view may be taken of the practice of religion: if it is not inherent in the way we go about the ordinary daily business of life, there is something amiss. Now you might say that if the Egyptians had been really balanced themselves, they would not have needed temples, but this is to take an inappropriately modern view of the function of temples. For the Egyptians the gods were real, and the temples were simply where they lived and where people served them. In ancient Egypt, to be religious was not a particular style of life, nor was religious activity something to be superimposed upon ordinary life.

This principle is one of the themes of Lao-tzu in his Tao-te-ching. Just as Lao-tzu would call the development of a code of morality a degeneration, so we may look askance at the idea of specifically religious acts. If you have some money and someone else has none, it should be possible to share that wealth between you with no more thought than a flower gives to blooming. Instead, however, there is so often the tendency to practise religion in the manner of—to borrow Dr Johnson's famous, or possibly infamous, image—a dog walking on his hind legs. Trained for years, he probably does it quite well—he probably totters about on his hind legs better than any dog in town, and is a credit to his master—but it remains a highly artificial performance. It is just no use putting our unredeemed doggy nature on its hind legs and stalking along in front of an admiring crowd, thinking 'Well, so this is the spiritual life.' There is no point in making a big thing of being a great Bodhisattva practising great virtue. It is because we have got ourselves into such a profoundly irreligious, unskilful state that we have to think in terms of religion and morality at all.

For, Subhūti, the Bodhisattva, the great being, should give gifts in such a way that he is not supported by the notion of a sign.

'Notion' is a translation of *saṃjñā*, which is one of the five *skandhas*[23], and means in that context something more like 'recognition'. Suppose for instance you were to perceive in the distance something green and of a certain recognizable shape and size, so that you were able to identify it, on the basis of your previous perceptual experience, as a tree. That is *saṁjñā*: not simply perception, but rather the identification of the perception as a perception *of* a particular item. Of course the actual process of perception and recognition is usually so swift as to make it impossible to distinguish between the purely perceptual element and the element of recognition, but moments of ambiguity do occur, especially in unfamiliar surroundings or light conditions, when you can be quite clear what your perception is without being able to label it securely.

So from the point of view of the Pāli Canon *saṁjñā* means 'recognition'. The Mahāyāna, however, points out (much as does Bishop Berkeley) that we do not rest content with mere perception, or perception-cum-identification, but that we mistakenly posit behind what we perceive an actual, definite, fixed entity, to which the particular colour, shape, smell, sound, and touch that we recognize pertain as attributes.

SOMETIMES PEOPLE IMAGINE THAT THERE IS JUST ONE BARRIER BETWEEN US
AND REALITY, A BARRIER BUILT OUT OF LANGUAGE OR SIGNS.
BUT EVEN APART FROM LANGUAGE WE HAVE A PERCEPTION OF THINGS AS THINGS

The Buddhist position is thus essentially a nominalist one. Realism, by contrast, maintains that a tree is more than the sum total of the percepts you experience and interpret as a tree. Buddhism does not quite hold that the tree only exists in your own mind, but it does predicate that even if there were a real tree existing independently of your own, or anyone else's, perceptions, there would be no way of verifying the fact. From the Buddhist perspective therefore, further speculation on the matter is futile.

What we are left with is awareness, and within that awareness or perception a kind of differentiation into opposite poles, one of which can be identified as the object, the other as the subject. Clearly, however, these objects and subjects cannot be looked upon as discrete, separate, and independent. If the object were *really* separate from the subject, how would you be able to perceive it—or even know it was there? Buddhists tend to think not in terms of a world of discrete objects perceived by discrete subjects, but in terms of a world of perception, a world of experience, a world of awareness, luminous and radiant, which here and there darkens, thickens, or coagulates into varying degrees of polarization (though we must guard against realist assumptions as we speak in these terms).

'Being supported by the notion of a sign' is, therefore, relying on a fixed idea. In the case of giving gifts, it amounts to acting in accordance with a fixed idea of what *dāna* is supposed to be. We could relate it to the third fetter, reliance on rules and rituals as ends in themselves:[24] if we do such-and-such then it signifies—it is the sign—that we are practising *dāna*. This way of proceeding is fine as far as it goes, but it is hardly free, spontaneous, creative, or natural in the way that *dāna pāramitā* is.

If we rely on rules and rituals as ends in themselves, we build a barrier between us and reality—and in fact this is a *second* barrier. Sometimes people imagine that there is just one barrier between us and reality, a barrier built out of language or signs. But even apart from language we have a perception of things as things: language just embodies, and in general arises out of, that perception. It is not that if there were no language we would perceive things as they really are. We would still be perceiving *things*, and things are not realities. So there is a *double* barrier between us and reality. Not only do we perceive things; we also use *words* in relation to things, and indeed to beings, and that simply reinforces our view of those things or beings as representing realities.

And why? Because the heap of merit of that Bodhi-being, who unsupported gives a gift, is not easy to measure. What do you think, Subhūti, is the extent of space in the East easy to measure?—Subhūti replied: No indeed, O Lord.—The Lord asked: In like manner, is it easy to measure the extent of space in the South, West or North, downwards, upwards, in the intermediate directions, in all the ten directions all round?—Subhūti replied: No indeed, O Lord.—The Lord said: Even so the heap of merit of that Bodhi-being who unsupported gives a gift is not easy to measure. That is why, Subhūti, those who have set out in the Bodhisattva-vehicle, should give gifts without being supported by the notion of a sign.

So why should the Bodhisattva give without any ulterior motive? This is the question the Buddha asks. The answer he gives himself—because the merit that accrues to the Bodhisattva in this way is immeasurable—is an example of the short-circuiting logic of this sūtra. It is, in a sense, inconsequential. The argument does not develop in a linear manner at all: that you are going to be rewarded with unlimited merit cannot be the motivation for an act essentially characterized as being unspotted by self-interest. Words like 'why', 'therefore', and 'because' appear here like ghosts of a reason-bounded world that this text has left far behind.

Reason is left behind, however, not because it is unnecessary, but because ultimately it has its limitations. There is no devaluation of reason being implied here. The intellect does not have direct access to absolute truth, but at no point does the Perfection of Wisdom suggest that the intellect can be dispensed with. And yet sometimes the impression one gets from Zen, or rather from Western interpreters of Zen, is that one first of all works oneself up into a state of intellectual confusion and then just jettisons it all with the introduction of a droll little Zen story. This is offered as the way the intellect gets into difficulties and the way Zen transcends them. But real dichotomies, real intellectual kōans that bring one to the frontiers of the intellect, need to be distinguished from the sort of mental confusion which is certainly not inherent in the intellect itself— strictly speaking, 'intellectual confusion' is a contradiction in terms—but which arises from playing around with reified concepts.

If you want to see how a real thinker works out his antinomies you must go to Kant. But you don't solve bad metaphysics with irrationalism. If this seems daunting, you have to remind yourself that it is your own intellect that you have to transcend, not Kant's or Nāgārjuna's! The point is that you overrun the positions of reason—you don't retreat from them. It is not as if you can just kick away your intellect because you don't want to have to cope with it any more—if you kick it away, you are kicking the ladder from under you. An Enlightened being is not an intellectual capon. This might all seem quite obvious, but the effects of pseudo-Zen have been wide-ranging and disastrous, so it is perhaps necessary to say it.

GIVING IS INNATE. WE ARE INNATELY VOID, INNATELY PURE, INNATELY GENEROUS. LOOKING BEYOND THE REALM OF INDIVIDUAL PSYCHOLOGY, WE MAY RELEASE OUR INNATE GENEROSITY AT A METAPHYSICAL LEVEL OF BEING WHEN WE ALSO REALIZE OUR INNATE VOIDNESS

Within a traditional Buddhist context, merit (*puṇya*) is thought to be the result of good deeds performed in former lives, and to manifest in terms of your appearance, your health, your complexion, your beauty, the effect you have on other people, the fact that things come easily to you, and so on. Some people seem to be just 'lucky', while others fall over as soon as they set foot outside the door. According to popular Buddhist belief you may actually build up a store of merit for the future. The most effective way of doing this is by making offerings to monks, by feeding them— usually over-feeding them—giving them robes, and performing pujas. A good bhikkhu is regarded in some countries as a sort of merit-making machine—put a rupee in the slot, and out comes a little packet of merit. If you feel that you have a great deal of catching up to do, you may even start constructing monasteries and stupas. *Puṇya* is personified in popular Theravādin Buddhism in the form of the *puṇyadevatā* or 'merit god', a sort of personal guardian angel hovering over you. I doubt whether it is a canonical conception, although there is always the possibility with the Theravāda of an essentially poetic idea being taken literally.

To be fair, the Theravādins are generally not as literalistic as the Brahmins, while the Brahmins in their turn are, as a rule, no match for the Jains when it comes to missing the point in this way. There was an Indian Jain ascetic I heard about once who woke up one day, and decided he'd had enough of being an ascetic. Having accumulated a great deal of merit over the years, he sold it to another ascetic, and set himself up in business with the proceeds.

Putting aside the idea of merit as producing objective consequences for a moment, it is more than feasible that the idea of merit from good deeds performed in this life would have a strong psychological pay-off in terms of building self-confidence. But on a *spiritual* level it means essentially the positive emotional experience that comes to you as a result of living a thoroughly skilful life quite apart from any expectation of future rewards. Merit modifies your being; you become a better person. It is like doing physical exercise: it is not that bigger muscles are your *reward*. You are just left with the natural result of your actions, which is that you have changed; your muscles are bigger. The amount, so to speak, of merit you acquire from giving is related to the degree to which you act without being 'supported anywhere': the more disinterestedly you function, the more positive your emotional state becomes.

A straightforward way to begin this apparently sophisticated practice of responding generously but disinterestedly to a situation—that is, without being determined by that situation—would be to transfer our giving from conventional occasions like Christmas or Mother's Day, when gifts are expected or even demanded of us, to occasions when we can respond to a more genuine and positive desire to give. At the same time, this is not to say that we have to wait for some inner urge to arise before starting to give. If this practice is to work we have to put the objective needs of people before the authenticity or otherwise of our generosity; it is more important that someone who is cold or hungry should get what they need than that we should feel good about giving it to them.

When someone who is not a Bodhisattva gives, however, there will eventually be a reaction. The altruism turns sour, or at least becomes strained, if one is not appreciated; one gets a little resentful, hurt, and disappointed. So then one knows that one is not yet a Bodhisattva. The Bodhisattva experiences no tension of this kind because there is no real experience of giving anything to anyone.

So long as we look upon the Bodhisattva as a fixed, separate individual in the same way that we look upon ourselves, there is clearly going to be no possibility whatsoever of such a being giving gifts in such a way that he or she 'is not supported by the notion of a sign'. The more merit you gain, the less of a separate person there is to collect it; and when you hit the jackpot—infinite merit—there is no one there at all to scoop it up. We are standing in the way of our own accumulation of merit all the time; we only have to get out of the way for the merit to come pouring through.

Giving is innate. We are innately void, innately pure, innately generous. Looking beyond the realm of individual psychology, we may release our innate generosity at a metaphysical level of being when we also realize our innate voidness. If to be a Bodhisattva is natural, to practise *dāna* is natural.

Chapter Four

HOW TO RECOGNIZE A BUDDHA

THE BUDDHA INHERITED SOMETHING OF THE NUMINOUS QUALITY OF
THE ANCIENT FIGURE OF THE 'COSMIC MAN' IN THE MINDS OF PEOPLE WHO THOUGHT
IN TERMS NOT OF EVOLUTION FROM THE APES BUT IN TERMS OF A DIVINE PATTERN
OR ARCHETYPE OF HUMANITY, A SUPERMAN

*The Lord continued: 'What do you think, Subhūti, can the Tathāgata be
seen by the possession of his marks?'—Subhūti replied: 'No indeed, O Lord.
And why? What has been taught by the Tathāgata as the possession of
marks, that is truly a no-possession of no-marks.' The Lord said: 'Wherever
there is possession of marks, there is fraud, wherever there is no-possession
of no-marks there is no fraud. Hence the Tathāgata is to be seen from
no-marks as marks.'*

The basic theme of this chapter is that the Buddha is not to be recognized
by the thirty-two marks which he possesses, even though these distinguishing physical features would be striking and even grotesque enough
to set him very clearly apart from the rest of humanity. But this is not the
conundrum that exercises us immediately. First we must ask what the
Buddha is doing with these thirty-two marks—or to be strictly accurate,
thirty-two major marks and eighty-four minor ones—at all, and where
he gets them from. The traditional answer is that they are the fruit of merit
earned through his practice of the Perfections—or rather the first five of
the Perfections—in his previous lives. If you look at Tibetan thangkas
depicting the Buddha, you will see that he has two haloes, the one round

the body representing the *puṇyasambhāra* or the accumulation of *merit*, and the one around the head symbolizing the *jñānasambhāra* or the accumulation of *wisdom*—wisdom of course being the sixth Perfection.

Looking at this more critically though, the whole idea of the thirty-two marks is much more difficult to fathom. It is put forward in the Pāli Canon as being, so to speak, pre-Buddhistic: learned Brahmins turn up in the Pāli suttas who are well-versed in what the marks consist in, and who immediately recognize them on the Buddha himself. However, you would be hard put to find a reference to these marks in pre-Buddhist Vedic literature; many Brahmins of today have not even heard of them unless through Buddhist texts. So if this idea did once figure within the Brahminical tradition there is virtually no extant record of the fact outside of the Buddhist scriptures.

Mrs Rhys Davids suggests that some of the thirty-two marks seem to have an aesthetic justification, while others have a purely symbolic function. Some of them are also attributes of Agni, the Vedic god of fire. The most fruitful interpretation of them, however, would appear to be that they are left over from the Vedic conception of the 'cosmic man'. This is not some primordial progenitor or original ancestor of the human race, like Adam. It is more like the concept, found in the cabbala, of the *Adam Kadmon*, the heavenly Adam—what you might call the archetype of humanity—which also features in Vedic literature as the *purusha*. In Vedic hymns, for example, the creation of the universe is described in terms of the sacrifice, the dismemberment, of the cosmic or archetypal man (a fairly persistent theme in early myth and legend).

What may well have happened is that some of the attributes of this cosmic man were gathered together into a tradition about a superman, or *mahāpurusha*, and that by the time the Buddha appeared Brahmins were equipped with lists of these thirty-two major marks, but did not know what the ancient Brahmins originally knew about their significance. To gain a thorough understanding of what the thirty-two marks are all about one would probably have to investigate Vedic literature and the whole concept of the *purusha* quite closely.

What we do know is that these mysterious marks came to be associated with the Buddha—or rather were superimposed on him. As a result the Buddha inherited something of the numinous quality of the ancient figure of the cosmic man in the minds of people who thought not in terms of evolution from the apes but in terms of a divine pattern or archetype of humanity, a superman, whose lineaments they aspired, if not exactly to conform to, at least to discover within themselves. From this point of view, the Buddha, in becoming Enlightened, became a sort of model, archetype, or pattern for other human beings—but in a spiritual rather than a mythological sense.

To what extent, however, can the Buddha have been recognizable in any straightforward sense by these marks? There is one obvious reason why a Buddha could not, on the face of it, be recognized solely from the evidence of the thirty-two marks—or even the eighty-four marks—and that is because the same evidence is supposed to be borne on the body of a *cakravartin rāja* or 'universal monarch'. This point is actually made much later on in the sūtra, in chapter 26:

> *The Lord said: If, Subhūti, the Tathāgata could be recognized by his possession of marks, then also the universal monarch would be a Tathāgata. Therefore the Tathāgata is not to be seen by means of his possession of marks.*

The following chapter brings another perspective, the attitude of the Buddha himself, onto this same issue:

> *The Tathāgata could surely not have fully known the utmost, right and perfect enlightenment through his possession of marks.*

The Buddha himself is not going to infer that just because he has the thirty-two marks as a result of previous good deeds he is therefore Enlightened. In other words, he knows the difference between a *cakravartin rāja* and a Buddha—which, no doubt, is only to be expected.

This is logical enough. What might seem a little odd, if by the way, is that a political ruler should come so close to being a Buddha that the two appear to be indistinguishable. They may both be leaders of humankind, but a ruler is ideally concerned with the setting up of external conditions, with encouraging the observance of the ten *kusala dharmas* in society, while a Buddha is predominantly concerned with inciting each individual to make an individual spiritual effort. It is difficult for one person to fulfil both functions—though not, if we follow the Mahāyāna, impossible. In the case of Amitābha and his Pure Land, the same being both sets up the ideal situation and teaches the Dharma within that context. On a more down-to-earth level we can point to the theocracy of Tibet, where the Dalai Lamas are iconically represented both as being Bodhisattvas and as holding in their hands the golden wheel of the *cakravartin rājas*. However, discounting these developments, a pinch of common sense would probably be enough to enable one to note whether the possessor of all thirty-two marks (in some later traditions, great disciples and even Arhats are said to possess a number, though not all, of these marks) appeared as a monarch or as a renunciate.

But even assuming that the Buddha could hardly be mistaken for a ruling prince, it is evident from some episodes that he is not recognized by certain people until his status becomes evident from his teaching. There are some marks, including those which commonly adorn traditional images of the Buddha, like the *ushnīsha* (the 'Bodhic protuberance' on the crown of the head), the curl above the eyebrows, and even the *svastika* on the chest, that might simply give him an unusual and even distinguished aspect amongst the common run of humanity. There are others, for instance arms that reach below the knees, which are a little grotesque, even if symbolically suggestive (the long arm of compassion?). But none of these peculiar deviations from the normal physical features by which we recognize a male member of the human species seems to elicit a double-take or any kind of wonder or surprise in the people he meets. It is sometimes said that the Buddha bears these marks not on his physical body but on his *subtle* body, the astral counterpart of his physical body.

Conze sensibly identifies these marks as attributes of the Buddha's 'glorified body' or *sambhogakāya*. But in distinguishing between the *sambhogakāya*, endowed with marks and perceived with the eye of faith, and the *dharmakāya*, the higher body or aspect of the Buddha's Enlightened mind, which is not endowed with marks and is conceived only with the eye of wisdom, Conze is perhaps being a little too schematic. The doctrine of the *trikāya*, the three bodies of a Buddha, may certainly be expressed in terms of body, speech, and mind—the *nirmānakāya* representing his Enlightened body, the *sambhogakāya* his Enlightened communication, and the *dharmakāya* his Enlightened mind.[25] We need, however, to skirt around any quasi-theosophical idea of there being three separate entities, or three different processes going on. Indeed, there is a fourth *kāya*, the *svabhāvakāya*, which seems to have been developed to furnish a unification of the other three, when it was felt that the three *kāyas* were turning into three Buddhas rather than three *kāyas* of one Buddha.

At the risk of possibly straying into heresy—not that taking this sort of risk is necessarily such a bad thing—we might even find quite a useful parallel for these *kāyas* in the Upanishadic *kośa* system, as expounded in the Taittiriya Upanishad. According to this teaching, a human being consists of layers rather like an onion. First there is the *annamayakośa*, made up of food (i.e. the physical body); then there is the *prāṇamayakośa*, the body made of breath—to speak literally—which means something like energy or vitality, and corresponds to the subtle, or astral body; thirdly there is the *manomayakośa*, the body made of mind (the Buddha himself spoke of a *manomayakāya*); fourthly comes the *prajñāmayakośa*, the body made of wisdom; and finally the *ānandamayakośa*, the body made of bliss. As if Buddhism were recapitulating these *kośas* in the course of its development, the Vajrayāna produced a fifth *kāya*, the body of great bliss, the *mahāsukhakāya*—bliss which has gone through the fires of *śūnyatā*. Although there is this correspondence between *kośa*, sheath, and *kāya*, body, in the Hindu and Buddhist traditions respectively, we might find the term *kośa* the more helpful of the two in this context, in that it suggests differing degrees of externality in our perception of the Buddha nature rather than actually separate bodies.

There is simply no way of inferring that someone is Enlightened, or even that there is such a thing as Enlightenment. There is no way to spot a Buddha

We can now understand how it is that the Buddha is not to be recognized by his marks. It is all a question of looking deeper. The Victorian art critic Ruskin made the point that if we imagine that we know who Apollo is through looking at a statue of him, we are mistaken. Apollo is not that particular shape at all; indeed, the shape of Apollo can never be captured in sensuous terms. Apollo is a significance, a spiritual force, that can never be represented. The more we rely on external appearances, the more likely we are to be misled, although close *attention* to appearances will take our perceptions deeper.

Perhaps the clearest way of coming at this point is through the concept of the 'five eyes'. There were people who were able to set eyes on Gautama the Buddha because they happened to be around at the time; there were people whose *divine eye* may have been sufficiently open for them to see his thirty-two marks; and there were those who saw the Unconditioned in the depths of the conditioned, and could see the Buddha with their *Dharma-eye*. Going even deeper, an Arhat would have seen the greater part of the Buddha's being, so to speak, with his *prajñā eye*. But give up being an Arhat, become a Bodhisattva, become yourself a *samyaksambuddha*, and you will see the Buddha as he actually is, with your Buddha-eye.

At a much lower level, we can apply the same idea of layers to our responses to other people. Clearly, just because someone can put a name to your external appearance does not mean that they recognize you in any real sense. Even in the case of ordinary folk, first impressions can be both deceptive and superficial. In fact, no one is to be known by their marks. It generally takes a good few years and some empathic effort to get to know someone well—except on the rare occasions when there is an immediate rapport, that sense of having known someone all your life when you have only just met them. It is always a question of penetrating deeper and deeper into a person's nature, encountering them at ever deeper and deeper levels. So we may imagine how much more this is the case in encountering the Buddha. The thirty-two marks do not denote wisdom or compassion. Nor is the Buddha to be known even by his discourse, his teaching, in the sense of the words or the ideas through which his teaching is communicated. You can only know the Buddha's mind through your own experience of it, either because you are in direct contact with that mind, or because you yourself develop an Enlightened mind.

It is peculiarly difficult for someone born and brought up in the West to get this category of Buddhahood, or Enlightened humanity, into focus. Conze sets out the challenge presented by the first of the Three Jewels very pithily: 'Our conception of the Buddha must do justice to him as the unconditioned Absolute.' It is all too easy on the one hand to fall short of the mark and think of the Buddha as a more or less exceptional human being (or even as a superman), and on the other hand to over-shoot the mark by deifying him, or imagining him as an incarnation of some higher principle, like Jesus Christ. The reality of Buddhahood consists in a third, quite different category. Of course as a Buddhist you do need to have some accurate, if provisional, conception of what it is that you are aiming at, but this is probably best established not through a lot of subtle theorizing, but by reading the Pāli scriptures to get an impression of the Enlightened human being in action as he goes about his daily business.

Similarly it is a mistake to suggest, as Conze appears to do, that to recognize the Buddha by the possession of the thirty-two marks represents the limited vision of the eye of faith in contrast to the superior and deeper vision of the eye of wisdom. The error arises from giving precedence to the conceptual mode over the imaginative or imaginal approach. It assumes that wisdom finds more adequate expression in concepts than it does in images. It sets wisdom—in the true sense of a direct, intuitive perception of the truth of things—against faith—in the popular sense of an unsophisticated belief in Buddhas and Bodhisattvas as supernormal beings who listen to prayers and confer blessings. But what if you were to visualize the form of the Buddha not simply in terms of the thirty-two marks but in terms of a figure that expresses wisdom and compassion, peace and energy? That sort of image would be an appropriate object for a faith that is the emotional counterpart of wisdom. Where there is true wisdom there will be true faith. At the other end of the scale, in the case, say, of the Buddhism of Sri Lanka, you find quite scholarly, learned monks who have well-developed, sceptical minds, but not much faith or devotion amongst lay people who have a large-hearted but somewhat undiscriminating faith that all too generously embraces Hindu deities and Muslim saints.

The achievement of the Mahāyāna was to bring faith and wisdom together, largely with the help of the Bodhisattva Ideal, although it is an integration that Nāgārjuna, for example, did not manage, even though he is credited with the authorship of devotional hymns as well as the dialectical analysis for which he is celebrated. He seems to have kept his wisdom and devotion in separate compartments. The most successful union of the emotional and intellectual is probably to be found in Śāntideva's *Bodhicaryāvatāra* and in the *Songs of Milarepa*. In a rather different way a strong emotional, archetypal content is fused together with a lofty—not intellectual or even cognitive, but *gnostic*—element in the *Vimalakīrti-nirdeśa*.

In fact, to infer Buddhahood from the evidence of the thirty-two marks might just as well be construed as an intellectual fallacy as an error arising from the devotional approach. One might argue that because a Buddha is one who possesses the thirty-two marks (or whatever other external evidence you like—the ten powers, the eighteen special qualities of a Buddha, and so on) and Gautama fulfils these conditions, therefore Gautama is a Buddha. Such a syllogism is specious, however, because the premise is false. There is simply no way of inferring that someone is Enlightened, or even that there is such a thing as Enlightenment. There is no way to spot a Buddha. You could have been around the Buddha every day, watching him, listening to him, and altogether miss seeing what he was and what he was saying. There were people who did, who got bored with him endlessly going on about the same old stuff. There was at least one monk who was pleased when Gautama died, saying 'Well, he was always telling us to do this and to do that, and not to do this, and not to do that. Now he's dead, at least we'll be free from all that.'

In the end your ability to see the Buddha, to perceive the *mahāprajñā* and the *mahākaruṇā* in the possession of which the Buddha essentially consists, is related to your own spiritual capacity; it depends on an experience of direct, intuitive perception.

The *Diamond Sūtra* says 'What has been taught by the Tathāgata as the possession of marks, that is truly the no-possession of no-marks.' In other words, if you say that a Buddha does not possess marks it is as though you are actually perceiving the Buddha. If you do not perceive him you cannot even say that he does not possess any marks. But are you actually perceiving him? In fact, when you say that you are perceiving him, even though you say that he cannot be perceived by the possession of marks, you are actually perceiving him by the possession of marks. So you have not seen him as not possessing marks. You have to see him as not possessing no-marks. Marks are not a real thing indicated by the word 'marks'. The word cannot be a sign for something which is not there. So it is not that the Buddha does not possess marks; he does not possess no-marks. It is not that there is no real possession of real marks—the marks themselves are not real. So there is no real possession of marks which do not really exist anyway.

Perhaps the Mahāyāna is becoming a bit much for us here.

Chapter Five

THE RAFT OF THE DHARMA

IT WOULD SEEM THAT—PERHAPS GENERALIZING A LITTLE SWEEPINGLY—

IF YOU ARE BORN AND BROUGHT UP AS A BUDDHIST, YOU CAN HARDLY HELP BUT

HAVE WRONG IDEAS ABOUT THE DHARMA

Subhūti asked: Will there be any beings in the future period, in the last time, in the last epoch, in the last 500 years, at the time of the collapse of the good doctrine who, when these words of the Sūtra are being taught, will understand their truth?—The Lord replied: Do not speak thus, Subhūti! Yes, even then there will such beings.

In any given world period the teaching does not last, but taking the cosmos as a whole, it does survive, because it is discovered and rediscovered again after being lost. The Dharma is not taught once and for all. So what's the use if it's all to be done again? Well, you might say, What's the use of combing your hair in the morning? You are only going to have to comb it again at night. The whole idea of teleology, that everything is leading up to the glorious final catastrophe, is a very Western concept. Buddhism, by contrast, offers a way to transcend an endless cycle of existence, which means that there are some things that just have to be continually restored by repeated efforts. The Dharma, so far as it survives in the world as Buddhism, just has to be kept up, revived, and brought back again and again and again. You could say it's what Bodhisattvas are for.

This note of impermanence, which was first sounded by the Buddha as a warning and a spur to practice, developed in later Buddhist texts into a despondent drone of determinist resignation to the inevitable disintegration of the Buddha's teaching. According to this pessimistic scheme of things, the year 1956 marked the end of the so-called 'last five hundred years'. There is certainly no doubt that the whole trend of modern life is against these wisdom teachings. Every advertisement that you see is in effect an advertisement against Buddhism, because it promotes greed, hatred, delusion, or all three. But although our conditions may seem unfavourable, they may have the effect of stimulating some people to seek some higher wisdom. We may put the current cultural decline down to television, but in the Buddha's day they probably said similar things about the introduction of writing. It is really very difficult to say for certain that one age is absolutely more conducive to spiritual growth than another. The earliest Buddhist teachings do certainly conceive of the possibility that the teaching of a Buddha would eventually disappear, and that it would decline by gradual stages, but we need not—indeed, apparently, we must not—think in terms of an inevitable, universal, and accelerating decline.

The flaw in such a schematic attitude is that it takes no account of the fact that as a spiritual principle the Dharma, the absolute truth, cannot possibly decline. It is possible to reify Buddhism too much. Is there such a thing as Buddhism, that is conditioned and can therefore decline after a while? Does the concept of the decline of Buddhism really make sense? If there are five hundred Arhats in this generation, why shouldn't there be five hundred or even more in the next generation? Why shouldn't the number of Enlightened beings increase by exponential progression? Perhaps if we look at what is actually happening when we speak of the decline of Buddhism we can understand how it is that the Buddha asserts so confidently, indeed categorically, that there will always be 'beings who, when these words of the Sūtra are being taught, will understand their truth'.

If it does not decline in an absolute sense, in what sense does Buddhism decline? What tends to happen is that the Dharma as a purely spiritual phenomenon crystallizes, with the appearance in the world of a Buddha, into a system of methods and teachings which we call 'Buddhism'. There is a passage in the Pāli Canon where the Buddha says that his *sāsana*, his teaching, will last longer than the *sāsana* of previous Buddhas because he has established a Vinaya.[26] Nowadays, in the Theravāda, Vinaya usually means 'monastic discipline', but as used by the Buddha in the sense of Dharma-Vinaya it means the expression of the Dharma in terms of a carefully formulated way of life. So there is no question that you need an appropriate form to bear the spirit of the teaching. Without this formal crystallization the Dharma will make very little headway in the world.

Indeed, however one may criticize the Theravādins for tending to lose touch with the spirit of Buddhism, at least they have a firm grip on the forms of practice and doctrines irrefutably laid down by the historical Buddha. While you have those, you always have the possibility of getting back to the spirit of the teachings. But once you jettison the form in favour of the spirit, you have to be very careful indeed that you never lose sight of the spirit, because if you do you have nothing at all to fall back on. This is the danger inherent in the more radical schools, like Zen, in which terms like karma and rebirth, nirvāṇa, Buddha, and even ethics are put on the sidelines, and can sometimes seem to disappear from view. Or you can find—in Nepal, for example—Buddhism getting mixed up with Hinduism to the extent that it is not just assimilating creative elements of Hindu culture in order to express the Mahāyāna spirit, but getting bogged down in the caste system and losing the spirit of Buddhism altogether.

Looking at it the other way round, people do tend to identify the Dharma with Buddhism, so that the fact that Buddhism has crystallized in one way—adequate for a certain time and for certain people—tends to prevent a different kind of crystallization in the future. It is as though the options are limited by the nature of the original crystallization. The Dharma crystallized in India in 500BCE, the phenomenon of monasticism arose, and now it is very difficult to get away from these historical facts, from—in India at least—yellow robes and shaven heads. People really think that this is Buddhism, and they become intensely loyal to the old forms—to the Vinaya, to the disciplines which the Buddha originally formulated for the cultural and social conditions of his time. Enlightened beings may try to swim against these old forms, but people will very often follow the old tradition rather than the Enlightened being—and quite rightly so, if it is not clear to them that this iconoclastic person is in fact Enlightened, or at least a creative iconoclast. In this way Buddhism itself, as a culture, may sometimes obstruct the attempts of an Enlightened being to spread the Dharma. Buddhism eventually gets so weighed down by its different cultural forms that even the most heroic attempts of the most gifted teachers cannot make headway on behalf of the Dharma against what passes as Buddhism. Hence the 'decline' of Buddhism, and the need for the arising of a new Buddha from time to time to make a fresh start.

It would seem that—perhaps generalizing a little sweepingly—if you are born and brought up as a Buddhist, you can hardly help but have wrong ideas about the Dharma. The mere fact that the Dharma crystallizes in a certain way becomes an increasingly limiting factor as more crystallizations take place in consequence of that original one. At every stage you have a growing weight of accumulated tradition to deal with. Even Zen, so iconoclastic in the beginning, became quite rigid, particularly in Japan. It is like someone throwing ink at a wall and making a blotch and then saying to someone else 'Come on, throw some ink in just the same way as I have, to make the same-shaped blotch … whoops … no, that isn't the same at all. Have another go…. Tsk, tsk. I did it so easily—why is it you can't?' What was originally a free and spontaneous act becomes a laborious and mechanical chore, like trying to copy a painting by Jackson Pollock.

So is it possible to have a perpetually self-renewing tradition? Can we guard against crystallization and decline? In setting up any new direction for Buddhism, the best thing is to plan it in such a way that when things do go wrong they can be clearly seen to go wrong—and go wrong so badly that someone has to do something about them. What you do not want is the pseudo-success of a Buddhist school which expands and enjoys popular support without being properly centred in any experience or development of insight. The corollary of this is equally true. Being Enlightened in no way guarantees that you are going to be able to reach people in any numbers or to any depth. Either the skilful means may not be there, or the times may just be unpropitious, the Buddhist tradition in which you find yourself just not to people's taste. You can try being devotional or intellectual, ascetic and puritan, or hedonistic and hippyish (you will look undependable and vague if you do not take a consistent line) but there is no guarantee of spiritual results, however skilfully you match your style to the prevailing fashion or zeitgeist. It is just no use looking for rules and procedures for disseminating the Dharma. Zen masters, for example, seem often to have communicated their Enlightenment effectively with very little personal contact, their cultural circumstances allowing a brief encounter with an Enlightened mind to go a very long way. We simply cannot insist that the Dharma crystallize in one particular form.

The laws by which Buddhism declines are simply the laws that govern Buddhism as a group activity. There will always be exceptional individuals who are not governed by those laws, true individuals who are not affected by the general decline. This means that, in principle at least, Buddhism, the knowledge of the Dharma, could continue indefinitely. Its decline is by no means inevitable.

For even at that time, Subhūti, there will be Bodhisattvas who are gifted with good conduct, gifted with virtuous qualities, gifted with wisdom, and who, when these words of the Sūtra are being taught, will understand their truth. And these Bodhisattvas, Subhūti, will not be such as have honoured only one single Buddha, nor such as have planted their roots of merit under one single Buddha only. On the contrary, Subhūti, those Bodhisattvas who, when these words of the Sūtra are being taught, will find even one single thought of serene faith, they will be such as have honoured many hundreds of thousands of Buddhas, such as have planted their roots of merit under many hundreds of thousands of Buddhas. Known they are, Subhūti, to the Tathāgata through his Buddha-cognition, seen they are, Subhūti, by the Tathāgata with his Buddha-eye, fully known they are, Subhūti, to the Tathāgata. And they all, Subhūti, will beget and acquire an immeasurable and incalculable heap of merit.

To understand the truth of this sūtra individuals will need to have accumulated, as the Buddha says here, a lot of merit and wisdom. Perhaps more significantly, they will also need to have honoured the Buddhas of the past, which means that the devotional, emotional element cannot be left out of consideration in preparing to become receptive to this Perfection of Wisdom teaching. Activities such as studying the Dharma and practising the precepts are not enough; you also need a devotional attitude. When the aspiring Bodhisattva thinks of the Buddha, the Buddha, we can say, thinks of the Bodhisattva, establishing a communication which is a source of strength and inspiration to the individual attempting to engage with the Perfection of Wisdom. The ability to rise to such elevated communication—for to be in contact with the Buddha is surely to be in contact with the *dharmakāya*—in itself implies a measure of transcendental insight, whether or not it is carried to the point of Stream Entry.

Contact with the *dharmakāya* is, of course, contact with the Unconditioned, and it can occur under very mysterious conditions indeed. I remember that when I was at the Maha Bodhi Society in Calcutta, a Muslim turned up one day. This would have been memorable enough in itself as Muslims in India will never usually enter Hindu or Buddhist places of worship. But this particular Muslim had a strange story to explain this anomalous action, a story that he had come all the way from Assam to tell. He came because on a great number of occasions he had been visited by visions of the Buddha. What made this so mysterious was that he had not at first known that it was the Buddha he was seeing. He had described his visions to people and they had said 'Well, that's the Buddha you're seeing.' He had not practised meditation—he was just an ordinary Muslim. Eventually he converted to Buddhism—an extraordinary thing, because apostasy is, as we know, not to be undertaken lightly if one is a Muslim. We had to smuggle him out of the city because when they got wind of what he was doing the Muslims were after his blood.

How does one interpret visions powerful enough to drive an individual to change the direction of his life so dramatically? It is of course possible that he had seen a picture of the Buddha in a school book, but this would not explain why the image was activated in such a powerful manner.

ACTUALLY, THE BODHISATTVAS HAVE THE SAME PERCEPTIONS, THE SAME SENSE IMPRESSIONS, AS EVERYONE ELSE, ONLY THEY DO NOT MISTAKE THEM FOR REALITY ... JUST AS WHEN YOU SEE A RULER INSERTED IN WATER YOU KNOW IT IS STRAIGHT EVEN WHEN IT APPEARS TO BE BENT

And why? Because, Subhūti, in these Bodhisattvas (1) no perception of a self takes place, (2) no perception of a being, (3) no perception of a soul, (4) no perception of a person.

In his translation, Conze numbers the eight ways in which we may misunderstand or misinterpret our experience and in which the Bodhisattvas who understand this sūtra will not. The first four are variations on a wrong view about the self held by non-Buddhists.

The first of these variations is that you have the impression of constituting a self that somehow exists outside or within or above the five *skandhas*, even though every detail of your experience may be classified into these five 'heaps'—of forms ('the objective constituents of perceptual situations ... and bodily feeling'),[27] feelings, perceptions or thoughts, choices or volitions, and changing states of consciousness. Because these categories all comprise what are essentially processes rather than bits and pieces that might add up to something solid, there is in fact, when they are exhaustively examined, nowhere within them or outside them for a self or ego to be able to stop and say 'Here I am—all this is me.'

The second wrong view—perception of a being—is wrong because the five *skandhas* cannot be said to add up to a being (*sattva*) that co-exists in space with the *skandhas*. They do not make up a being that persists unchanging despite whatever changes are happening outside it.

Neither does the Bodhisattva hold any perception of a soul—the third of these wrong views—because the life force that holds things together from birth until death does not persist unchanging. It would of course be included in the five *skandhas*, under *vijñāna* or 'consciousness'.

Likewise, there can be no perception of a person, because whatever passes from one rebirth to the next does not persist unchanged as something separate from the five *skandhas*.

Nor do these Bodhisattvas have (5) a perception of a dharma, or (6) a perception of a no-dharma. (7) No perception or (8) non-perception takes place in them.

These last four wrong views are specific to Buddhists.

The Hinayanist may have 'a perception of a dharma', viewing the 169 (according to the Theravāda) or 72 (as reckoned by the Sarvāstivādin School) material and mental constituents into which the Abhidharma analysed all phenomena as absolutely existent entities. Bodhisattvas, however, perceive all *dharmas* as provisional intellectual constructions.

Of course, one has to be careful that in perceiving the non-existence of *dharmas*, one is not subtly reifying the non-existence of *dharmas* by offering it as a truer version of reality; this is how 'a perception of a no-dharma' arises. It is not that the *dharmas* absolutely do not exist; they cannot be negated to become non-existent. They have no *ultimate* existence, but they do have a qualified, relative existence.

We commonly imagine, when we perceive a concentration of attributes which we can identify as a single item, that we are perceiving a thing to which those attributes belong, but this imagining of ours is in fact the seventh of the wrong views which the Bodhisattva avoids. There is really no thing there which can be distinguished from its attributes; there is not a thing right inside that the attributes are, as it were, stuck onto. To take a simple example—remove the greenness, the spikiness, and the smoothness, and where is the holly leaf? This of course is Buddhist nominalism. All we have are the names of things; we do not have the things themselves.

Actually, these Bodhisattvas have the same perceptions, the same sense impressions, as everyone else, but they do not mistake them for reality, hence the fact that 'no non-perception takes place in them'. They do not take their perceptions as being absolutely valid; they are not misled by appearances—just as when you see a ruler inserted in water, you know it is straight even when it appears to be bent.

> *And why? If, Subhūti, these Bodhisattvas should have a perception of either a dharma, or a no-dharma, they would thereby seize on a self, a being, a soul, or a person. And why? Because a Bodhisattva should not seize on either a dharma or a no-dharma.*

The Abhidharma analysed so-called persons and so-called things into *dharmas* in order to prove that what you think of as yourself and what you think of as objects to be grasped are not separate or fixed entities. The Mahāyāna demonstrated that even *dharmas* must be seen as empty; and, further, that *śūnyatā* itself has to be discarded. Nothing can be taken as an end in itself. Whatever our interpretation of reality, it is always simply a means, a remedy, a raft. As long as we insist on perceiving an object, even *śūnyatā* itself, then we are still carrying a notion of a subject, a self, or some such subjectivity—however subtle or faint—to do the perceiving.

> *Therefore this saying has been taught by the Tathāgata with a hidden meaning: 'Those who know the discourse on dharma as like unto a raft, should forsake dharmas, still more so no-dharmas.'*

According to the Pāli version of this discourse, which is recorded in the *Majjhima-Nikāya*,[28] the Buddha tells his disciples that they must leave *dhammas*, or righteous ways, behind them along with unrighteous ways when they achieve their goal. In other words, their practice of ethics is simply a means to an end, a raft to take them to the further shore. Ethical discrimination is the business only of unenlightened beings. Enlightened beings do not have to try to act skilfully—it is simply their nature to do so. According to the *Diamond Sūtra*, this discourse also carries a more esoteric teaching wherein the word *dharmas* is to be interpreted as the 'ultimate entities' of the Abhidharma. Whether this metaphysical interpretation is justified or not historically is another matter, but it was a general Mahāyāna tendency to read deeper meanings into some of the teachings they had inherited from the Hīnayāna in its

Sarvāstivādin form. The point is, whether one understands the parable in ethical terms or metaphysically, that one must not settle down at any stage.

This said, the fact that the Dharma is only a raft must not be allowed to work as a surreptitious devaluation of the Dharma. There is a problem here inasmuch as people seem to be able to develop faith in something only to the degree that they absolutize it. It is difficult to have faith in something without regarding it as an end in itself. So it is not easy to regard Buddhism as provisional—and it is because it is not easy to do this that Buddhism develops a sort of spiritual hardening of the arteries and declines.

> *The Lord asked: What do you think, Subhūti, is there any dharma which the Tathāgata has fully known as 'the utmost, right and perfect enlightenment', or is there any dharma which the Tathāgata has demonstrated?*

The basic point here is quite simple. When we want to talk about something which transcends our experience we can still only talk about it in terms of our experience. When we speak of the Buddha as knowing Enlightenment, what we say is based on the analogy of our own ordinary knowledge, and so far as we are concerned knowledge involves a subject—the knower—and an object—the thing known. In other words, the whole framework of our knowledge is dualistic, so that we cannot but conceive of the Buddha's knowledge of Enlightenment as being of that dualistic kind. We think that on the one hand there is the Enlightened knower, the Buddha, and on the other there is the object of his knowledge, Enlightenment, and conclude that becoming Enlightened consists in 'knowing' that object. In the state of Enlightenment, however, there is of course no division of subject and object.

We can even see a double meaning in the word 'dharma'—it can be understood as 'teaching' of course, but also as 'object'. This is because there is no possibility in Sanskrit of using a capital letter to distinguish between the two meanings as we would usually do in English. The way a word like 'Dharma' may be highlighted is by the Sanskrit or Pāli version of quotation marks—by the little indeclinable word, *iti*, put in usually at the end of a direct quote. By eschewing a capital letter for the word 'dharma' in this context, Conze retains the ambiguity of the original in his translation. So the sentence could be understood as starting in two different ways: 'Is there any object …' or 'Is there any Dharma …'.

To return to the essential point being elucidated here, even the doctrinal categories of Buddhism are not to be taken literally, as ends in themselves. All they can do is point towards experience. There is no specific experience known as 'utmost, right, and perfect Enlightenment' that you may take or treat as an object, and then present as an object to other people, whether in the form of verbal communication or in any other form. We must not transfer to the Unconditioned the various categories that we have derived from our experience of the conditioned. The Buddha's experience of Enlightenment cannot be conceived of in terms of our own experience of things that we have discriminated as separate objects—which means that it is quite literally inconceivable.

TRANSCENDENTAL INSIGHT IS NOT A THOUGHT, AND COMPASSION AS THE EXPRESSION OF THAT INSIGHT IS NOT AN EMOTION

Subhūti replied: No, not as I understand what the Lord has said. And why? This dharma which the Tathāgata has fully known or demonstrated —it cannot be grasped, it cannot be talked about, it is neither a dharma nor a no-dharma.

At about this point one might be forgiven for wondering if we might not be flogging a dead horse here. To get some idea of the sort of mental attitude that the Perfection of Wisdom teachings are hammering at in this way, we probably have to go back to the sort of highly-trained Catholic theologian who has satisfied himself that St Thomas Aquinas got everything sewn up, cut and dried, and neatly disposed of once and for all. The excessively intellectual emphasis, or conceptual approach, that needed to be vigorously counteracted by the Perfection of Wisdom school is not, perhaps, a major problem in the West today. The English in particular are not over-intellectual or prone to metaphysics.

This is not to say, however, that we in the West are in the clear. In fact, the whole idea of achieving a balance, of balancing reason or intellect with faith or emotion, is not a useful one as far as the spiritual life is concerned. In the West we find it difficult to see beyond the idea of balance because we see intellect and emotion, reason and faith, as belonging to entirely separate realms, one of which has been colonized by science, and the other by religion. The whole trend of the Semitic faiths, and especially of the Judaeo-Christian tradition, has been to identify religion rather too closely with ideas about the material order. When those ideas about the material order started to be challenged during the Renaissance, religious faith was set irrevocably in opposition to intellectual growth. The industrial revolution, and the lack of integration that has persisted at all levels in the world ever since, can be fairly plausibly traced back to this split in the European psyche. The split between religion and science is in reality a split between very old-fashioned, even ancient, science and modern science, but as a result of it religion has come to be identified with emotion and faith as opposed to, and vulnerable to, reason. But positive, healthy emotion and real faith should never have anything to fear from any amount of knowledge.

In Hinduism the split does not reach into the psyche, but one is still expected to follow one of four alternative paths: *rāja-yoga*, *jñāna-yoga*, *bhakti-yoga*, or *karma-yoga*. The Buddha, however, introduced the teaching of the Five Spiritual Faculties specifically to integrate and unify faith and wisdom, energy and concentration, with mindfulness as the unifying factor. There is not some kind of separate religious faculty that we bring to our spiritual practice. A spiritual consciousness is simply a concentration and co-ordination of all one's faculties in a certain direction which one recognizes to be ultimate. A very important aspect of the meaning of the word 'spiritual' is that of unified being, unified energy. When we get onto the spiritual path—and this is still on the mundane level—any conflict between the rational and the emotional has been resolved.

As a result of the deep split we have inherited, however, we can hardly help thinking of the development of the Five Spiritual Faculties in terms of a *parallel* development—rather than as a unification or harmonization. Consequently we tend to take Buddhist doctrines as abstract meta-physical ideas, as if the Buddha propounded them for our intellectual consideration—especially if we look at Buddhism as if it were the product of a particular intellectual climate. But if we do this, what do we do with our emotions? What do we turn to in order to meet our emotional needs—or rather, who do we turn to? The fact is that if one splits intellect from emotion one is almost bound to demand the existence of a personal God in some form or other. There is no God in Buddhism—and by the same token there are no abstract metaphysical principles running the universe either. If the Buddha uses conceptual language, it is still the product of an Enlightened mind, and it is addressed to our whole being. In the end there is nothing intellectual about wisdom, and nothing emotional about compassion. Transcendental insight is not a thought, and compassion as the expression of that insight is not an emotion.

And why? Because an Absolute exalts the Holy Persons.

A more literal translation than Conze's here would be 'Because the Holy Persons are made influential by the Uncompounded'. Conze in his notes comments 'The *Absolute* is literally "the Unconditioned". With an obvious and deliberate disregard for logic the sūtra claims that this unrelated Absolute can enter into a relation with certain persons.' In fact, the literal translation of *asaṁskṛita* is 'the Uncompounded'. Although this might amount to the same thing as 'the Unconditioned', substituting 'the Uncompounded' for 'the Unconditioned' would restore logical coherence, because there is no contradiction in the Uncompounded, the incomposite, entering into a relation with something else which is compounded or put-together—or even with something else which is also Uncompounded.

Conze translates the term *prabhāvita* as 'exalted', but this is not quite the right word. The idea of *prabhāva* is definitely that of 'influence', and if we were to make a choice out of the alternative translations that Conze offers in his notes, 'draw their strength from' would probably be the closest to being accurate. The function of the word 'because' here is one of emphasis—the emphasis being on 'Absolute' (or preferably 'Uncompounded').

Anyway, the idea being put forward here is, as Conze puts it, that the Holy Persons have 'arisen' from the Unconditioned. It is reminiscent of something the Buddha says to the monks quite often in the Pāli texts: 'You are my own true sons, born of my mouth, born of the Dharma; the heirs to the Dharma, not heirs to worldly things....' You become one of the 'Holy Persons' when you become a Stream Entrant; and to the extent that you participate in or identify with the Unconditioned, by so much do you become influential.

The Holy Persons are empowered by something that defies categorization or definition, even if you can see whatever it is in action in their lives. So this 'Absolute' cannot be thought of as an object out there with which you are in contact. It is only too easy to think of Enlightenment as some sort of object waiting to be realized. If you think in those terms, it will seem to you that when someone becomes Enlightened, an inactive Enlightenment or Absolute becomes active and manifests through that person. This is, however, only a way of thinking and speaking, and not to be taken literally. The Holy Persons are exalted, or empowered, but there is no Unconditioned to exalt them—although it might lead to misunderstandings if we were to say that they exalt themselves.

The Lord then asked: What do you think, Subhūti, if a son or daughter of good family had filled this world system of 1,000 million worlds with the seven precious things, and then gave it as a gift to the Tathāgatas, Arhats, Fully Enlightened Ones, would they on the strength of that beget a great heap of merit?—Subhūti replied: Great, O Lord, great, O Well-Gone, would that heap of merit be! And why? Because the Tathāgata spoke of the 'heap of merit' as a non-heap. That is how the Tathāgata speaks of 'heap of merit'.— The Lord said: But if someone else were to take from this discourse on dharma but one stanza of four lines, and would demonstrate and illuminate it in full detail to others, then he would on the strength of that beget a still greater heap of merit, immeasurable and incalculable. And why? Because from it has issued the utmost, right and perfect enlightenment of the Tathāgatas, Arhats, Fully Enlightened Ones, and from it have issued the Buddhas, the Lords.

Any amount of giving of material things in the ordinary worldly sense, however appropriate, necessary, and beneficial it may be on its own level, or however meritorious in a traditional Buddhist sense, is completely incomparable with even the smallest amount of giving of the Dharma, and especially with the gift of the Perfection of Wisdom. The whole heap (so to speak) of the conditioned cannot be compared with even the smallest grain (so to speak) of the Unconditioned. So what is the implication here for us?

IF YOU GO AND GIVE JUST ONE TALK ON THE DHARMA TO AN AUDIENCE OF PEOPLE WHO HAVE NEVER HEARD THE DHARMA BEFORE ... THE AMOUNT OF MERIT YOU THEREBY GENERATE IS FAR GREATER THAN IF YOU HAD SPENT, SAY, TEN THOUSAND LIFETIMES AS A SOCIAL WORKER

The Buddha is effectively saying that if you go and give just one talk on the Dharma to an audience of people who have never heard the Dharma before, disclosing to them perspectives which have never been disclosed to them before, the amount of merit you thereby generate is far greater than if you had spent, say, ten thousand lifetimes as a social worker in ten thousand different worlds. It is almost impossible to overestimate just how meritorious teaching the Dharma is—even in the ordinary sense, apart from any direct disclosure from your own experience of the Perfection of Wisdom.

Quite simply, going for Refuge does involve a responsibility to others. Are we genuinely reticent at the prospect of talking about something beyond our experience, or are we just afraid of exposing our inadequacies? If one is giving a talk introducing Buddhism, there is no need to discourse on the thirty-two different kinds of emptiness, but one can certainly speak plainly about the impact of the Dharma on one's own life, about one's own experience of going for Refuge. One can talk about ideals even if one has not fully realized those ideals. Just giving a basic talk on the Dharma to some sixth form or Women's Institute may well drop a seed into a small patch of fertile ground in that audience. This is an action that needs to be distinguished very plainly from other activities, however therapeutic or consciousness-raising. We can hardly go for Refuge without having some glimmering of an idea of Enlightenment that we can pass on. In the end it comes down to making the effort—an effort that is inseparable from the spiritual life and the Bodhisattva Ideal. It is perhaps worth adding that we need to take care to nurture any seeds we have sown in the context of the spiritual community.

The seven precious things are gold, silver, lapis-lazuli, coral, gems, diamonds, and pearls. First it has to be understood that these commodities are precious in themselves, and not a whit devalued by being amassed in such quantities as to fill a galactic system. Then, having discounted market forces, one might well imagine that the most meritorious way of disposing of all this wealth would be in such a way as to confer the greatest good on the greatest number of beings. But one would be wrong. Traditionally speaking, the merit accrued from giving is commensurate not only with the quality of the gift but also with the spiritual virtue of the recipient. Convenient for spiritually virtuous-looking monks one might think, but what possible use could Fully Enlightened Ones have for the seven precious things, in whatever quantities? Well, none at all of course. And how, practically speaking, could one present such a gift anyway?

The greatest material gift is one offered in a spirit of genuine devotion and commitment to the spiritual ideal, as distinct from a regard for mundane ends, however wholesome or praiseworthy those mundane ends may be. It comes down to, for example, creating a beautiful shrine-room before setting up a soup-kitchen for the poor. Purely spiritual values must be placed unequivocally above all others. To build a stupa dedicated to world peace, for example, probably suggests that you are not convinced of the overwhelming importance for humanity of the spiritual ideal of Enlightenment over mundane ideals like world peace, freedom, and equal rights. A stupa dedicated to the Buddha has no justification on the mundane level at all—it is totally useless, which makes it a much clearer statement. A Buddhist 'peace pagoda' makes, frankly, a pleasant bromide out of the challenge of Buddhism. Why not build a stupa dedicated to the Buddha—and not just an agreeable little folly bringing a bit of oriental charm to a public park, but a gigantic one covering a couple of acres? If it can be adorned with the seven precious things, so much the better.

Even such a stupa would still, however, be a material thing; and a material gift, even one dedicated to spiritual ideals, is finite, and therefore capable of producing only a finite quantity of merit. By contrast, the harvest from dropping the seed of the Dharma into the mind of one person is literally incalculable. What is Unconditioned is of quite a different order from that which is conditioned.

Notice that Subhūti's answer to the Buddha's question here, even though he does string it together as though it made logical sense—'And why? Because ...'—does not really contain a logical connection. Subhūti's tone of progressive reasoning is ironic, as he is actually driving back over his tracks to guard himself against any possible accusation by the Buddha that he has not really understood. It's as if he is saying 'You're not going to catch me out. All right, I'm talking that language if you insist, but I'm not fooled by it any more than you are.' There is a constant switching back and forth between the Absolute and the relative points of view. Dealing with and talking about the exigencies of the practical spiritual life requires us to take our stand on the relative plane, but as soon as we have crystallized an idea in language we have to dissolve it. The Perfection of Wisdom literature attempts an impossible task. If it is to be true to itself, it cannot say anything at all. So there is a continual, almost violent, oscillation between the provisional and the Absolute, creating quite a peculiar atmosphere. No sooner are you told to do something than the text hastily adds that you mustn't do it, or that you haven't done it, or that you must think that you haven't done it.

Of course, we need to bear in mind that the negative version of a word in Sanskrit is not the same as a negative in English, and can sometimes mean something positive; but even so, it can only be positive in relation to a negative. Sanskrit cannot go beyond the relativity that is inherent in even the most refined language; it just exploits its limitations more successfully, which in a sense makes it a more dangerous instrument. Sanskrit is so articulate a language, it expresses subtle differences so clearly and beautifully, that one may be tempted to forget that even the language of the gods, the *devabhāshā*, as the Brahmins like to call Sanskrit, cannot express the Unconditioned. It is only *devabhāshā*, not *Buddhabhāshā*.

The Law of Identity states that A is A; the Law of Contradiction, that A cannot be both B and not-B; and the Law of the Excluded Middle, that a thing must be either B or not-B. The *Prajñāpāramitā* flagrantly and insistently disregards these irrefutable laws of logic so that one's intellect finds itself oscillating between contradictory statements, trying vainly to determine which of them is true, and unable to conceive of a dimension—the dimension of emptiness—in which the opposites are identical.

And why? For the Tathāgata has taught that the dharmas special to the Buddhas are just not a Buddha's special dharmas. That is why they are called 'the dharmas special to the Buddhas'.

The eighteen special attributes of a Buddha, known as *Buddhadharmas*, which make up the *dharmakāya* are features of the conduct of body, speech, and mind like 'The Tathāgata does not stumble', 'His vigour never fails', 'He is not rash or noisy in his speech', and 'His cognition and vision regarding the past, present, and future proceeds unobstructed and freely.' They are a transcendental counterpart of the thirty-two marks, and they are brought in here because they are the product, or the issue, of *prajñā*, rather than, as with the thirty-two marks, of *puṇya*, merit. At the same time, of course, the Buddha is not actually perceived or comprehended through these qualities, any more than through the thirty-two marks, which is why 'the dharmas special to the Buddhas are just not a Buddha's special dharmas'.

Chapter Six

INSIGHT WITH A CAPITAL I

IF YOU ARE OBSERVING SILENCE OR CELIBACY OR FASTING OR INDEED ANY PRACTICE,

IT IS ABSOLUTELY CRUCIAL TO THE PRACTICE THAT IT BE PERFORMED

IN A CHEERFUL AND EASY-GOING MANNER

*I am, O Lord, the one whom the Tathāgata, the Arhat, the Fully Enlightened
One has pointed out as the foremost of those who dwell in Peace. I am, O
Lord, an Arhat free from greed. And yet, O Lord, it does not occur to me,
'an Arhat am I and free from greed'. If, O Lord, it could occur to me that I
have attained Arhatship, then the Tathāgata would not have declared of me
that 'Subhūti, this son of good family, who is the foremost of those who
dwell in Peace, does not dwell anywhere; that is why he is called "a dweller
in Peace, a dweller in Peace"'.*

It is not that as an Arhat Subhūti is not aware of being an Arhat; but
although he is aware of being an Arhat, he is, at the same time, not
conscious of it. He does not see it as an object, so there is no question of
his making it an object of grasping. If he has to present it to other people
as an object which he has attained he does so only to conform to linguistic
usage. He does not really think or feel himself that he has attained to
anything at all in that way—which is why he has attained it.

The idea of testifying to your attainment is clearly a risky procedure. It
does, however, seem to have become expected in certain traditions almost
as a matter of politeness to announce one's spiritual 'grade'. In the Zen
tradition this is taken to extremes: at the end of a retreat the Master

announces the names of all the good boys who have attained *kensho*, and they go to the top of the class. Sometimes they even get certificates. It is difficult to refer to one's personal spiritual attainment or insight naturally and unselfconsciously, without appropriating it or exploiting it in some subtle way; recognizing this, the central Buddhist tradition encourages a healthy reticence. If you are observing silence or celibacy or fasting, or indeed any practice, it is absolutely crucial to the practice that it be performed in a cheerful and easy-going manner.

The point is that if you grasp too strongly at a spiritual state, what you are grasping at is not a spiritual state at all. You just cannot have a possessive attitude towards even the concept of Enlightenment. To insist on your attainment too strongly is clear proof that you haven't got it at all. Robert Burns satirizes an extreme example of this serious spiritual defect—within what is obviously quite a warped tradition anyway—in his famous poem 'Holy Willie's Prayer', which purports to represent the grateful orisons of a Scottish Calvinist that he is so much more pious than other men—barring a few minor slips into drunkenness and fornication.

But if we are here slating spiritual pride, where does the positive quality of 'Buddha pride' fit in? The simple answer is that it is a Vajrayanic concept. Inasmuch as the Vajrayāna presupposes the Mahāyāna, and as, technically speaking, the whole of the Vajrayāna takes place within the last of the ten *bhūmis* or 'grounds' of the Bodhisattva's progress, so any specifically Vajrayanic idea applies only to a fully-fledged Bodhisattva. At that level 'Buddha-pride' is an unselfconscious awareness of belonging to the Buddha family, and a natural feeling for how to behave in a way that is appropriate to a member of that family. Actually, however, within the Buddha family the idea is inapplicable, strictly speaking, as there is literally no question of behaving inappropriately. There is here no conflict or even distinction between desire and duty.

When Subhūti says that he is one the Buddha has pointed out as 'the foremost of those who dwell in peace', he is alluding to a well-known passage in the *Aṅguttara-Nikāya* of the Pāli Canon in which the Buddha praises each one of his eighty foremost disciples for the particular quality or achievement in which they are foremost.[29] It would seem from this that as people develop they become more individual, more distinctive in their abilities and endowments. Buddhist art quite often fails to do justice to this efflorescence of individual talents and qualities within the Sangha. Monks are depicted around the figure of the Buddha as little rubber stamp miniature versions of him minus the *ushṇīsha*—not an impression that is borne out by the scriptures themselves.

Now Bodhisattvas, as opposed to Arhats, are expected to develop some versatility, but it has to be said that even the Buddha was not good at everything. The thousand arms of Avalokiteśvara, each with its weapon, tool, or emblem, depict the Sangha in its diversity of skills as well as the diversity of skills required of each Bodhisattva. They represent the ideal of co-operation, of abilities working together and complementing one another—as opposed to people jostling to be top dog and insisting that their own field of endeavour has a much greater weight or distinction than the unimportant things that other people get up to.

Among the eminent company of the Buddha's disciples, with all their individual attributes, there was clearly no shortage of possible deuteragonists for the *Diamond Sūtra*. The obvious person to play the leading role with the Buddha would have been Śāriputra, 'foremost in wisdom'—but this wisdom in which he is so pre-eminent is the intellectual, analytical wisdom of the Abhidharma rather than the transcendental wisdom of the *Prajñāpāramitā*; so instead the compiler (if we may designate the author or authors in this historical way) of the *Diamond Sūtra* names Subhūti as the disciple best equipped to receive the Perfection of Wisdom.

Subhūti became an Arhat, the *Aṅguttara-Nikāya* tells us, on the basis of—which is not, of course, necessarily by means of—his practice of the mettā bhāvanā, the meditation in which he develops universal loving kindness. The Buddha also commends him as the one who, 'teaching the Dharma without distinction and limitation, is the chief of those who live remote and at peace.' 'Remote and at peace' translates the word *araṇa*, which is the negative form of the term *raṇa* meaning 'violence', but it also suggests the word *araṇya*, or 'forest', which carries the connotation of remoteness—which is possibly why it is used instead of the more strictly positive term for peace, *śānti*. The combination of qualities that Subhūti embodies is suggestive of the Bodhisattva Ideal more than of the Arhat Ideal (the Arhat Ideal as conceived by the Mahāyāna, that is), and in the *Diamond Sūtra* he comes across as quite the Mahayanist.

The Lord asked: What do you think, Subhūti, is there any dharma which the Tathāgata has learned from Dīpaṅkara, the Tathāgata, the Arhat, the fully Enlightened One? Subhūti replied: Not so, O Lord, there is not.

According to tradition the Buddha-to-be, then called Sumedha, as a disciple of the twenty-fourth Buddha previous to him, Dīpaṅkara, was assured by Dīpaṅkara of ultimate Buddhahood. What the *Diamond Sūtra* is saying, however, is that nothing at all took place between Dīpaṅkara and Sumedha, and that the great succession of Buddhas in which Dīpaṅkara descries his own disciple is empty.

In other words, strictly speaking, there is no such thing as Buddhist tradition in any literal sense. There isn't a 'deposit of truth'—as the Bible is called by some Protestants—delivered for all time to the faithful and simply handed down from generation to generation, even if the Theravādins do sometimes think of the Pāli Canon in this way. Buddhism is not a 'revealed religion' in this sense. It does involve revelation in the sense that all knowledge is a species of revelation, but there is not some *thing* that is revealed and then passed on unchanged.

In this regard, even the Zen insistence on the concept of transmission—Zen being traditionally defined as 'a special transmission outside the scriptures'—can be misleading. No doubt the best Zen masters interpret this key concept precisely as a succession based on having your understanding verified by someone who has had their understanding verified … and so on, all the way back to the Buddha. But there is no doubt also that many Zen students do conceive of this transmission in quite literal, even materialistic terms—and this despite the fact that the *Diamond Sūtra* is especially cherished by the Zen tradition.

A cultural tradition there may be, but not a spiritual tradition, if by this we mean some unchanging thing actually handed on or transmitted, like a precious vase passed down from generation to generation (until someone drops it). The only satisfactory image for the Buddha's transmission would be a relay of flaming torches, some flickering, some dwindling to a spark, and some blazing and roaring, but all capable of lighting the next torch.

Another, simpler way to explain it is just to say that what the Buddha reveals is himself, and in so doing he inspires the disciple into being his own Enlightened self.

The Lord said: If any Bodhisattva would say, 'I will create harmonious Buddhafields', he would speak falsely. And why? 'The harmonies of Buddhafields, the harmonies of Buddhafields', Subhūti, as no-harmonies have they been taught by the Tathāgata. Therefore he spoke of 'harmonious Buddhafields'.

A Bodhisattva speaking of creating harmonious Buddhafields 'would speak falsely' just as a musician becoming too conscious of the beautiful music he is playing is apt to strike a false note. A good performance depends on the complete absorption of the player in the music, with no such lapses in concentration. The same goes for one's practice of meditation, as you may know from your own experience. If in the middle of meditating you suddenly think 'Gosh, I'm really getting on well today … really concentrated … Oh yes, I'm really getting deeply into it … hardly any thoughts there at all …'—well, there goes your meditation. On an infinitely loftier, transcendental level, the same goes for being a Bodhisattva and creating Buddhafields. (These are fields of influence within each of which a Buddha is personally responsible for the spiritual evolution of the inhabitants.) Whether you are meditating or creating Buddhafields, you can only do it successfully if you do it naturally and spontaneously.

THE SPIRITUAL LIFE IS A COMMON, EVEN A CO-OPERATIVE VENTURE, UNDERTAKEN IN UNBROKEN ASSOCIATION WITH OTHER BEINGS

What, however, is actually being created when, by the perfection of skilful means, you create a Buddhafield? What is its ontological status? In what sense can it be said to exist? What is it? Conze pronounces it to be 'no material or perceptible fact … in reality … no more than a mental construction'. Buddhist tradition on the other hand does represent it as actually existing in exactly the same way as this world exists—equally material, equally perceptible, and at the same time equally void. Looking at it the other way round, this world itself is no less of a mental construction than a Buddhafield or Pure Land is, although we perceive it as real, as existing. The only distinction to be drawn between them is that a Buddhafield is more archetypal, and, from a relative standpoint, nearer to reality, nearer to the transcendental, than is this world of ours, inasmuch as from this world (the *kāmaloka*) you have to pass through the *rūpaloka* and the *arūpaloka* to arrive at the transcendental. If, therefore, worlds were to be classified into three ontological categories—the absolutely real, the relatively real, and the apparent or illusory—Buddhafields would come into the second one. If you were in a Buddhafield, you would experience it as you experience this world—as a spatial reality. In an absolute sense, however, a Buddhafield is no nearer to reality than this world is, because in an absolute sense the conditioned in *any* form is *infinitely* remote from the Unconditioned.

But can we accept the impression we get from many Buddhist texts (an impression which Conze himself does not examine) that Bodhisattvas work all on their own to set up Buddhafields, creating them entirely out of their own merits so that a lot of other beings can come along afterwards and inhabit them? Can a Bodhisattva establish his or her own Buddhafield irrespective of what other beings are up to? No. On the contrary, your rebirth depends on the spiritual choices you yourself have made, on your own spiritual evolution, which must contribute to the quality of the Buddhafield in which you arrive. Bearing in mind that Conze warns us not to press too closely the idea of a Bodhisattva 'creating' a Buddhafield—as the Sanskrit *nishpādayati* means also 'accomplish, perfect, achieve, ripen and mature'—it would surely seem that what brings you to one Buddhafield rather than another is a strong connection with the Bodhisattva responsible for establishing that Buddhafield. So from a certain stage, maybe even from the initial stage, the Bodhisattva is most probably working in successive lives with a host of other beings; and when the Bodhisattva does eventually come to establish the Buddhafield into which they are all born, he or she does so in conjunction with them. The Buddha of a Buddhafield has simply taken the leading part in its creation.

This supposition fits well with Buddhist tradition. In the Jātaka tales, the same group of people—Devadatta, Rāhula, Ānanda, and the rest—are reborn with the Buddha-to-be time after time, or rather lifetime after lifetime. When he becomes Enlightened, they all turn up as his disciples and all (except Devadatta) become Enlightened after him. So in the context of the Hīnayāna you have the concept of a whole group of people under the leadership of one powerful personality traversing life after life together until they eventually emerge in the world in their last lives of all and gain Enlightenment all together. The Mahāyāna version of this sodality is of a group of beings being reborn again and again in different worlds, even in different world systems, but always together, and ending up in a world of their own, as it were—one which they have created by their joint efforts. And unlike the Hīnayāna idea of the world you end up in—which is this impure one—the world which, according to the Mahāyāna, you have helped create, is not just a Buddhafield, but a *pure* Buddhafield. Where the two traditions do agree is on the important point that the spiritual life is a common, even a co-operative venture, undertaken in unbroken association with other beings.

The Buddha's repetition here—'The harmonies of Buddhafields, the harmonies of Buddhafields'—is an example of an idiom found also in the Pāli scriptures, and evidently employed for emphasis. It obviously provides a reliable way of recording emphasis both in the oral communication of the Dharma and in the written texts, *devanāgarī*, the script used, lacking printing conventions such as capital letters, underlining, and italics; but it also seems likely that it represents the way people actually spoke.

> *Therefore then, Subhūti, the Bodhisattva, the great being, should produce an unsupported thought, i.e. a thought which is nowhere supported, a thought unsupported by sights, sounds, smells, tastes, touchables or mind-objects.*

This refers, as Conze says, to *apratishṭhita-nirvāṇa*, the final nirvāṇa of a Bodhisattva, unfixed and unsupported. Although free from saṁsāra, the Bodhisattva does not settle down in nirvāṇa, and can continue to appear in the realm of saṁsāra without belonging there in any way. We must not imagine the Bodhisattva stuck in a Buddhafield looking after lots of disciples; at this level a Bodhisattva is not limited in any way whatsoever, and is even able to emanate different bodies to perform different functions in different parts of the universe. The term 'unsupported' is not to be taken too literally, however; in this context it means 'not identified exclusively as this or that', 'not one-sided'. In other words the Buddha, or a Bodhisattva of the tenth *bhūmi*, is not to be thought of dualistically.

Hui Neng, sixth patriarch of the Southern Zen School, recounts in the *Platform Sūtra* how he gained Enlightenment upon hearing these words. While Zen literature tends to use the word 'enlightenment' in quite a loose, liberal way for the kind of insight that might come to you over the course of your first weekend retreat, Hui Neng's experience certainly amounted to Insight with a capital I. On the other hand, it is also true to say that real Insight is sustained on the basis of a number of small insights. The same small insight repeated often enough to effect the kind of change that will shift the balance of your being to the point of Stream Entry, by that token becomes real Insight. It is like hammering at a rock until on the twentieth blow it splits. The previous blows have each contributed to splitting the rock—but only if the twentieth blow actually comes to be struck. So in a way it is difficult to determine whether an insight on its own is just an insight or whether it is actually part of the rock-splitting process. What we can say is that for Hui Neng it was at this point in the *Diamond Sūtra* that the rock split.

Chapter Seven

HALLOWED GROUND

Suppose, Subhūti, there were a man endowed with a body, a huge body, so that he had a personal existence like Sumeru, king of mountains. Would that, Subhūti, be a huge personal existence? Subhūti replied: Yes, huge, O Lord, huge, O Well-Gone, would his personal existence be. And why so? 'Personal existence, personal existence', as no-existence has that been taught by the Tathāgata; for not, O Lord, is that existence or non-existence. Therefore is it called 'personal existence'.

At first glance the idea of a man with a body as huge as Mount Sumeru seems quite grotesque. But it is only a huge personal existence because it is a lone existence. The point would be lost if *everyone* were as big as Mount Sumeru—i.e. towered eighty-four thousand leagues (a league is generally computed to be about three miles) above sea level.

Conze, perhaps following one of the Indian commentaries, states that this passage is 'meant to stress the all-pervading greatness of the Dharmabody', but offers no compelling reasons for accepting what he presents as an incontrovertible interpretation. Indeed, he concludes by rather shuffling off his responsibility as translator and commentator, saying 'the whole passage loses its point in translation....' This is really just a smoke-screen, for the translation is no more obscure than the original—no play upon words is lost in it, for example.

There may well be the implication that the whole universe is the *dharmakāya*, but there does not seem to be any definite connection. What is clear is the general principle that whatever you identify yourself with, even if—following some forms of the Vedanta—you regard the whole universe as yourself, that personal existence is still a no-existence. The Buddhist view is that this—whatever it is—does not belong to me; this is not my self. In at least one form of Vedanta, however, the approach is rather to expand the self as much as possible, to expand consciousness to the extent that you become one with everything in the universe. This is a perfectly legitimate procedure up to a point: the practice of the four *brahma-vihāras*, the 'abodes of the gods', involving the development of mettā, sympathetic joy, compassion, and equanimity, provides a not dissimilar path, involving an expansion of feeling, if not of being. But to regard all beings as yourself, all bodies as your body, and whatever you see as yourself is not a Buddhist but an Upanishadic strain of thought. According to the Upanishads, within, you identify your *ātman* with the *Brahman*, and without, you identify the whole of the universe with your own body.

It is against such cosmic pantheism that this passage in the sūtra is perhaps directed. Even if your body is a cosmic body, as a personal existence it is still a no-existence. What the Vedanta does not realize is that this universal cosmic body is still essentially *śūnya*. You do not solve the problem of self merely by expanding yourself. However extensive the thing with which you identify yourself, there is still a limit to it if you do not regard 'personal existence' as 'no-existence'. According to the 'logic' that runs throughout the sūtra, even an existence as huge as Mount Sumeru would be huge *because* it was a no-existence.

However, it is perhaps appropriate at this point to remind ourselves of Candrakīrti's warning: 'It is better to have a belief in the self as high as Mount Sumeru than to have a false view of *śūnyatā*—because if you are sick, medicine can cure you, but when the medicine has become poison, then what hope do you have?'[30] He is saying in effect that it is better to follow Vedanta and believe in the Absolute self than to think that you and everything you experience is illusion. We can have a great time as Buddhists knocking down the ultimate truths of other religions like ninepins, saying 'there's no God', 'there's no soul', and so on, but these things at least symbolize something above and beyond the material and the mental. We have to be careful that we never allow a reduction of Buddhism to a form of materialism or nihilism to gain currency through misunderstanding *śūnyatā*.

We may even go so far as to say that the classical form of the *anātman* doctrine, stated baldly and literally, is beside the point, and quite unhelpful. We may read about it in books on Buddhism, but if we are practising Buddhists, the issue simply does not arise in this abstract form. The *ātman* that is being denied by this doctrine is our present being *conceived as something ultimate*, beyond which there is no wider or higher possibility, or which we are never going to transcend. *Anātman* means that the empirical self is not ultimate. What the doctrine is getting at is that beyond our present mode of existence and experience there are other dimensions of being which we can grow towards in a way that is inconceivable to our present sense of individuality. In denying the soul the *anātman* doctrine is not denying something deeper. It is saying that we shut ourselves off from anything deeper by asserting 'No, *this* is me'. So to deny the 'soul' in its poetic sense, as an expression for the deeper emotional aspect of one's existence, would put Buddhism in a completely false light.

If the concept of *anātman* has to be handled with care, it does have the positive value that it clears the way for a much more radical and far-reaching development than does the concept of soul. Mystics get into notorious difficulties when they try to interpret their experience in terms of God and soul.

One of the great difficulties which confronted the Indian Buddhists was how they could give some idea, at least to the rational mind, of some higher level of consciousness which one can actually experience in the future—which one can in a sense actually become—without the ego appropriating it and using it to designate itself. Vivekananda, when he came to the West, used to say 'You are not sinners, you are divine, you are God'—which of course was all very refreshing at the time, and is fair enough as a statement if one understands it to mean that if one breaks down one's present individuality, one will emerge into a dimension which is God but which is nevertheless oneself. But what tends to happen is that one takes it to mean that 'I' am in some respects God. What is meant to be the substance of the self is taken as an attribute of it—and it is very difficult to avoid a mild inflation of the ego at this suggestion. So Buddhism does not encourage one to imagine 'I am the Absolute', 'I am Buddha', or 'I am Enlightened', except perhaps in very advanced Tantric practices, when one identifies oneself with the deity at the centre of the mandala. Even then, this takes place only under very special circumstances and with all sorts of safeguards and supports, including the watchful eye of one's teacher.

The Buddha was concerned to deny the Brahminical *ātman* doctrine because the idea of an immortal, unchanging, autonomous self—implied by the connotation of *ātman* with autonomy—had to be rejected as a species of the extreme view of eternalism. But he was also concerned to guard against the opposite extreme, annihilationism. So when Vacchagotta the Wanderer asked him 'What have you to say about the existence of the self?' he remained silent. After his visitor had left in disgust, the Buddha explained to Ānanda that if he had replied that the self does not exist 'It would have added to the bewilderment of Vacchagotta the Wanderer, already bewildered. For he would have said, "Formerly I had a self, but now I have one no more."'[31]

The fact is that we *do* have a self as the sum total of our activities, our thinking, our seeing, our feeling, our willing, and our imagining. This 'self' may be termed *svabhāva*, 'own-being'. The *anātman* doctrine simply warns us not to abstract an entity apart from and somehow activating these processes. There *is* something else behind them—there is another dimension of consciousness, there is even Enlightenment—but it is not to be designated as a 'self'. So when we assert that the self is empty, we must be clear what we are talking about. On the one hand, our 'own-being' as the sum total of our activities is empty in the sense of being subject to the law of conditionality. On the other hand, the self as an abstracted entity behind those processes is empty in the sense of being illusory, of not existing at all.

In actual experience, of course, one cannot be quite sure where one's illusory self ends and one's real empirical self begins. The law of *anātman* could therefore be stated thus: the self is illusory to the extent to which it claims to be absolute. That is, it is illusory to the extent to which it makes absolute demands or has absolute expectations, to the extent to which it expects the whole universe to revolve around it. There's an element of this in everyone—'Why should this happen to me?' 'Why shouldn't I be happy?'—which is what prompts the arising of neurotic craving and hatred. It is this self which has to be discarded as illusory; it is neither healthy nor helpful to attempt to destroy the empirical self. A better model for our practice is one that involves the refining of the empirical self—making it ever more positive—until it evaporates (as it were) in some higher dimension. Associated with the real empirical self is a healthy desire and even a healthy anger or energy which is neither good nor bad, but just happens to be the raw—even crude—materials that we need to work on and transform into something beautiful. The empirical self is as necessary to the Buddhist as clay is to the potter.

We are on altogether safer ground if we speak not in terms of the classical *anātman* doctrine, but in terms of growth. We can even speak of 'something' that grows, and sort out the metaphysics of that 'something' afterwards. At the appropriate time we will appreciate that this development of consciousness involves transcending our present individuality, and becoming part of something much larger. After all, we have the capacity to experience dimensions of consciousness in dreams or under the influence of drugs that are hardly suspected or even recognized by our everyday self, so it should not be too difficult—without thinking of these analogies as equivalent to spiritual experience—to accept that our present sense of personal identity is not ultimate but can be transcended.

ANY SORT OF CONCENTRATED MENTAL ACTIVITY CAN PRODUCE SOME UNUSUAL PHYSICAL EFFECTS

Moreover, Subhūti, that spot of earth where one has taken from this discourse on dharma but one stanza of four lines, taught or illumined it, that spot of earth will be a veritable shrine for the whole world with its gods, men and Asuras. What then should we say of those who will bear in mind this discourse on dharma in its entirety, who will recite, study, and illuminate it in full detail for others! Most wonderfully blest, Subhūti. they will be! And on that spot of earth, Subhūti, either the Teacher dwells, or a sage representing him.

Chapter 11 rehearses the theme of chapter 8, the incalculable merit deriving from the exposition of this sūtra. Chapter 12 goes further and extols the virtue of the very earth upon which the sūtra is expounded.

The word translated as 'shrine' is *caitya* which literally means something heaped up. Perhaps it was originally no more than a little heap of stones to which some sort of sacredness was attached, but the word came to be applied to any object of veneration, including sacred buildings, relics, images, and trees. In India today you can often see stones that have been set up at the foot of certain trees. There are altogether five species of tree considered especially sacred in the Hindu world, including the banyan tree, the bel tree, sacred to Shiva, and the peepul or bo tree, known by arborists as *ficus religiosa*, but called by Buddhists the bodhi tree because it was while sitting under such a tree that the Buddha gained Enlightenment. These trees are often found on the outskirts of a village, sometimes five of them planted as a group with stones piled at their feet, and people come to anoint them and make offerings of flowers. There may be some source of this sacredness—like a dryad or *devata* living in the tree—made explicit, but more often than not there is just a vague, instinctive sense of power emanating from that particular tree. In the Pāli scriptures there are many *caityas* mentioned, and the Buddha seems to have spent many pleasant hours here and there amongst them.

When discussing the stability of societies, the Buddha advised the Vajjians to keep up the offerings at their ancient shrines.[32] It is surely a symptom of general cultural decline when people cease to respect their own traditions and culture. As long as the birthplaces of great national figures, or the places where they lived and worked, or other places associated with significant contributions to the community, like war memorials, are maintained at the national expense as a focus for our appreciation of great deeds and works—so long there remains at least some vestige of cultural vitality in the national community.

Whether or not something of these great figures literally rubs off onto their immediate surroundings, whether there is some objective virtue or power that pertains to a sacred spot, or whether the atmosphere of a place is just a matter of association, is not easy to establish. In creating a sacred spot you would probably choose a place that was already auspicious anyway—which is why churches were often built on the sites of old temples. There is no doubt, however, that places can develop an atmosphere of their own, certainly as a result of meditation or devotional practices taking place in them—and objects can be affected in the same way. When I was living in Highgate, I had two rūpas which I had brought from India, one of Śākyamuni, and the other of the four-armed Avalokiteśvara. They sat on a big, heavy bookcase at the back of the room; and when I was working I definitely felt that there were two people sitting there behind me. I was not worshipping the images myself all that much, but perhaps they had been the objects of much veneration in the past.

I had another, more extraordinary confrontation with a rūpa in the early sixties, when I visited a friend in Bombay. This was an elderly lady who had become a Buddhist and had picked up a number of Buddhist images, one of them being a little Buddha image made of semi-translucent greenstone. As soon as I arrived, my friend sat me in a low armchair facing a window which looked out over the Arabian Sea, with this green rūpa on the window-sill, and asked me to tell her what I could see. She was obviously quite excited. So I sat and looked for a while, and in the end I saw around the image a sort of green aura. It was not a circular halo—the figure was edged with a band of green light which gradually expanded, filling the entire room with bright green light. Of course, I kept looking round for some straightforward source—a reflection from the sky or the sea perhaps—but the light was definitely coming from the image, and there was nothing delicate or subtle about it. It was almost crude, a bit like powerful fluorescent lighting. After a while it just faded.

Apparently my friend's Christian servants had been quite frightened by the whole phenomenon. But according to popular Indian—though not Buddhist—belief, the image would simply be regarded as being particularly lively, or *jagrat*, 'awake'. Indeed, Vajrayāna Buddhists, as well as orthodox Hindus, conduct 'life-establishing' ceremonies over images, sometimes coinciding with the painting in of the eyes, which supposedly bring them to life. I suppose it is understandable that an object upon which many people's thoughts have been focused should become in some sense alive.

This would seem to have been what happened to the relics of Sāriputta and Moggallana when they were being displayed to several thousand people once in Burma. My old friend Bhikkhu Sangharatana said that he and everyone else present saw the relics actually circling round inside their little hermetically sealed glass capsules, surrounded by rainbows. He himself did not regard this as anything supernatural, attributing it to the force of so many people's thoughts. To be frank, when I was involved with organizing receptions during their tour of India, I found the whole atmosphere surrounding these relics more fetishistic and commercial than strictly spiritual, even though they created some useful publicity for Buddhism on the popular level.

All this goes to show that any sort of concentrated mental activity can apparently produce unusual physical effects. There is no reason, therefore, why it should not have an effect on the physical surroundings, the 'spot of earth', where that activity takes place. We have been considering fairly short-lived effects, but what about a transcendental effect? The *Diamond Sūtra* would seem to suggest here that the transcendental can produce effects—via the human body, presumably—that would be perceptually different from, let us say, the powerful mundane effect of someone in the dhyānas.

It is also fair to say that the whole thing is an exercise in skilful means. Hallowed places become focal points of national piety—witness the pilgrimages to Canterbury in the Middle Ages, or the pilgrimages made to cultural monuments like Shakespeare's birthplace today. The Buddha is perhaps just trying to enlist some of this kind of piety and popular devotion—in a refined and sublimated form—to the cause of the Dharma. In claiming such power for the Perfection of Wisdom as to make holy any place where even a few lines of it have been expounded, he is stressing its significance and value. So perhaps this passage is simply what is called *prasamsa*, a sort of hyperbolical praise which is not to be taken too literally. After all, from a purely spiritual point of view all places are equally sacred. The sacred cannot really be delimited in this way. It is probably not very healthy if we start to conform to norms of good behaviour within the confines of some consecrated place (as Christians do in a church—and some Buddhists do in a shrine-room) simply in order to be able to let ourselves go when we get outside again.

Still, we are most of us drawn to visit the Buddhist holy places in India, and it is perhaps not just because some of the places where the Buddha lived and taught are much the same as they were in the Buddha's day. It is not just a question of getting nearer to the Buddha as an historical personality. These places are, for us, hallowed ground.

Chapter Eight

STRETCHING THE MIND TO ITS LIMITS

**YOU COULD SAY THAT THE DIAMOND SUTRA IS A SORT OF ELABORATE KOAN
DESIGNED TO GRADUALLY STRETCH THE MIND TO BREAKING POINT**

*Subhūti asked: What then, O Lord, is this discourse on dharma, and how
should I bear it in mind?—The Lord replied: This discourse on dharma,
Subhūti, is called 'Wisdom which has gone beyond', and as such should you
bear it in mind!*

This is the end of the first part of the sūtra. The first chapter of Part Two
goes on hammering away with the same principle, applied to a number
of different cases:

*And why? Just that which the Tathāgata has taught as the wisdom which
has gone beyond, just that He has taught as not gone beyond. Therefore is it
called 'Wisdom which has gone beyond'. What do you think, Subhūti, is
there any dharma which the Tathāgata has taught?—Subhūti replied: No
indeed, O Lord, there is not. The Lord said: When, Subhūti, you consider
the number of particles of dust in this world-system of 1,000 million worlds
—would they be many?—Subhūti replied: Yes, O Lord. Because what was
taught as particles of dust by the Tathāgata, as no-particles that was taught
by the Tathāgata. Therefore are they called 'particles of dust'. And this
world-system the Tathāgata has taught as no-system. Therefore is it called a
'world system'. The Lord asked: What do you think, Subhūti, can the
Tathāgata be seen by means of the thirty-two marks of the superman?—*

Subhūti replied: No indeed, O Lord. And why? Because those thirty-two marks of the superman which were taught by the Tathāgata, they are really no-marks. Therefore are they called the 'thirty-two marks of the superman'.

When you come to express translogical matters in terms of logic you can only express them in terms of contradictions or paradoxes. Something is what it is because it is what it is not; or, everything is what it is because of emptiness. You have something because you do not have it. The Buddha has the thirty-two marks of the superman—why does he have them? Because he does not have them; his having them is a no-having them.

Really, we need to reflect upon this. It is not going to become immediately obvious. We can understand what is being said—except that it is quite evident nonsense on the level of logical discourse. Does this nonsense, however, convey any glimmer of translogical meaning? Is it possible to draw some small faint insight into what the Buddha might be getting at? Sometimes perhaps, but as soon as you start thinking about it the glimmer of meaning evaporates. It is just not susceptible to any kind of brain-teasing; it is something to be taken up in the context of meditation and reflection.

Śūnyata is no kind of substance or thing, not even a metaphysical or transcendental thing, and we have to appreciate that language compels us to speak about it as though it was. In speaking about *śūnyatā* we have to do continual violence to language; and when we stop doing violence to language, when we start taking what we say about *śūnyatā* literally, then we are no longer speaking about *śūnyatā*. The basic point made by the Mādhyamika School and by the Mahāyāna generally is that *śūnyatā* is not to be thought of in terms of existence or non-existence. Intellectually speaking, that statement is as far as we can go. We have to transcend it intuitively, as it were, with the eye of wisdom, and see what *śūnyatā* 'is' without seeing it as something that is; and at the same time see what *śūnyatā* 'is not' without seeing it as something that is not.

It is very easy to go on like this and allow the intellect to get busy playing around with *śūnyatā* in a way that is not basically serious. All the time we imagine that we are beginning to get a clearer idea, but the purpose of the Perfection of Wisdom is to baffle the intellect completely, so that we experience the need for some other faculty to come into operation. The *Diamond Sūtra* seeks to cut off every avenue of escape, to bring the intellect up against a sheer, insurmountable wall so that it collapses and accepts that it can make no sort of impression. In the Zen tradition they say that trying to penetrate *śūnyatā* with the intellect is like a gnat trying to penetrate a great ball of steel with its little proboscis. There are no metaphysical statements in Buddhism; it denies us anything to understand on the metaphysical level. When you say 'Ah yes, now I understand what *śūnyatā* means', you have understood the words and their particular meaning, but the words have nothing to do with *śūnyatā*.

The danger with all this is that one may feel inclined to give up trying to understand before the sūtra has done its work. You could say that the *Diamond Sūtra* is a sort of elaborate kōan designed to gradually stretch the mind to breaking point. Indeed, the real purpose of Buddhist speculative philosophy is to stretch the mind to its limits. It certainly stretches the mind more effectively than minds have been stretched in the West, and it therefore transcends the mind more effectively and 'cleanly'. But the mind is not going to be stretched if it has already cottoned on to the fact that it is on a hiding to nothing. A kōan is not going to work if you know what the real kōan is right from the start. It is only after you have already struggled to understand it that it dawns on you what the kōan is—and then you get a glimpse of something beyond. If a Zen student is given the kōan of 'the goose in the bottle', for example, the kōan he has to wake up to is not the kōan of 'the goose in the bottle' but the kōan of himself working on 'the goose in the bottle'.

> *The Lord said: And again, Subhūti, suppose a woman or a man were to renounce all their belongings as many times as there are grains of sand in the river Ganges; and suppose that someone else, after taking from this discourse on Dharma but one stanza of four lines, would demonstrate it to others. Then this latter on the strength of that would beget a greater heap of merit, immeasurable and incalculable.*

'Personal existence' would be a better translation of *ātma-bhāva* than 'all their belongings'. To say 'suppose a woman or a man were to renounce their personal existence'—in other words to sacrifice their life—would make better sense as well as being more literal. This is of course one of the main themes of the sūtra: the incommensurability of *puṇya* and *prajñā*, or, if you like, of quantity and quality. Even an interminably repeated sacrifice of your very heart's blood—and we must presume that in this context this means such a sacrifice made without having realized Perfect Wisdom—produces less merit than simply teaching a little of this sūtra. In other words, no amount of conventional religiosity can ever make up for a lack of genuine spiritual insight.

This is in no way to belittle the importance for the individual of skilful behaviour. The general point, in terms of the spiritual community, is that however rich your cultural tradition, however intellectually profound your soteriology, however widespread and influential your religion, unless there is present in that tradition some experience of insight, you have not got very much. Buddhism as a cultural phenomenon, without the Dharma in its true sense, is not really all that helpful.

Chapter Nine

A SENSE OF THE SUBLIME

**WE BEGIN TO UNDERSTAND THE DIAMOND SUTRA, NOT WHEN WE IMAGINE THAT WE
HAVE WORKED OUT WHAT IT MEANS, BUT WHEN, AS WE CONTEMPLATE IT,
WE ARE MOVED—EVEN TO TEARS—BY A SENSE OF THE SUBLIME**

*Thereupon the impact of Dharma moved the Venerable Subhūti to tears.
Having wiped away his tears, he thus spoke to the Lord: It is wonderful, O
Lord, it is exceedingly wonderful, O Well-Gone, how well the Tathāgata has
taught this discourse on Dharma. Through it cognition has been produced
in me. Not have I ever before heard such a discourse on Dharma. Most
wonderfully blest will be those who, when this Sūtra is being taught, will
produce a true perception.*

The teaching put forth in the *Diamond Sūtra* may seem quite abstract in
form, but for Subhūti it is not abstract at all. His emotional response
demonstrates a distinctive emphasis of the Mahāyāna. It is well known
that when the Buddha died, the Arhats that were there—and Subhūti is,
according to this text, an Arhat—exhibited no particular emotion. Only
those who were relatively unenlightened felt any separation or loss at the
removal of the Buddha's physical body. Thus arose the general Hīnayāna
view of Arhats as cool, impassive figures. The Mahāyāna, however,
recognized that there were appropriate objects for the expression of
powerful emotion—even, and indeed all the more so, at the highest levels
of spiritual development. In the *Aṣṭasāhasrika Sūtra*, the 'Perfection of
Wisdom in 8,000 Lines', for example, there is a Bodhisattva called

Sadāprarudita—*sadā* meaning 'always', and *prarudita*, 'weeping'—and he is always weeping because he is constantly moved by the Dharma.

Subhūti is of course only an Arhat, so he just sheds a few tears—but the important thing is that he is deeply moved by the Dharma. It is essential that we feel strongly and deeply about the Three Jewels, and also about the particular context within which we practise, our Buddhist Order, and indeed about the local spiritual community within which we live or work. It comes down to fidelity, staying true to your friends and keeping faith with the Dharma. It is quite significant that in Tibet the Bodhisattva Tārā is known as 'the faithful Tārā'.

In the modern West, our social mobility gives us a kind of freedom, but at the same time it tends to limit our ability to develop close, deep, and strong relationships. The ease with which we can move on to pastures new tends to blunt our appreciation of our experience. We can always go off and make new friends when a situation or a relationship begins to make deeper demands upon our emotions, and this means that we seldom expose ourselves to any experience deeply and lastingly enough for it to move us. But to be strong and healthy, emotions need to be rooted in loyalty and commitment. When people are moving from one place to another, from one relationship to another, from one religion to another, and when the idea of not being tied down, of not limiting our options, of not identifying with a particular set of values, is understood as freedom—when it no longer seems clear at what to weep and at what to rejoice—then a situation develops in which there is no longer any outlet for the natural expression of strong emotion.

Of course, this has not always been the case in our society. We have only to go back to the nineteenth century to find the whole country, even hard-boiled politicians, awash with tears over the death of Little Nell or Paul Dombey. Dickens himself apparently used to laugh and cry and behave rather like a madman when he was writing, quite carried away by the events his imagination was conjuring up. Even fifty years ago, my mother and her friend would come back from the cinema on a Thursday night saying how much they'd enjoyed it—'We had a really good cry.' Perhaps these days we are afraid of seeming sentimental. We are increasingly uneasy about responding naturally to what may seem to our social consciences rather less than worthy demands upon our emotions. Also, perhaps, the emotions gradually become constrained within a social context of increasing control and security.

But Subhūti does weep. He weeps because the Dharma has touched something in him that has not been touched before. Weeping when you hear the Dharma is a sign that something has got through to you. It is as though the Dharma touches some spring in you, opens something up that was hitherto blocked, melts something that was congealed, frees up energy that was imprisoned. And you are touched, you are moved, you are stirred. There is a powerful expression for this sort of state in Pāli: *samvega*—to be shaken by the Dharma. There is even quite a powerful word in English which gives some idea of the sort of emotional response we need to discover in ourselves before we can claim to have taken in even a little of this teaching—and that is the adjective 'sublime'. We begin to understand the *Diamond Sūtra* not when we imagine that we have worked out what it means, but when, as we contemplate it, we are moved—even to tears—by a sense of the sublime.

What the sublime represents is something vast and grand and over-whelmingly powerful which gives us a terrifying sense of our own smallness, but which at the same time allows us—and this is what moves us, even exhilarates us—the realization that on another level it is no greater than us, that there is that within us which resonates with that grandeur. The sublime moves us in a way that the simply beautiful cannot. It is there in the works of Michaelangelo and Beethoven; among the *rāgas* of traditional Indian music it is expressed in the *bhairava*, the 'terrible' mode; and in the *Tibetan Book of the Dead* it is embodied in the wrathful deities, who are not beautiful like the peaceful forms, but sublime and awesome.

Subhūti is shaken by a revelation of something even more sublime than the nirvāṇa that he has, presumably, so far attained. It is as though he was standing on a mountain peak imagining that it was the highest peak of all, and then, the mist clearing, he looked up, and there was another peak still, towering above him. As the Buddha carefully removes the Dharma beyond the reckoning of the most extravagant scale of values, it is the sublimity of the perspective revealed to him that moves Subhūti to tears.

It is not difficult for me to accept and believe this discourse on Dharma when it is being taught. But those beings who will be in a future period, in the last time, in the last epoch, in the last 500 years, at the time of the collapse of the good doctrine, and who, O Lord, will take up this discourse on Dharma, bear it in mind, recite it, study it, and illuminate it in full detail for others, these will be most wonderfully blest. In them, however, no perception of a self will take place, or of a being, a soul, or a person. And why? That, O Lord, which is perception of self, that is indeed no perception. That which is perception of a being, a soul or a person, that is indeed no perception. And why? Because the Buddhas, the Lords have left all perceptions behind.

Subhūti's understanding has moved on. Just seeing the greatness of the Dharma in a new way gives him a new vision of things. And at once his mind turns again to people who will come to this teaching in a less auspicious era. He already knows, from the exchange recorded in chapter 6, that there will be individuals at that time who will be able to respond as he has done, so the issue does not need to be raised in the form of a question again. He does raise it again however—because the original question came from a slightly more limited perspective—but this time in a spirit of wonder. The same question calls for the same answer, but at the same time elicits a slightly different, slightly deeper, emotional emphasis than before, because Subhūti himself is a little different.

The Lord said: So it is, Subhūti. Most wonderfully blest will be those beings who, on hearing this Sūtra, will not tremble, nor be frightened, or terrified.

J.M.W. Turner, a great painter of seascapes, and especially storm-swept seascapes, used to go out in a boat during a storm and have himself lashed to the mast so that he could make notes on his sketchpad. Obviously if he had allowed himself to be frightened out of his wits by this experience, he would have been unable to make proper use of it. Instead, he found the courage to be impressed and inspired by the sublimity of the wild natural forces seething around him. If you are over-preoccupied with your own safety, the sublime appears to be simply threatening and destructive. To open yourself to an experience of the sublime, you need to rise above being concerned only with your own continued existence. To take another example, if you contemplate the forms of the wrathful while in an unskilful state of mind, you see them as wrathful and threatening, whereas if you are in a more positive state, they are awe-inspiring, heroic, wonderful, sublime. And, as the Buddha says here, the same principle applies to the *Diamond Sūtra*.

All this is not to say that there is anything wrong with being frightened—quite the reverse. There are people who remain stolidly impervious to any hint of danger, say in a storm at sea, through a kind of blind faith in the ship, the captain, and the impossibility of their own demise. This is lack of imagination. In a way it is quite a healthy sign if you are terrified by the teaching of the sūtra, because it shows that you have understood it to some extent. Speaking schematically, we could say that to worldly people the Dharma appears terrifying, while to Bodhisattvas it appears sublime and awe-inspiring. But if the Dharma appears to you as beautiful—well, this means that you have just risen to the level of a Buddha.

This applies, at a much lower level, to the question of living in spiritual communities. The idea of living in a single-sex community would make the man on the Clapham omnibus run a mile; they would be terrified at the prospect. Someone who has begun to meditate and reflect on the Dharma might find the idea somewhat awe-inspiring. But if you are actually living in a community, it is just beautiful, because you realize from your own experience that it is the best possible way to live.

> *And why? The Tathāgata has taught this as the highest (paramā)*
> *perfection (pāramitā). And what the Tathāgata teaches as the highest*
> *perfection, that also the innumerable (aparimāṇa) Blessed Buddhas do*
> *teach. Therefore is it called the 'highest perfection'.*

The play on words here gives this straightforward statement the momentarily enigmatic look of another Perfection of Wisdom riddle. In fact, etymologically speaking, the words *parama* and *aparimāṇa* are not at all closely linked to *pāramitā*, but they do throw some light on the term. The point being made is simply that all Buddhas teach the same thing (i.e. Perfect Wisdom) because they have all realized the same reality.

Chapter Ten

THE PERFECTION OF PATIENCE

Moreover, Subhūti, the Tathāgata's perfection of patience is really no
perfection. And why? Because, Subhūti, when the king of Kalinga cut my
flesh from every limb, at that time I had no perception of a self, of a being, of
a soul, or a person. And why? If, Subhūti, at that time I had had a
perception of self, I would also have had a perception of ill-will at that time.
And so, if I had had a perception of a being, of a soul, or of a person. With
my superknowledge I recall that in the past I have for five hundred births
led the life of a sage devoted to patience. Then also have I had no perception
of a self, a being, a soul, or a person.

Here a new subject is being introduced, the *kshānti pāramitā*, the Perfection
of Patience, and the Buddha refers to a classic example of patience from
one of his previous lives.

The Buddha is saying that there are two kinds of patience. One, the
mundane virtue, is where you just grit your teeth stoically and turn the
other cheek even though you would like to give the other person a sock
on the jaw. The other, the transcendental kind, is where you are not, in a
sense, conscious of anything being done to you by anybody. You are not
fostering a notion of a self or a non-self, nor of the other person as being
bound to either of these categories. With the one you are doing your best
not to act upon your anger; with the other there is simply no possibility
of anger. You see somebody doing something but there is no trace in your
mind of the idea that '*he* is doing this to *me*'.

This does seem a very lofty level of attainment indeed. By some stretch
of the imagination it might seem possible to practise *dāna pāramitā*, but

the Perfection of Patience seems more difficult to conceive of, especially under such trying circumstances as those on which the Buddha is here reminiscing. After all, the absence of any trace of anger does not entail any lessening of purely physical suffering. Perhaps we can get some idea of the nature of this experience by considering the relationship between a mother and her child. A child may quite deliberately hit and hurt his mother, but quite often the mother will not have much sense that '*he* is hurting *me*', because she has a residual feeling of oneness with the child. In a sense, it is her own flesh and blood that is hitting itself.

A third kind of patience is that practised by the Hinayanist, who by analysing beings and things into their constituent *dharmas,* realizes the folly of becoming angry with a parcel of material and mental states. This is a proven method of controlling and even eradicating the grosser forms of anger, but unfortunately it does not stop you from thinking of the *dharmas* themselves as realities, which makes it impossible to get rid of the subtler forms of anger. This is why the Hīnayāna practice of *kshānti* is said to be supported by *dharmas.*

At a lower level still, you may exercise a degree of genuine patience relatively easily when you make the effort to perceive clearly the reasons for apparently unreasonable behaviour. Someone may be, if not exactly sawing the flesh from your bones, still causing you a lot of trouble and inconvenience, but you may be able to see why it is happening, and why that person is in that state. 'To understand all is to forgive all', as the French saying goes.

> *Therefore then, Subhūti, the Bodhi-being, the great being, after he has got rid of all perceptions, should raise his thought to the utmost, right and perfect enlightenment. He should produce a thought which is unsupported by forms, sounds, smells, tastes, touchables, or mind-objects, unsupported by dharma, unsupported by no-dharma, unsupported by anything. And why? All supports have actually no support. It is for this reason that the Tathāgata teaches: By an unsupported Bodhisattva should a gift be given, not by one who is supported by forms, sounds, smells, tastes, touchables, or mind-objects.*

The Bodhisattva should produce a thought which is not derived from anything, not imputable, referable, or traceable to ordinary sense experience or to any dualistic thinking. All we can say is that this thought arises from the deepest possible level within him quite spontaneously.

'All supports have actually no support' is not quite right. A better translation would be: 'That which is supported has no support.' Basic Perfection of Wisdom. It is—perhaps surprisingly—obvious as well as true. If something depends on being supported by something else, it is not ultimately supported at all, because it is supported by something outside itself, a support which can be taken away at any time. So that which is supported is, in reality, or in absolute terms, unsupported. The only way you can be supported in any real sense is by being unsupported.

> *And further, Subhūti, it is for the weal of all beings that a Bodhisattva should give gifts in this manner. And why? This perception of a being, Subhūti, that is just a non-perception. Those all-beings of whom the Tathāgata has spoken, they are indeed no-beings. And why? Because the Tathāgata speaks in accordance with reality, speaks the truth, speaks of what is, not otherwise. A Tathāgata does not speak falsely. But nevertheless, Subhūti, with regard to that dharma which the Tathāgata has fully known and demonstrated, on account of that there is neither truth nor fraud.*

This carries an echo of a passage in the Pāli scriptures, in which the Buddha says that although he uses ordinary language—speaking, that is, in terms of 'I' and 'you'—he is not misled by it. And again, turning to the *Laṅkāvatāra Sūtra*, there is the famous and arresting declaration that from the night of his Enlightenment to the night of his *parinirvāṇa*, the Buddha did not utter a single word. Another, less provocative way of putting this would be to say that no word that could be uttered could do justice to reality. As the Buddha did in fact speak out of his experience of reality—as everything he said, if you take the real meaning of it, was in accordance with reality—then in truth he did not say anything. And this is because 'he speaks the truth, he speaks of what is, not otherwise. A Tathāgata does not speak falsely.'

There is, however, the inevitable rider to this, that we must not apply our dualistic notions of truth to the fact that the Buddha speaks the truth. He speaks not the truth that is opposed to falsehood, but the truth in the sense of the ultimate reality that must be understood in a deeper, non-dualistic sense. This does not mean that the Buddha might tell a lie; it means that on a metaphysical level there is no distinction between truth and untruth to which the Buddha conforms.

> *In darkness a man could not see anything. Just so should be viewed a Bodhisattva who has fallen among things, and who, fallen among things,*

renounces a gift. A man with eyes would, when the night becomes light and the sun has arisen, see manifold forms. Just so should be viewed a Bodhisattva who has not fallen among things, and who, without having fallen among things, renounces a gift.

Here are contrasted two ways of practising *dāna*, one conjoined with, or illumined by, *prajñāpāramitā*, the other not, and therefore blind. A Bodhisattva who has 'fallen among things' gives something thinking that it is a real thing that he gives, that he himself, the giver, is a real thing, and that the person to whom he gives is a real thing. Such a Bodhisattva is in darkness, blind to the Perfection of Wisdom.

The point has been made before. Only the language, the metaphor of sight, is different. The idiom 'fallen among things' probably calls to mind the parable of the good Samaritan, which speaks of 'the man who fell among thieves', but it is also echoed in the Gnostic expression 'fallen into the world'. 'Renouncing a gift' is also new. It does not of course mean 'refusing a gift'; it is simply a stronger version of 'giving a gift', suggesting a stronger sense of giving up any interests of your own whatsoever in the gift. In the sense of renouncing your own body, your *ātma-bhāva*, it may even be said to represent an aspect of *kshānti*.

THE BUDDHA LOOKING AT YOU IS AN ASPECT OF YOU LOOKING AT THE BUDDHA— AND THIS IS, IN A WAY, A VERY STRANGE EXPERIENCE

Furthermore, Subhūti, those sons and daughters of good family who will take up this discourse on Dharma, will bear it in mind, recite, study, and illuminate it in full detail for others, they have been known, Subhūti, by the Tathāgata with his Buddha-cognition, they have been seen, Subhūti, by the Tathāgata with his Buddha-eye, they have been fully known by the Tathāgata.

Here is another passage that sounds familiar. In chapter 6 the Buddha avers that Bodhisattvas living in an age of decadence, 'who when these words of the sūtra are being taught will find one thought of serene faith', will be seen and fully known by the Tathāgata. Here, however, it is those who will take up the steady practice of reflection, recitation, study, and communication who have been fully known and seen by the Tathāgata. The past perfect tense used for this last verb might suggest that the Buddha is jumping the gun, but in fact he has already fully known and seen these people because one of the powers of a Buddha is the faculty of direct perception into the future.[33]

The point being made here is to do with communication. By virtue of being a Buddha, the Buddha sees you with his Buddha-eye, or at least knows you with his Buddha-cognition. Being a Buddha, that is how he sees and knows. When you see the Dharma, you see the Buddha with your Dharma-eye, and then there is a much more direct communication between you and the Buddha than when you were looking at some thought or idea or even image of the Buddha rather than at the Buddha himself. Now that you are really looking at the Buddha, well, now he can really look at you. So the Buddha looking at you is an aspect of you looking at the Buddha—and this is, in a way, a very strange experience. It is rather like the eyes painted on the sides of the *harmikās* of Nepalese stupas: if you look at them, you find that they are looking at you.

This mutual seeing reflects a sort of duality, but also a sort of non-duality. You are not 'one' with the Buddha, because, after all, he is looking at you and you are looking at him; but in a way he sees himself reflected in you and you see yourself reflected in him, so you are moving in the direction of non-duality (always remembering that non-duality does not exclude duality).

We could say that being seen by the Buddha is another aspect of Going for Refuge. We use various terms to indicate different aspects of one and the same fundamental spiritual experience: entering the stream, going forth, the opening of the Dharma-eye, and the *parāvṛitti* (a term taken from the *Lankāvatāra Sūtra*), 'the turning about'. To these we may add the idea of being seen by the Buddha with his Buddha-eye.

Chapter Eleven

A Breath of Nonsense

There needs to be some element of the Dharma which is not relevant to our spiritual development at all. When it comes to transcending conditioned existence the last thing we need is something useful

And if, Subhūti, a woman or man should renounce in the morning all their belongings as many times as there are grains of sand in the river Ganges, and if they should do likewise at noon and in the evening, and if in this way they should renounce all their belongings for many hundreds of thousands of millions of milliards of aeons; and someone else, on hearing this discourse on Dharma, would not reject it; then the latter, would on the strength of that beget a greater heap of merit, immeasurable and incalculable.

As we have seen, the temptation to reject this teaching is so great because it is so threatening, and the merit coming from resisting that temptation is commensurably great. Not rejecting it is tantamount to accepting it, or at least being open to it.

There is another reason, however, for rejecting the *Diamond Sūtra*, a reason which is perhaps closer to home for most of us. The gravamen of our resistance to it is likely to be that it hardly seems relevant or useful to our predicament. We can answer this charge in the language of the Perfection of Wisdom itself. Its usefulness is in its uselessness; it is relevant because it is so irrelevant.

As seriously practising Buddhists we do need to be able to relate traditional teachings to our own personal experience. We need to work out how the Dharma bears upon our own lives, how it applies to the world we live in, and how to interpret ancient texts so as to be of practical and immediate concern to the situation in which we find ourselves. But on another level we should not be over-concerned with what is relevant to 'me', interesting to 'me', applicable to 'my' situation in the West. It is all very well to expect Buddhism to be meaningful to where we are, here and now—but where is here and when is now? Is our conditioned existence all we are? In the end there needs also to be some element of the Dharma which is not relevant to our spiritual development at all. When it comes to transcending conditioned existence, the last thing we need is something useful. In fact it takes something quite irrelevant to transcend conditions—and then the pointless becomes the most relevant thing of all.

So in the *Diamond Sūtra* we are still concerned with the Dharma, but we are not concerned with any of the things that we usually think of as constituting the Dharma—the things that we settle down and feel comfortable with. We are taking a rest from looking at ethics or meditation or impermanence; instead we are getting a breath of nonsense, a touch of Lewis Carroll or Edward Lear (without suggesting by this analogy that *'Alice in Wonderland'* is some kind of Zen text, of course).

The Perfection of Wisdom is like salt. An exclusive diet of it probably wouldn't do you much good, but you need a pinch of it in your spiritual diet all the time. It gives it a little flavour—the flavour of irrelevance. Otherwise, if it all becomes too relevant, well, you take it all too seriously—you think too much in terms of yourself as you are now. It's refreshing to have something which in a way you understand, but which in another way you don't understand at all.

What we have in the *Diamond Sūtra* is a comprehensible but irrelevant meaning, with a further significance or purport that *is* relevant but is *not* comprehensible. It is not difficult to get at the meaning of the sentences, but to get at what I am calling the purport, the direction in which the words are pointing above and beyond the verbal meaning, is much more difficult. It may also sometimes be difficult to explain the connection between the meaning and the purport. What we may be sure of is that we can only get at the purport by constantly bearing the meaning in mind. One way to do this is to recite the words constantly, as one does in some visualization practices, repeating certain short verses over and over again. If we repeat the comprehensible but irrelevant words often enough, as monks have been doing for hundreds of years in the monasteries of Japan and the lamasaries of Tibet, something of the purport will begin to dawn on us.

> *Those who will take up this discourse on Dharma, bear it in mind, recite, study and illuminate it in full detail for others, the Tathāgata has known them with his Buddha-cognition, the Tathāgata has seen them with his Buddha-eye, the Tathāgata has fully known them. All these beings, Subhūti, will be blest with an immeasurable heap of merit, they will be blest with a heap of merit unthinkable, incomparable, measureless and illimitable. All these beings, Subhūti, will carry along an equal share of enlightenment.*

This 'cake' model of Enlightenment, in the English at least, seems odd, not to say clumsy. The point being made is that all these beings will have much the same spiritual status. They will all partake equally in Enlightenment, you could say. 'Those who will take up this discourse on the Dharma, bear it in mind, recite, study, and illuminate it in full detail for others' will basically have a lot in common—quite a reasonable inference.

IF YOU HAVE GOT AS FAR AS TAKING UP THE DIAMOND SUTRA, YOU HAVE ACTUALLY COME A VERY LONG WAY

> *And why? Because it is not possible, Subhūti, that this discourse on Dharma could be heard by beings of inferior resolve, nor by such as have a self in view, a being, a soul, or a person. Nor can beings who have not taken the pledge of Bodhi-beings either hear this discourse on Dharma, or take it up, bear it in mind, recite or study it. That cannot be.*

We know by now that the word 'because' is likely to signal an inconsequential hop in the argument—and so it proves here. The reason is no reason at all. But the sūtra evidently means this surprising assertion to be taken literally. If you hear this sūtra, recite it, or study it, you have to infer that you must have taken the Bodhisattva Vow. It is not saying that someone who does not have some sort of spiritual resolve will not understand the discourse; it is saying that such a person will not even hear it. If you have full faith in the sūtra you have to conclude that the mere fact that you are able to hear it in this life means that you must have taken the Bodhisattva Vow in a previous life. Well, is this idea so difficult to take seriously? Why should certain people be reading and studying a text that apparently makes no sense at all? It is by no means a bestseller. Conze's definitive translation has not, to my knowledge, set the publishing world alight. So how is it that we should come to be engaged with such a baffling and bewildering work as this?

How is it that some people do take to certain things so very readily, like the proverbial duck to water? They just plunge in as though whatever it is were already quite familiar to them. They are in their element. And how often have we come across a book—apparently by accident—at just the time we needed it, as though there were some kind of law of magnetic attraction working on some unseen plane? I am not suggesting a sort of linear causality in operation here, but something more like a web of interrelationships spanning—I will not say transcending—both time and space: you touch one part of the web, and there is a response from another corresponding part.

In this way we may start to wonder if we might not have some kind of mysterious affinity with this Perfection of Wisdom teaching that goes back to a previous life. Perhaps we are tempted to believe that we are coming back to something we have known before, and taking up the threads once again. We may even decide that the temptation *not* to believe that this may be so is the one to be examined.

At the bottom of all this is the general principle that you are drawn to a teaching when you are ready for it. It is as though the teaching is moving toward you at the same time that you are moving towards it. It is perhaps an encouraging thought—and perhaps also a sobering one— that merely coming into contact with the teachings of the Perfection of Wisdom means that you have a certain spiritual capacity, that the ground has been prepared to some extent. If you have got as far as taking up the *Diamond Sūtra*, you have actually come a very long way.

This kind of optimistic perspective on one's spiritual condition is an unfamiliar one for anyone brought up within the Christian tradition of original sin. The taint of Adam's fall may be purified by baptism, but how long does that state of purity last? Does it survive the first time the baby clutches its little fists, or gives Mother a nasty look? Not according to St Augustine. It has surprised me in the past how many people brought up as Christians, whether Protestant or Catholic, have appeared to know very little about actual Christian teaching; instead, they just seem to have absorbed a sort of gloomy presence.

The Mahāyāna perspective is simply more encouraging—if also more demanding, inasmuch as we have that much more to live up to. There is no excuse for apathy or unskilful mental states—and no cause for complacency either. The responsibility for our condition is our own, and the means of improving it are also in our own hands. This less oppressive atmosphere needs a bit of getting used to; we probably need to remind ourselves to take a few deep breaths of it from time to time. Buddhism is not saying that we definitely have exalted spiritual antecedents, but only that we cannot rule out the possibility. If we find ourselves, for whatever reason, studying the Perfection of Wisdom, this must be accounted a very propitious circumstance indeed. We are not doing too badly at all with our lives. We probably have more merit working for us than we think.

If you do still feel like a miserable sinner, well, perhaps you are just a backsliding Bodhisattva, an Arhat on the skid, a down-at-heel incarnate lama. Perhaps your present incarnation is just a hiccup in an otherwise rather distinguished spiritual progression. This particular world system is supposed to be a tough one, where the influence of Māra is dominant, and attachments are very strong. So why not be optimistic? Taking up the *Diamond Sūtra*, you are perhaps simply back where you belong.

Of course, there are people who would feel quite uneasy if they were told that they had taken the Bodhisattva Vow, and who would contemplate the prospect of becoming a Buddha with a certain amount of dismay. This is certainly the conclusion of the *Saddharma-puṇḍarīka*, in which the Bodhisattva who goes about telling people that they are all due for Buddhahood fails to meet with a very favourable response. I am also reminded of a passage from a Chinese opera translated by Lin Yutang, a long declamatory song from a young girl who is running away from a nunnery and who says, among some other rather strong things, that she does not want to be a nun, indeed she does not want to be a Buddha, and she is not going to be a Buddha. She is going to run down the hill away from the nunnery and find herself a handsome young lover. And no, she is not going to be a Buddha.

On the other hand, it was once said of my friend and teacher, Dhardo Rimpoche, that although he did not at first *feel* like an incarnate Bodhisattva, he believed those who had told him that this was what he was, and simply acted accordingly. In the same way, if having come into contact with the *Diamond Sūtra* convinces you that you have taken the Bodhisattva Vow, there is then just the simple matter of acting as if you had. It makes everything terrifyingly simple: you know who you are, so you know exactly what you have to do.

Chapter Twelve

CUT DOWN TO SIZE

**IT IS AS WELL NOT TO STUDY THE DIAMOND SUTRA IN ISOLATION,
AT LEAST NOT WITHOUT KNOWING WHO AND WHERE OUR SPIRITUAL FRIENDS ARE**

*...those sons and daughters of good family, who will take up these very
Sūtras, and will bear them in mind, recite and study them, they will be
humbled,—well humbled they will be! And why? The impure deeds which
these beings have done in their former lives, and which are liable to lead
them into the states of woe,—in this very life they will, by means of that
humiliation, annul those impure deeds of their former lives, and they will
reach the enlightenment of a Buddha.*

Maybe we have taken the Bodhisattva Vow in a previous life; nonetheless
we may also have committed unskilful actions. But taking up the study
of these sūtras we will be humbled, and in this process our impure deeds
will be annulled. This is why this sūtra is sometimes recited in the context
of a purification ceremony. Chih-i refers to one such in *Dhyāna for Beginners*, saying that if we become conscious of any breach of the precepts,
we can confess it in front of an image of the Buddha, burn incense, light
candles, and recite Mahāyāna sūtras until such time as we feel that we
have freed ourselves from the ill-effects of that particular transgression.[34]

It seems a bit of a mystery, though, that the sūtra should have the power
to humiliate us. But the fact is that when you come into contact with the
teaching of the Perfection of Wisdom, you come into contact something
very powerful indeed. If you allow yourself to be affected by it, there

arises a tremendous incompatibility between your response and the way you usually are, and that tension needs to be dispelled. The parts of yourself that remain on the sidelines while the aspiring element in you engages with the Perfection of Wisdom need to catch up very, very quickly. Something drastic needs to happen. Just feeling humble on account of previous unskilful deeds is not going to be enough. The discrepancy could be dangerous, even schizophrenic, were it not for the immense amount of *puṇya* (merit) that you generate when you plug into the Perfection of Wisdom. Thanks to your merit, things will actually happen to humiliate you. Circumstances will arise to bring humiliation on your head, and with that suffering much that is unskilful in you will very quickly be purged away, so that more of you can rise to the challenge of the Perfection of Wisdom.

Here opens a singular perspective on the incidence of suffering. Things may start going badly for us not as a result of unskilful behaviour, but in consequence of our exposing ourselves to a higher vision. We may even find ourselves thinking that everything was going rather well for us until we took up the spiritual life. We tend to expect that adopting the spiritual life should make everything go much more smoothly for us, but that certainly does not always happen. The spiritual life may be a happy one, but it is by no means necessarily easy or free from difficulties and suffering. A properly functioning spiritual community will help to carry us over these hurdles. It is as well not to study the *Diamond Sūtra* in isolation, at least not without knowing who and where our spiritual friends are.

This new perspective calls for a complete shift in the way we respond to circumstances. If it does happen that we are brought low, especially in such a way that we are humbled, we should not just react, reassert ourselves, and limit the damage. We need to understand what is happening, and appreciate that the process of purgation is at work. This process is well known to anyone who practises the Vajrasattva *sādhana*; the purificatory process manifests itself in various experiences, sometimes in dreams, which indicate that we are expelling, in a manner of speaking, whatever is unskilful within us.

We like to read books about destroying the ego; the idea of it is inspiring and even attractive. But when the ego becomes subject to the buffets and belabourings of actual circumstances, when our self-esteem does actually get brought down a peg or two, well, that is quite another matter. It takes some effort to accept certain disagreeable experiences as positive, to realize that we are sometimes actually fortunate to be having a hard time—particularly the kind of hard time in which our ego comes up against the fact of its own egohood, when it is forced to recognize itself for what it is, and to do something about itself. This is not to say that any old suffering is good for us, but we need to be very careful about identifying certain situations as good or bad, and therefore as correspondingly the result of good or bad *karma*—because it works the other way round too. You could, for example, be born the healthy scion of a wealthy family and conclude that this circumstance was the result of *puṇya* (merit), not *pāpa* ('sin'). But would that necessarily be the case? Certainly not, for example, if that family had no respect for the Dharma.

There are some traditional ways of setting up humiliating conditions. You cannot but be humble while begging for food; and even when you beg on behalf of a charity, you will soon see whether your pride makes you feel uncomfortable and inferior in such a role. Traditionally, it is the guru who is supposed to humiliate you, especially in the Vajrayāna—though people in the West, and I suspect even in the East nowadays, cannot any longer take such treatment, perhaps for lack of faith.

The classic case of a guru's kind humiliation of a disciple is Marpa's treatment of Milarepa, a disciple who had committed so many unskilful deeds that he was well on course for the hell-realms. The only hope for Milarepa was to gain Enlightenment in one lifetime, so that he would not be reborn at all within the saṁsāra, and it was quite a forlorn hope for someone as overloaded with evil *karma* as he was. Marpa could see no other way of lifting this burden from his disciple than by humiliating him by making him build towers and pull them down, over and over again. In setting up a very positive situation for Milarepa as a result of which he would be well and truly humbled, Marpa seems to have been functioning like the Perfection of Wisdom itself (and his wife's name was Dagmema, Tibetan for *nairātmya* or 'not-self').

It is sometimes said that hard gurus are in a way better and more effective than soft ones (you generally have to be one or the other, otherwise your disciples get confused and upset) but that soft gurus are better for larger numbers of people. So paradoxically, you could say, the fewer the disciples, the better the guru. Another guru who ran a school of hard knocks, as it were, and whom I met in Bangalore in about 1950, was the ferocious, one-eyed Yalahankar Swami, who was said to be at least six hundred years old.[35] He had only a few disciples, and concentrated on trying to eradicate their egotism. He would send them to visit any sādhus who were passing through the district, in order to perform before them a very lengthy and elaborate form of prostration which took several minutes to complete, and which had to be repeated a number of times. He felt that you could carry a lurking pride quite intact through a casual observance of the conventional prostration, so that it just did not do the job properly. One very important thing he taught me was that humility is just as much a form of egotism as pride. With those who were proud he behaved more proudly still; with those who were humble, with even greater humility. 'However high you go', he said to me once, 'I shall always be above you. However low you go, I shall always be below you.'

Dr Johnson too, on a more worldly level, had little time for self-deprecation: 'all censure of a man's self is oblique praise. It is in order to shew how much he can spare. It has all the invidiousness of self-praise, and all the reproach of falsehood.' Humility can also be a strategy for specifically avoiding humiliation, as Boswell himself observed: 'Sometimes it may proceed from a man's strong consciousness of his faults being observed. He knows that others would throw him down, and therefore he had better lie down softly of his own accord.'[36]

This goes to show that humility is not enough. You need to take risks. If you don't ever face the possibility of failure, then you don't ever face the possibility of humiliation, and therefore of growth. Failure will only have meaning for you if you have made a tremendous effort to succeed. The terrible temptation is to venture nothing. But in fact, the less you risk, the greater your fear of failure, and the greater the potential humiliation. So much becomes invested in the imperative of success that you cannot even give a lecture in case it should not be an astounding success. You become paralysed. You haven't gone beyond success and failure; you are beneath them. If you're not careful, you become someone with a great future behind them.

Your pursuit of success is going to invite humiliation in the degree to which your motivation is personal success rather than the success of the project itself. To the extent to which your ego has identified with the success of that particular project, to that extent you risk being humbled. But if you throw yourself into a worthwhile project, you win whether you succeed or fail. Your motivation doesn't really matter—it will get knocked into shape anyway in the course of an ambitious and meritorious undertaking; and if you fail, you are humbled, which is, of course, not a bad thing at all. Humiliation may even be counted amongst the ways in which Perfect Vision might arise—being cut down to size by reality itself—so it can be a very positive experience indeed. If you can take it as such, you find you can survive it. Life goes on. You pick yourself up, dust yourself down, and start all over again.

On an ordinary social level you take a risk every time you make any kind of advance towards another person. If social success is too important to you, you will never dare to approach anyone. You just have to get used to an occasional rebuff. It can also be humiliating to be in a foreign country with a limited command of the language—the natives speak to you as if you were a child, or very stupid, or deaf—but the alternative is just to stay at home. If you make a fool of yourself in public—you forget your notes for a lecture, or you realize you are at the wrong meeting—you feel disgraced. You can be humbled by being open to criticism. If you become ill and no longer have control of your own body, or if you lose your looks, or if you become old and people start patronizing you, or if you are ridiculed, all these things can be quite mortifying. There are so many potentially humiliating situations, and you need to be able to make the most of them.

The great Zen master Hakuin was scorned for many years by other pious Buddhists because he stood accused of being the father of an illegitimate child. 'It's yours. You keep it,' the indignant parents of the mother said to him. 'Is that so?' was all he replied as he accepted the child from them. Some years later the mother confessed that she had falsely accused him to protect someone else, and her parents came to collect the boy again. 'Well, we're sorry', they said, 'It's all been a terrible mistake— we realize now you weren't the father after all.' As he surrendered the boy, Hakuin just said 'Is that so?' False accusation is one of the most difficult things to accept without making a fuss. Losing your reputation in that way, and being scorned by people who once respected you, seems to take the meaning out of life; it is so unfair and unjust, and you have right on your side. But the ego is also on your side. It is Hakuin's 'song' that he accepted this humiliation—which for him, of course, was no humiliation, so little of selfhood was there in him to be crushed.

A little nearer home, the poet John Milton saw the failure of his whole life's work—or rather the overthrowing of the Republican cause to which he had devoted his life—with the restoration of the Crown in 1660. Everything he stood for, personally and politically, was lost. And yet he evidently did come to terms with that failure, as he had done with his blindness ten years before, and he shifted his outlook. Within a few years the crushing of all his ambitions had fructified, and he had produced the only truly epic work in English literature, *Paradise Lost*.

These are fairly extreme examples of people who have taken life on the chin and thereby achieved a deeper harmony. The humiliation that springs from *puṇya* is never more than you can take—but it is of course possible to be so humiliated, perhaps through the malice or unskilfulness of others, as to be harmed or damaged by the experience. There is no need to go about deliberately humbling other people, even if you can persuade yourself that it is for their own good. That would be quite a suspect procedure. Honest criticism, yes, by all means—in the interests of good communication and spiritual friendship—but the business of humbling can safely be left in the hands of the Buddhas and Bodhisattvas.

On the other hand, it is not the office of a friend to salve wounded pride, to reassure someone who has been humiliated, and thereby minimize the experience. To take that most hair-raising of human experiences, public speaking, if someone forgets their notes and gives such a lame performance as to be embarrassing to listen to, don't console them. Don't deprive them of their humiliation. Allow them to derive some benefit from the experience.

Chapter Thirteen

THE REALITY OF THE BUDDHA

He who has set out in the Bodhisattva-vehicle—he is not one of the dharmas.

The Bodhisattva comes into a different category from any other kind of being. He—or she—just does not belong among the *dharmas*. With the arising of the bodhicitta, a new note has been struck, a new, purely transcendental element has been introduced, a seed has been sown that is not native to the soil at all, but comes from somewhere else altogether. In the Gnostic tradition a sage is referred to as the 'stranger', or even the 'Stranger', one who essentially does not belong. The Bodhisattva is something like this—except that we cannot really think of the Bodhisattva as an individual, because the term 'individual' as we usually use it stands for a mundane category. We can add that the spiritual community, like the Bodhisattva, does not belong among the *dharmas*. In the midst of society it does not belong to society. It is not part of the social group, though it may appear to be so. What it represents is the introduction—even the invasion—of a foreign body, in the strict sense of the term.

HOW DOES A BUDDHA FORETELL FUTURE EVENTS?

What do you think Subhūti, is there any dharma by which the Tathāgata, when he was with Dīpaṅkara the Tathāgata, has fully known the utmost, right and perfect enlightenment?—Subhūti replied: There is not any dharma by which the Tathāgata, when he was with the Tathāgata Dīpaṅkara, has fully known the utmost, right and perfect enlightenment.— The Lord said: It is for this reason that the Tathāgata Dīpaṅkara then

predicted of me: 'You, young Brahmin, will be in a future period a
Tathāgata, Arhat, fully Enlightened, by the name of Śākyamuni!'

Here is a restatement and an extension of the argument of chapter 10.
The Buddha-to-be, whatever quantities of merit he accumulated, actually derived nothing from his experience with the Buddha Dīpaṅkara that
would enable him subsequently to realize Enlightenment for himself.
The Buddha says that Dīpaṅkara's prediction took place *because* there
was no way that the Buddha-to-be's future Buddhahood could be in-
ferred from, ascribed to, or predicated upon, any perceived conditions.

The faculty of prediction exercised by Dīpaṅkara is one of the Six
Abhiññās (Sanskrit *abhijñās*), the supernormal powers of a Buddha. Five
of them, including the power of prediction, represent the higher and
more refined kinds of mundane attainment, which pave the way, so to
speak, for the sixth, genuinely transcendental power: knowledge of the
destruction of the *āsavas*—the *āsavas* being craving for sensuous
pleasure, craving for existence, and ignorance. The general principle
here seems to be that Enlightenment is approached by a progressive
refinement of the mundane, from the *kāmaloka* through the *rūpaloka* and
the *arūpaloka* to the *lokottara*. So the first five *abhiññas*—or the first two of
a briefer version of them, the Three *Ñānas* or Knowledges—do not
constitute part of the Enlightenment experience proper.

How then does Dīpaṅkara's predictive power, mundane though it is,
operate? How does a Buddha foretell future events? The temptation is
to try to skirt round the sort of contradiction that racks Christian theol-
ogy—how to reconcile human free-will with God's foreknowledge of
what human beings will do. So one might assume that Sumedha had
attained Stream Entry and that (to follow Hīnayāna dogmatics) it was a
simple matter then for Dīpaṅkara to predict full Enlightenment for him
within seven lifetimes by straightforward inference. What Sumedha was
actually assured of, however, was *samyak-sambuddhahood*, which meant
that he was on the path of the Bodhisattva, not that of the Arhat, and so
had—according to Mahāyāna dogmatics—not just seven, but an innumerable succession of rebirths awaiting him over three *kalpas* before
he got there.

Now you could, if you liked, step outside the historical framework
within which these divergent doctrines developed, and try to reconcile
the two paths. You would have a job doing it though. Some later
Mahāyāna traditions place the paths end to end, as it were, but certainly
in the Perfection of Wisdom sūtras the path of the Arhat and the path of

the Bodhisattva are considered to exclude one another: if you enter upon the one, you do not enter upon the other. So there is no question of Stream Entry for Sumedha, because he is not going to be an Arhat, and thus there is no straightforward inference for Dīpaṅkara to make.

The way Dīpaṅkara's predictive power works is clear enough if we take into consideration the workings of karma, which are also laid open in all their details to the supernormal vision of a Buddha. The karmic results of any action are actually quite open and uncertain: there is no way whatever of knowing in advance the results of any particular action. Some karmas are quite weak and may not come to fruition at all. Only time will tell. So if the Buddha sees that what beings are experiencing now is the direct result of particular karmas performed in the past, and that karmas which they are performing now will have definite and specific results in the future, this cannot be through any drawing of inferences. The Buddha does not infer that this is happening because of that, and that it will necessarily produce such and such results. He sees these causes and results only through direct supernormal perception, operating independently of time; that is, he sees the past and the future in the present. Dīpaṅkara perceives Sumedha's future Buddhahood not as an inference from, say, Sumedha's Stream Entry—because this cannot be done—but simply through direct perception. Dīpaṅkara even perceives that the young Brahmin ascetic standing before him in Nagpur will be named Śākyamuni.

Śākyamuni, incidentally, is a patronymic meaning 'a muni of the Śākya tribe'. *Muni* means 'one who is silent' and also 'one who is wise', so it is sometimes translated as 'silent sage'. In fact, the basic meaning is 'one who is silent', but one who is silent is assumed to be wise—like the wise old owl in the nursery rhyme:

A wise old owl sat in an oak,
The more he heard, the less he spoke,
The less he spoke, the more he heard,
Wasn't he a wise old bird?

'All dharmas', Subhūti, have as no-dharmas been taught by the Tathāgata.
Therefore all dharmas are called the Buddha's own and special dharmas.

You cannot tie the Buddha down to being this or that specific thing; therefore it is as though anything and everything belongs to the Buddha. The Buddha is, you might say, identical with emptiness. All *dharmas* are empty, so it follows that the Buddha, being empty, possesses all *dharmas*.

The Buddha possesses all *dharmas* by virtue of his realization of that *śūnyatā* which is the essential nature of all *dharmas*. This idea is personified in the figure of Māmakī, the consort of the Buddha Ratnasambhava. *Māmakī* means 'one who considers all as "mine"'. All things are hers because she does not claim anything as hers. She represents an attitude of delight in and appreciation for everyone and everything. Seeing them as being not different from herself, she holds them all equally dear, equally close to her heart.

> *The Bodhisattva, however, Subhūti, who is intent on 'without self are the dharmas, without self are the dharmas', him the Tathāgata, the Arhat, the fully Enlightened One, has declared to be a Bodhi-being, a great being.*

There are two kinds of *nairātmya* or 'emptiness of self': the Hīnayāna conception of *pudgala-nairātmya*, or 'no soul', and the Mahāyāna extension of this principle, the *dharma-nairātmya*, or 'without self are the dharmas'. The Buddha is saying that it is a preoccupation with *dharma-nairātmya* or *dharma-śūnyatā*, the deeper level of *śūnyatā* which goes beyond the *pudgala-nairātmya*, that is the mark of a Bodhisattva.

As we have seen, the Sarvāstivādin School recognized that the *pudgala*, the 'self', was not something solid or impartite, but composite, and therefore conditioned, transitory, and unsatisfactory. Having broken the self down into a number of psycho-physical elements, they then regarded these elements—*dharmas*—as ultimate, thus simply transferring the notion of an entity from the *pudgala* to the *pudgala*'s constituent *dharmas*.

What the Mahāyāna proposed was that the *dharmas* were conceptual, almost arbitrary constructions, just as much as was the *pudgala*. You don't have to stop with *dharmas*, said the Mahayanists. You can go further, on and on, indefinitely. That possibility of going on indefinitely is represented by the idea—it cannot be other than an idea to begin with—of *dharma-nairātmya* or *dharma-śūnyatā*. Further to denying the label 'self' to the various processes that make up the individual subject, and that are governed by *pratītya-samutpāda*, the law of conditionality,[37] the Mahāyāna insisted that the same principle must apply to *dharmas*. There is no unchanging 'dharma-entity', just as there is no 'tree-entity' or 'jug-entity' standing behind these things—or the processes that make up these things—and constituting their real nature. Yes, there *is* something standing behind them, but it is reality, the One Mind, nirvāṇa—and we cannot apply to *that* the word we have used for something quite different which we refer to when we speak of 'tree', 'jug', or 'dharma'.

What do you think, Subhūti, does the fleshly eye of the Tathāgata exist?—Subhūti replied: So it is, O Lord, the fleshly eye of the Tathāgata does exist.—The Lord asked: What do you think, Subhūti, does the Tathāgata's heavenly eye exist, his wisdom eye, his Dharma-eye, his Buddha-eye?—Subhūti replied: So it is, O Lord, the heavenly eye of the Tathāgata does exist, and so does his wisdom eye, his Dharma-eye and his Buddha-eye.

What is going on? Can this be the Perfection of Wisdom—allowing an assertion like this to pass without pinning it to a contradiction of itself? Surely the five eyes exist because they do not exist? Is Subhūti letting up a little? Is the Buddha letting up a little?

In fact there is no reason to assume that the Perfection of Wisdom is nodding off for a moment here. First of all, mundane reality has to be allowed to exist on its own level, for its own purposes; the transcendental does not negate the mundane. Secondly, this sudden affirmation of the existence of the Buddha's attributes in the midst of a relentless and ruthless dismantling of anything the mind might seize upon has the effect of throwing into bold relief the reality of the Buddha himself as the ultimate refuge. For devotional purposes the Buddha's attributes have to be allowed to stand. Finally, the fact that we are brought up short at this point shows that we should be able by this time to understand exactly in what sense something may be said to exist. We don't have to go on being told that mountains are not mountains, and that trees are not trees. As the lesson sinks in and becomes second nature to us, mountains are once again simply mountains, and trees are just trees.

The Lord said: As many beings as there are in these world systems, of them I know, in my wisdom, the manifold trends of thought. And why? 'Trends of thought, trends of thought', Subhūti, as no-trends have they been taught by the Tathāgata. Therefore are they called 'trends of thought'. And why? Past thought is not got at; future thought is not got at; present thought is not got at.

It is a commonplace of early Buddhist thought that as one of his attainments the Buddha knows the psychological characteristics, the tendencies, and the temperaments of all other living beings. The Mahāyāna goes further and argues that the Buddha knows these trends of thought because they are no-trends, because thought, whether of the past, future, or present, cannot be apprehended as a real, objectively existing thing, any more than can anything else of the past, present, or future.

> *What do you think, Subhūti, is the Tathāgata to be seen by means of the*
> *accomplishment of his form-body? Subhūti replied: No indeed, O Lord...*

'The accomplishment of his form body' refers to the particular psycho-physical organism that the Buddha attains to in his last life as a result of skilful deeds performed in previous lives. This is the *rūpakāya*. In the Hīnayāna it is differentiated simply from the *dharmakāya*, which, just referring to the sum total of the teaching, has nothing very metaphysical about it. In the Mahāyāna, however, the *dharmakāya* comes to mean the Buddha's transcendental personality, as distinguished from his mundane or phenomenal personality, the *rūpakāya*.

> *The Lord asked: What do you think, Subhūti, does it occur to the*
> *Tathāgata, 'by me has Dharma been demonstrated'? Whosoever, Subhūti,*
> *would say, 'the Tathāgata has demonstrated Dharma', he would speak*
> *falsely, he would misrepresent me by seizing on what is not there. And*
> *why? 'Demonstration of dharma, demonstration of dharma', Subhūti, there*
> *is not any dharma which could be got at as a demonstration of dharma.*

Just occasionally in this sūtra we can get a grip on what is being said at a slightly more accessible level than the purely metaphysical. Here, it does seem understandable that it should not occur to the Buddha 'by me has Dharma been demonstrated'. In a way, it is like the child's view of the adult: driving the car and going to work seem like very special, wonderful, mysterious activities until they become part of the normal, everyday business of living. In the same natural way, perhaps the Buddha doesn't think of himself as teaching something called the Dharma. He just thinks of himself—if he thinks in these terms at all—as talking to people, and sharing his vision with them. His 'doing' is inseparable from his 'being' in a way which is perfectly natural, although to us it may seem quite extraordinary. But for us too, the more our practice of the Dharma deepens, the more it becomes our ordinary way of living.

Note again that the distinction between 'the Dharma' and 'a dharma' made by the use of upper or lower case is not available in Sanskrit. Ideally you want to imagine that you are *hearing* the sūtra rather than reading it, so as to retain the ambiguity of the word. The more meta-physical reading of this passage asserts itself when the meaning of 'dharma' is more plainly 'any object of the mind'.

Subhūti asked: Are there, O Lord, any beings ... at the time of the collapse of the good doctrine who, on hearing such dharmas, will truly believe?— The Lord replied: They, Subhūti, are neither beings nor no-beings. And why? 'Beings, beings', Subhūti, the Tathāgata has taught that they are all no-beings. Therefore has he spoken of 'all beings'.

Again, there are two levels at which we may take this. The simplest reading is also the deepest: all beings are equally identical to—that is to say, not different from—*śūnyatā*. More provisionally speaking, however, we may tie it up with chapter 17: 'He who has set out in the Bodhisattva-vehicle—he is not one of the dharmas.' It is as though some beings are more empty than others—at least provisionally. They will be able to believe because there is that in them which transcends existence and non-existence, which gives them an affinity for the teaching, and on account of which they cannot be classified as 'beings' or 'no-beings'. They are not separate individuals, but at the same time they are not actually non-existent. They belong to a new category, represented in its fullness by the Buddha himself.

What do you think, Subhūti, is there any dharma by which the Tathāgata has fully known the utmost, right and perfect enlightenment?—Subhūti replied: No indeed, O Lord, there is not any dharma by which the Tathāgata has fully known the utmost, right and perfect enlightenment.—The Lord said: So it is, Subhūti, so it is. Not even the least (anu) dharma is there found or got at. Therefore is it called 'utmost (anuttara), right and perfect enlightenment'. Furthermore, Subhūti, self-identical (sama) is that dharma, and nothing is therein at variance (vishama). Therefore is it called 'utmost, right (samyak) and perfect (sam-) enlightenment'.

There is a play on words here that gets lost in the translation but which in the original helps to undermine our faith in mere verbal constructs. There is a play firstly on *anu*, although one *anu* has a dot under the n, making it a nasal ṇ, so it is actually a different prefix; and secondly on *sama*—although again it is unlikely that there is any etymological connection between *sama* and *sam-*.

Self-identical through the absence of a self, a being, a soul, or a person, the
utmost, right and perfect enlightenment is fully known as the totality of all
the wholesome dharmas.

'Self-identical through the absence of a self' is another abrogation of the
law of contradiction: A is identical with A through the absence of A.
'Nothing is therein at variance' is simply a different way of saying
'self-identical'.

You could say that perfect Enlightenment consists in the totality of all
skilful mental states—including the understanding that these
'wholesome dharmas' are 'no-dharmas'.

Those who by my form did see me,
And those who followed me by voice
Wrong the efforts they engaged in,
Me those people will not see.

In other words, the Buddha is to be identified with his *dharmakāya* rather
than with his *rūpakāya*. The Buddha says as much in the Pāli Canon,
where he says 'He who sees the Dharma, sees me.'[38] These verses are
more than likely to be part of an older tradition; they do not, so far as I
am aware, crop up in the large Perfection of Wisdom sūtras.

From the Dharma should one see the Buddhas,
From the Dharmabodies comes their guidance.
Yet Dharma's true nature cannot be discerned,
And no one can be conscious of it as an object.

The Buddhas are essentially embodiments of the Dharma, embodiments
of *bodhi*, not just personalities. They are guided by the Dharmabodies,
the higher spiritual realities, so closely that they are not actually separate
from them. At the same time, this Dharmabody, this higher reality, does
not exist as an object as distinct from a subject. It is a 'pseudo-object'—
something which is essentially not an object, but which is perceived or
spoken of as an object.

Nor should anyone, Subhūti, say to you, 'those who have set out in the
Bodhisattva-vehicle have conceived the destruction of a dharma, or its
annihilation'.

You cannot conceive the destruction or the annihilation of that which in
reality does not exist. Reducing *dharmas* to *śūnyatā* does not mean that
you are destroying them: the mere fact that *dharmas* are reduced to
śūnyatā means that they are not entities to be destroyed anyway.

How does it feel to be an irreversible Bodhisattva?

*And again, Subhūti, if a son or daughter of good family had filled with the
seven precious things as many world systems as there are grains of sand in
the river Ganges, and gave them as a gift to the Tathāgatas, Arhats, fully
Enlightened Ones,—and if on the other hand a Bodhisattva would gain the
patient acquiescence in dharmas which are nothing of themselves and which
fail to be produced, then this latter would on the strength of that beget a
greater heap of merit, immeasurable and incalculable.*

The experience of the *anutpattika-dharma-kshānti*, the patient acceptance
of the non-arising of *dharmas*, is represented by the eighth *bhūmi* (reckoning the *bhūmis* according to the *Daśabhūmika*).[39] Seeing *dharmas* apparently
coming into existence and passing away, the Bodhisattva does not see
real entities, nor any arising or passing away. To take the old comparison
of the magician who makes you see an elephant, you do see what appears
to be an elephant, but no elephant is actually there. Even if the magician
conjures up a figure who kills the elephant, well, no killing has actually
taken place. This is a simile used throughout the Mahāyāna for seeing
things as essentially empty. What is particular about the level of insight
we are looking at here—the eighth *bhūmi*—is the element of *kshānti*. Any
lingering resistance to the idea of *anutpattika-dharma* has completely gone.

But there is still a question that remains unanswered, a question that
does not seem ever to have been looked at. Why should seeing things in
that way, and to *acquiescence* in seeing things in that way, constitute
irreversibility? Why *anutpattika-dharma-kshānti* in particular? What special connection does that have with *samyak-sambuddhahood*—as opposed
to Arhatship? To find this out we simply need to ask ourselves 'How does
it feel to be an irreversible Bodhisattva?'—or, to be realistic, 'Can we get
an idea of a feeling of what it might be like to be an irreversible
Bodhisattva?'

We can start by trying to imagine what it would be like not to take
anything seriously, ontologically speaking. Your experience is like a
dream, a vision—you see it all right, but you see through it, thoroughly
see through it. It is like a lucid dream, a dream in which you know you
are dreaming. Your experience of the world, of conditioned existence, is
vivid—more vivid than ever—but you are not misled by it. And of course,
most significant of all, you see that there are no beings to save. And
among these so-called beings there is yourself—so there is also no

question of any 'self' to save. The possibility of thinking in terms of individual emancipation no longer exists. From that point onwards, you genuinely see no difference between yourself and others. All are equally dream-like and, in a sense, illusory. It is like a game, and you don't mind any more what particular game you are playing; but it is also like the other kind of play—a spontaneous expression of creativity.

If we think of irreversibility in this way, and if irreversibility is at least broadly analogous to Stream Entry on the so-called Hīnayāna path, what bearing does this notion of *anutpattika-dharma-kshānti* have on the idea of Stream Entry? It is clearly connected with the first fetter, *sakkāyadiṭṭhi*, the mistaken belief in a fixed, unchanging self which is broken on Stream Entry.[40] The Hīnayāna does not follow the metaphysical implications of breaking this fetter as the Mahāyāna does—it is more practical, straightforward, almost psychological in its approach—and yet the implications are there, nevertheless. You are no longer thinking that there is anyone there to be saved at all—neither other people nor yourself.

> *Moreover, Subhūti, the Bodhisattva should not acquire a heap of merit.—Subhūti said: 'Surely, O Lord, the Bodhisattva should acquire a heap of merit?—The Lord said: 'Should acquire', Subhūti, not 'should seize upon'. Therefore it is said 'should acquire'.*

The Bodhisattva should acquire merit spontaneously, without thinking that merit is a real thing, or that the acquisition of merit is a real acquisition by a real person who really does acquire it.

> *Whosoever says that the Tathāgata goes or comes, stands, sits or lies down, he does not understand the meaning of my teaching. And why? 'Tathāgata' is called one who has not gone anywhere, nor come from anywhere. Therefore is he called 'the Tathāgata, the Arhat, the fully Enlightened One'.*

The Tathāgata is the one who is 'thus gone', 'gone in such and such a way'; or he is 'thus *come*'. It can be either, depending on how you divide the word: Tatha-agata or Tatha-gata. He is 'thus come' or 'thus gone', although he neither comes nor goes. The usual Theravāda interpretation is quite plain and straightforward: the Tathāgata is one who has gone to or come from the state of Enlightenment, as his predecessors did. The Mahāyāna, as you might expect, tries to put a little more philosophical spin on the concept: the Tathāgata both comes and goes in the sense that he goes out of the world—from the conditioned to the Unconditioned—

by means of wisdom; and he comes back to the world by reason of compassion. His going is his coming, his coming is his going. Wisdom is compassion; compassion is wisdom.

In *The Awakening of Faith in the Mahāyāna*, Aśvaghosha uses the term *tathatā* or 'suchness', which is an abstract noun but the same basic word. *Tathatā* is quite a strange term, expressing the indefinability of things, the impossibility of defining or describing anything. You can only say 'It is such as it is' or 'Thus it is.' Things are such as they are, and it is quite beyond the competence of words or concepts to express their nature.

The fact is—according to the *Diamond Sūtra*—that the Tathāgata is 'thus come' and 'thus gone' because he neither comes nor goes, nor stands, nor sits, nor lies down. We should by now be able to guess the reason for this, which is of course that the Buddha is not to be identified with his physical body, his *rūpakāya*, but with his *dharmakāya*. Obviously the *dharmakāya* does not come or go, stand, sit, or lie down.

But we can go a little deeper into what is being said here. Even the *rūpakāya* or phenomenal personality of the Buddha does not come and go in an ultimate sense, because ultimately there is no coming or going at all, no more than there is any arising or destruction of *dharmas*. Sometimes it is even said that ultimately everything remains in a state of immobility—though this is perhaps a rather difficult concept.

Chapter Fourteen

SEEING THROUGH ILLUSIONS

And what the Tathāgata taught as 'the world system of 1,000 million worlds', that he has taught as a no-system.

Conze's notes to chapter 30 need to be taken with a pinch of salt. He asserts that 'a universe is no more than a fortuitous conglomeration of various elements and therefore it is really a no-system'. He gives a 'scientific' reason, but it is not the reason given by the sūtra. In fact, it is not because it is fortuitous that the world system of a thousand million worlds is a no-system—it is because the various elements themselves have no existence, because the conglomeration is a no-conglomeration. Besides, the law of karma would be enough, you would have thought, to prevent things from being 'no more than fortuitous'.

Conze also suggests that 'our spirit is often weighed down by the mere thought of ... the enormous quantity of matter that we perceive around us.' But Blaise Pascal probably speaks for more of us when he writes, in the *Pensées*, 'The eternal silence of these infinite spaces terrifies me.' The mind actually takes comfort from a sense of material solidity.

And finally, Subhūti, if a Bodhisattva, a great being had filled world-systems immeasurable and incalculable with the seven precious things, and gave them as a gift to the Tathāgatas, the Arhats, the fully Enlightened Ones,—and if, on the other hand, a son or daughter of good family had taken from this Prajñāpāramitā, this discourse on Dharma, but one stanza of four lines, and were to bear it in mind, demonstrate, recite and study it, and illuminate it in full detail for others, on the strength of that this latter

would beget a greater heap of merit, immeasurable and incalculable. And
how would he illuminate it? So as not to reveal. Therefore is it said, 'he
would illuminate'.

There can be no directly conceptual revelation of the Perfection of
Wisdom. To *illuminate* it can only mean giving expression to it, or trying
to communicate it, by way of metaphor, simile, and poetry, which is
precisely what the sūtra goes on to do.[41]

> *As stars, a fault of vision, as a lamp,*
> *A mock show, dew drops, or a bubble,*
> *A dream, a lightning flash, or cloud,*
> *So should one view what is conditioned.*

This is the most famous part of the whole sūtra, and it is a very useful
verse on which to meditate and reflect in such a way as to provoke the
arising of insight. To take it image by image, first, one should view what
is conditioned as one views stars. Stars are hardly perceptible at all,
whatever their mass, within the vast empty reaches of space. They are
so far from our possessing as to be beyond the grasp of the imagination
itself. And they disappear with the first dawning of the sun.

Then, the conditioned is like a fault of vision. Things are not as they
seem to be. It is as simple as that. According to the traditional commentaries, what is meant here is the kind of affliction to the eyes that would
cause a monk to see imaginary hairs in his begging-bowl. This illustration is a bit extreme, suggesting as it does that the conditioned is as
illusory as are those 'hairs', whereas it is from a *metaphysical* point of view
that the conditioned is illusory. The conditioned is not *ultimately* real, but
it is real in the sense that it is perceived. It is not like so many spots before
the eyes.

The later Yogācāra philosophy elucidates this distinction by differen-
tiating three kinds of reality: *parikalpita*, *paratantra*, and *parinishpanna*.
The first of these, *parikalpita*, is what we usually mean by 'illusory': that
which is imputed or imagined. *Paratantra* refers to knowledge which is
'other-dependent'—*para* meaning 'other', and *tantra* 'that which is
woven or put together'. It applies to that which is not self-existent, but
dependent for its existence upon various causes and conditions that have
brought it into being. It stands for conditioned or relative knowledge, a
projection onto the world outside of our own mental structure. *Parinish-*
panna means 'perfect', and thus refers to absolute knowledge—
knowledge of that which exists without dependence upon conditions.
So the distinction is made between that which does not have even a

relative existence, *parikalpita* (to take a traditional example, a snake that turns out to be have been a rope all along) and *paratantra*, that which is real on a practical, common-sense level (you see that the 'snake' is really a rope) but which is itself an illusion when seen from the point of view of *parinishpanna* (which sees that the existence of the rope depends upon its constituent strands).

IF YOU CAN LAUGH AT MUNDANE ISSUES THAT WERE ONCE OF GREAT CONCERN TO YOU, IT MEANS THAT YOU ARE BEGINNING TO RELEASE THE ENERGIES THAT ARE LOCKED UP IN THOSE ANXIETIES, AND TO SEE THROUGH THE ILLUSIONS THAT ARE BOUND UP WITH THEM

There are really two kinds of illusion in the sense of *parikalpita*. The 'fault of vision' is only an analogy for the metaphysical or even psychological illusion of the *ātman*—we think we perceive an ego, but it isn't really there. This illusion of 'self' is said to be of the same kind, though not of the same order, as mirages and imaginary hairs in the begging-bowl. In a way it doesn't matter if we *perceive* the 'self'—just as it doesn't matter if we perceive those imaginary hairs. But if we *act* upon the assumption that this 'self' is an independent autonomous entity over and above, or behind, the sum total of our thoughts, words, and deeds, if any sort of emotional attitude arises from this illusion, we are in trouble. It is in this sense that we can say that the whole contemporary world view is based upon illusion.

We are also in trouble, however, if we fail to distinguish between the illusion of the 'self' as an independent entity on the one hand, and the reality of our empirical being, our thoughts and feelings—our experience of the five *skandhas*—on the other. All that these two different forms of knowledge have in common is *avidyā*, lack of transcendental knowledge. The relatively real *paratantra* is illusory, but only in relation to what is absolutely real.

Thirdly, we are urged to view the conditioned 'as a lamp'. A lamp burns on fuel: take away the fuel, and the lamp goes out. So it is with all conditioned things.[42] If we think of a candle in the wind—and the forms of lamp used at the time of the composition of this verse were scarcely better protected—this is how delicately contingent are conditioned things. It sometimes seems strange that anything should continue to exist at all, its coming into existence and its survival being dependent on so many different factors. That you come to be reading this particular book in this particular form, represents a marvellous concatenation of millions upon millions of conditioned *dharmas*, all co-operating in a particular way. So the continued existence of conditioned *dharmas* is all the time distinctly precarious.

Then, the conditioned is like a 'mock show'. The illustration of the magical illusion is a favourite one in Indian literature. Most of us are familiar with magic tricks on the level of pulling rabbits out of hats, but the kind of mock show referred to here is on a rather grander scale, like the famous Indian rope trick. A rope is thrown up into the sky and just hangs there; a boy goes up it and disappears, and a man goes up after him and also disappears; then bits and pieces of the boy start falling down and the man comes down again. Finally, the master magician puts all the bits and pieces under a cloth, and when he whips it away the boy is standing there bowing. And then of course they pass the hat round. It is said to be done through mass hypnosis.

Ordinary life presents us with an experience which is ultimately no more real than the Indian rope trick. Indeed, a really proficient magician will be able to deceive other senses than that of vision, conjuring up musicians playing instruments for example. Ultimately, what is happening is that we are all collectively hallucinating, as you might say. On an ordinary level people with the same sort of backgrounds will tend to 'see' things in the same way. Likewise, at a deeper level we share the same sort of reality because we have the same sort of *karma*. We all 'hallucinate' in much the same way, although it is very difficult to realize that we are hallucinating because we all agree that our hallucinations are real. What we tend to regard as real is that which is generally accepted to be the case. If a number of people in a room all see a pink elephant, then that pink elephant exists, unless someone like the Buddha comes along and persuades them that it isn't really there. Questions about the nature of reality arise because, despite this apparently identical experience, people actually experience and see things in different ways.

The English poet Robert Herrick put the comparison of conditioned existence to dewdrops as well as anyone. His poem 'To Daffodils' expresses a mournful but keen perception of impermanence, focusing in its conclusion on the image of dew drops:

Fair daffodils, we weep to see
  You haste away so soon;
As yet the early-rising sun
  Has not attained his noon.
    Stay, stay,
  Until the hasting day

> *Has run*
> *But to the evensong;*
> *And, having prayed together, we*
> *Will go with you along.*

> *We have short time to stay, as you,*
> *We have as short a spring;*
> *As quick a growth to meet decay,*
> *As you, or any thing.*
> *We die*
> *As your hours do, and dry*
> *Away,*
> *Like to the summer's rain;*
> *Or as the pearls of morning's dew*
> *Ne'er to be found again.*

For the comparison of conditioned existence to a bubble, again, over to the English poets: Francis Bacon this time. This is the famous opening to his one anthology piece:

> *The world's a bubble; and the life of man*
> *Less than a span.*

The whole idea of the impermanence of beautiful things is of course a commonplace amongst poets of all nationalities. They may include an injunction to 'seize the day' (Horace: *carpe diem*) or 'Gather ye Rosebuds while ye may' (Herrick again), but the overall mood is one of melancholy.

For the Buddhist, though, impermanence can be a source of exhilaration. If things are impermanent, it means that they change; and if they change, they can change for the better. If there were no changing, if things were not impermanent, there would be no development, no work, no progress, no evolution: nothing would ever happen at all. So the Buddhist is actually exhilarated by the openings and opportunities thrown up by impermanence.

The *Diamond Sūtra*'s verse goes on to exhort us to view what is conditioned as a dream. The point of this comparison is that when you truly wake up, when you are fully Enlightened, you find that all the emotional experiences of ordinary life, of relative existence, are as unreal as a dream, and they lose their potency. While you are in the dream you really are frightened or angry, and you really believe that there is something to be frightened or angry about. But when you wake up, well, you know that you are awake and that it was all a dream. The emotions die away and you find yourself laughing at what seemed so real when you were asleep.

And it is like this when you become Enlightened: all the passions, all the desires, all the annoyances of ordinary life just fade into insignificance; they no longer exist for you.

For a lot of people, becoming more committed in their practice as Buddhists can be like this too. You find that your motivations have changed, and that the goals that used to be very important to you—getting a good job, progressing in your career, getting married and making a home, raising a family—don't seem to matter all that much any more. They seem quite laughable, like the games that children can take so very seriously. If you can laugh at mundane issues that were once of great concern to you, it means that you are beginning to release the energies that are locked up in those anxieties, and to see through the illusions that are bound up with them. Particularly in the Zen tradition, though also in the records of Indian Buddhism, people very often burst out laughing when they come to see through their illusions.

Then, conditioned existence is like a lightning flash. However imposing and compelling conditioned things may appear to be, they are still as brief as lightning on a summer's night, when viewed from the aspect of the Unconditioned.

Lastly, we should view what is conditioned as a cloud. It is very easy to be affected by all sorts of passing trends or circumstances, particularly by a general *Zeitgeist*, or spirit of the age, that may cloud a whole society for a spell, but that eventually passes over and gives way to a different social atmosphere, a new economic climate. It is easy to allow your mood or spirit to be affected—even infected—by the ebb and flow of political currents. It is all too easy to come under the influence of the prevailing orthodoxies. But we can be aware of these mundane forces in the air, and ensure that they do not determine our fundamental emotional attitude. Our spiritual condition need not be dependent on temporal, mundane factors.

Thus spoke the Lord. Enraptured, the Elder Subhūti, the monks and nuns, the pious laymen and laywomen, and the Bodhisattvas, and the whole world with its Gods, men, Āsuras and Gandharvas rejoiced in the Lord's teaching.

Part Four

THE RATNAGUNA-SAMCAYAGATHA

Introduction

THE GREATER MANDALA

**IN THE DIAMOND SUTRA PERFECT WISDOM IS POWERFUL, THRUSTING, AND EFFECTIVE.
DON'T IMAGINE, HOWEVER, THAT YOU'RE GOING TO GET A GREAT POWERFUL BLAST
FROM THE RATNAGUNA-SAMCAYAGATHA.
HERE, PERFECT WISDOM IS GOING TO COME VERY SOFTLY, VERY GENTLY,
VERY UNOBTRUSIVELY**

The *Ratnaguna-saṁcayagāthā* is quite unlike the *Vajracchedikā*. It comes at the Perfection of Wisdom, we might say, from an entirely different direction. This is reflected in the title itself: we are contemplating not the 'Perfection of Wisdom that cuts like a diamond', but the 'verses on the accumulation of the precious qualities of the Perfection of Wisdom'. It is, of course, the same Perfection of Wisdom, but there is a markedly different emphasis. Before we look at the text, therefore, we need to take another look at our fundamental assumptions about the subject-matter of the *Ratnaguna-saṁcayagāthā*. Otherwise we are likely to be hampered by a subtle but critical misunderstanding right from the start.

Like the *Diamond Sūtra*, the *Ratnaguna-saṁcayagāthā* is concerned with one single subject. Indeed, this one subject provides the field of enquiry for the whole of the Perfection of Wisdom. The subject is the career of the Bodhisattva. What is a Bodhisattva? How does a Bodhisattva behave, practise, live? What does a Bodhisattva do? Now if we are not careful, we can pick up a false impression of the nature of the Bodhisattva from the laborious detail in which the texts answer these questions. If from their deliberations we start to form an impression of the Bodhisattva as a highly intellectual being, and of the Perfection of Wisdom as a highly intellectual teaching, then—to be blunt—we have got the wrong end of the stick.

The verses we are going to encounter may seem abstruse, but they are not *intellectually* abstruse—or at least, much less so than many other Perfection of Wisdom texts. The *Ratnaguna-saṁcayagāthā* is quite simple and intelligible in comparison with, for example, the *Diamond Sūtra*. If we still find it a little daunting, it may well be because in it we run up against the medieval Indian mode of communication, which, being excessively abstract and conceptual, is not very well suited to the spiritual genius of Buddhism. In particular, such a relentlessly conceptual approach is ill-suited for the task which the Perfection of Wisdom texts set out to achieve, the task of demolishing the whole conceptual framework they rest upon. Concepts are dismissed by means of other concepts—comparatively gross ones giving way to comparatively subtle ones.

Most Westerners—and certainly most English people—simply do not feel at home with this sort of thing. It may be a relief, therefore, to realize that this is not a standard approach which has to be followed by all Buddhists. We need to distinguish between the Indian mind at work and Buddhism itself, and develop a form of expression more natural to us. It may be difficult to see where we are going to find a more real and immediate form of expression into which this conceptual language might be translated, but we do have a precedent. In its progress from India to China, Buddhism did change its manner of expressing itself completely. Ch'an Buddhists took teachings like this and entirely recast them, so that instead of lengthy, abstract disquisitions you got a shout, or a slap, or someone holding up a flower. The same thing was meant, but the medium of communication was totally different. As translated into Chinese, the *Prajñāpāramitā* literature itself has a different, more concrete feel to it, as the Chinese title—'The Dark Wisdom'—indicates.

We could start to develop our own version of the teachings, as the Chinese did, by pruning some of the metaphysical exuberance of the Mahāyāna. Alternatively, we could perhaps go back and explore archaic Buddhist teachings like the *Udāna* and the *Sutta-nipāta*, which date from a time long before the Abhidharmists and the Mahayanists began their conceptual analysis, if we want a more down to earth approach. But we need not abandon the Perfection of Wisdom texts for fear of taking them the wrong way. Even while we grapple with the medieval Indian mind, there are still various basic and straightforward means we can use to derive great benefit from the teachings.

The first and most important thing is to recognize that the medium is not the message.[43] Otherwise, we should have no hope at all of getting in touch with Perfect Wisdom by reading books about it, or even by reading the scriptures. In fact, the message and the medium are so far from being the same thing that they actually undermine one another. The Perfection of Wisdom may speak a language which intellectuals understand, but its message actually has nothing to do with anything intellectual. If we pay more attention to the medium than the message we will get the idea that these teachings are an encouragement to think, but they are not. Rather, they use thought to undo thought. Of course, this very idea can cause us all sorts of problems, especially if we get caught up in thinking about how to think our way out of thought—as we are likely to do if we succumb to the baleful influence of the ever-burgeoning *literature* of Zen.

Having recognized that the medium is not the message, however, how can we free our minds from this tendency to convoluted thinking? One method is the practice of silence. When we stop voicing our thoughts, our thinking becomes less busy and more illuminating. At the same time we are coming more directly into contact with things, and even—perhaps surprisingly—with other people. A silence does not signal a break in communication; if anything, there is even more communication, at a more subtle level. We find more subliminal, and in that respect more expressive, modes coming to the fore, involving the eyes, the face, gestures, and posture. We may even find that we can communicate our awareness of someone without looking at them.

Another method which helps to lift the veil of discursive thought is chanting a mantra. This works by giving you something to think *of*, but not something to think *about*, because a mantra doesn't have a meaning in the ordinary sense. You may give it a meaning, but that will be quite secondary. Primarily it is a sound—a sound symbol. It is very important to be wholehearted about mantra-chanting, to make a conscious decision at the beginning of the practice that all your energy is going to go into that practice. If you don't gather yourself together at the start, you just sort of drift into it, and trains of thought tend to develop while the mantra is carrying on in another part of your mind.

Any serious student of the Perfection of Wisdom will, of course, practise meditation. It might seem that the obvious practice to concentrate on would be one that specifically developed awareness or mindfulness—the *ānāpāna-sati*, the 'mindfulness of breathing', perhaps—and this would not be a bad idea by any means. Very often, however, the word 'awareness' is used in a way that suggests some kind of dissociation from feeling, but this is what I would call 'alienated awareness', a cold, separated awareness, very different from the real, integrated awareness of the Bodhisattva. So if you want to develop Perfect Wisdom, an equally important practice is, perhaps surprisingly, the mettā bhāvanā, the cultivation of universal loving-kindness.

Why this should be so becomes clear when we take a fresh look at the word 'wisdom'. This is our workaday rendering of the Sanskrit term *prajñā*, but Herbert Guenther translates *prajñā* more precisely. According to Dr Guenther, wisdom consists in 'analytical appreciative understanding'. As we have seen, the reduction of all *dharmas* to *śūnyatā* is the analytical understanding that is an essential ingredient of *prajñā*—but it has to be united with quite another mode of understanding, described by Guenther as 'appreciative'.

THE BODHISATTVA, QUITE UNPURPOSEFULLY, REARRANGES THE WHOLE UNIVERSE AND TURNS IT INTO A GIGANTIC MANDALA

The appreciative aspect of *prajñā* opens up a perspective on the whole subject-matter of the *Ratnaguṇa-saṃcayagāthā*—and of the *Prajñāpāramitā* generally—that is all too easily overlooked. It represents such a significant dimension of the activity of the Bodhisattva, and offers such a useful counterbalance to the intellectuality with which we tend to approach *Prajñāpāramitā* texts, even such lucid ones as the *Ratnaguṇa-saṃcayagāthā*, that it is worth exploring some of its implications. Let us remind ourselves, therefore, of what the experience of a Bodhisattva (to whom the *Prajñāpāramitā* is specifically addressed) is really like.

The Enlightenment of the Buddha was not a cold, detached knowledge. He saw with warmth; he saw with feeling; what is more, he saw everything as being pure, or *subha*, which also means beautiful. The Buddha saw everything as pure beauty because he saw everything with compassion—just as, conversely, when you hate someone, they appear ugly. When, out of mettā, you see things as beautiful, you naturally experience joy and delight. And out of that joy and delight flow spontaneity, freedom, creativity, and energy. This flow from mettā to joy to freedom and energy is the constant experience of the Bodhisattva. The Bodhisattva's wisdom in the fullest sense therefore includes mettā. In a sense, we could even say that mettā *is prajñā*.

We may further dispel any impression a superficial look at the *Prajñā-pāramitā* may give that the Bodhisattva is a sort of glorified logic-chopper by looking at another word used to describe the Bodhisattva's experience: *vidyā*. *Vidyā* is the opposite of *avidyā*, 'ignorance', and is usually translated as 'knowledge'. However, Guenther renders it as 'aesthetic appreciation' (like *prajñā* but without the element of analysis), which comes much closer to its true meaning. *Vidyā* is a sort of relishing of things, a harmony with the world; and its opposite, *avidyā*, conveys a sense of alienation and conflict—certainly not an absence of *knowledge* in the usual sense of the word.

When one is said to *know* something, this carries the suggestion that the knowledge is utilitarian. One knows what the thing is good for; one knows what one can do with it. Sometimes this attitude to things can strike you quite forcibly. One evening, when I was living in Kalimpong, I was out for a walk and saw an enormously tall, beautiful pine tree growing at the side of the road. As I stood admiring it, a Nepali friend came along. 'Just look at this tree!' I exclaimed. 'Isn't it magnificent?' 'Oh yes', he replied, 'There must be at least twenty *maunds* of firewood there—enough for the whole winter!'

If what we see is the utilitarian value of something, we are relating to it from a need, which becomes desire, which turns to craving for the object conceived as fulfilling that desire. The tree is seen not as existing in its own right, for its own sake, but as something to fulfil our own need. If, however, we have no desires to be fulfilled, there is no subject and no object. That is the state of the Bodhisattva—empty of any desire to use things for any particular purpose. All that is left is aesthetic appreciation. If you are a Bodhisattva you enjoy the world much as you enjoy a work of art or an artistic performance—with the difference that you do not experience a division between yourself and something 'out there'. Normally—though less so in the cinema—people in an audience retain a sense of themselves as subjects separate from what they are experiencing as an aesthetic object, and to that degree remain alienated from it. But the Bodhisattva's experience of the world is more like

> *Music heard so deeply*
> *That it is not heard at all,*
> *But you are the music*
> *While the music lasts.*[44]

or like the experience of the woman in the stalls who gets completely carried away and shouts up at Othello 'You silly fool! Can't you see she's innocent?'

The 'purpose' of a Bodhisattva, if one may speak in that way at all, is in no degree passive, however. It is not unlike the function of the artist—except that a painter, say, can rarely just enjoy the world without starting to think of how to make a picture out of it. What the Bodhisattva creates is something different. The Bodhisattva, quite unpurposefully, rearranges the whole universe and turns it into a gigantic mandala.

What does this mean? Well, what is a mandala? Putting aside the more conventional descriptions, let us take this short definition by a Tibetan teacher, Rongzompa Chokyi Zangpo: 'To make a mandala is to take any prominent aspect of reality and surround it with beauty.' Why you should select one particular aspect of reality over another will be a matter not of attraction as a form of craving, but of spiritual affinity. It will be a facet of reality that you value and appreciate enough to want to surround it with a harmonious pattern of beautiful images. You take, say, a particular Buddha figure—one that you find particularly appealing, sublime, or precious—as the aspect of reality you want to focus on, and you decorate it with, for instance, other Buddha figures at the points of the compass. Then you might place the four elements in between, and use all the other things in nature as materials with which to fill the spaces so as to make a harmonious and pleasing configuration.

The Bodhisattva creates a mandala through a response to the world that is aesthetic and appreciative rather than utilitarian. To sustain life you have to engage in a certain amount of practical activity—you have to think about things and understand how the world works—but if you are a Bodhisattva all this takes place within an overall context of aesthetic appreciation. We usually think of 'aesthetic appreciation' as a little separate part of life within a much larger area that is utilitarian and 'practical', but really it needs to be the other way around. Our overall attitude, our overall response to life, should be purely aesthetic. We should not seek to use things, but just enjoy them, appreciate them, feel for them. We don't have to think of our mandala of aesthetic appreciation as something the size of one of those Tibetan *thangkas* sitting in a corner of the great big real world of important practical business. Instead, we can think of ourselves as living *within* a 'greater mandala' of aesthetic appreciation, of which all our practical mundane affairs, and the fulfilment of all our (non-neurotic) needs and wants, occupy just a tiny corner. The real values are aesthetic, not utilitarian.

There is a story of a Taoist sage who was sitting by a river with a fishing rod when someone came along and asked him how he could reconcile trying to catch fish with being a Taoist sage. He replied 'It's all right, I'm not using any bait.' He was just enjoying the fishing; he didn't need to try and catch anything. We don't *really* have anything to do—well, do we? Most of the time we could just be sitting back, as it were, and enjoying the universe. That's our major occupation. That's our real work—not to work. We need to get food to eat, clothing, a roof over our head, healthcare, a few books, transport of some kind ... but the rest of our time and energy we can just devote to the contemplation of the universe, simply enjoying it all. This is how a Bodhisattva lives, anyway.

I am not talking about some lotus-eating, day-dreaming, navel-gazing ideal here. The Bodhisattva is the greatest worker of all, constantly responding to the objective needs of a situation, but at the same time he or she operates within the greater mandala of aesthetic appreciation. It is not even as though the sphere within which the Bodhisattva operates is a sphere of 'practical activity' that exists apart from the greater mandala. Bodhisattvas do not absent themselves from the mandala of aesthetic appreciation when they carry on their practical activities. The greater mandala interpenetrates that limited sphere, so that those practical activities are an expression of the values of the greater mandala within a certain context and for the sake of certain people.

The Bodhisattva essentially courses between—and transcends—two unsatisfactory extremes. On the one hand, we can be so immersed in practical activities that we identify with them and consequently become rather harassed and worried, losing sight of the wider horizons of aesthetic appreciation. On the other hand, we can lose ourselves in a spaced-out—if vaguely positive—state of mind in which we are unable to get anything done. The ideal is the middle way. We need to carry on the cycle of practical activities—to which we are *not* attached, which does *not* harass us, about which we *don't* worry—within the much wider circle of the greater mandala. Then we can enjoy our work, because it is interpenetrated by this appreciative awareness. This kind of balance is not at all easy to achieve. All the time we are likely to be tending towards one or the other of these two extremes, so that we will need to make constant adjustments to keep to a middle way.

One antidote to the first extreme is to get into the country for a while, and allow the influence of nature to remind us of the higher reality of the greater mandala. But as well as taking breaks from the city—to go on retreat, for example—we also need to restore the balance a bit every day. This means making sure that the time we spend with friends is not devoted exclusively to practical matters. It also means using our meditation time creatively, not just to sort out the problems and difficulties of daily life.

The antidote to the second extreme is quite simply to plunge into some demanding project. The ideal situation is to live and work with other people, so that you are all working for the sake of a shared spiritual objective, and everything you do is—directly or indirectly—towards that end. You can get a lot of hard and even tough work done if you have an overall atmosphere which is relaxed, peaceful, and light-hearted (which may mean living and working with people of the same sex). Of course you inevitably lose perspective sooner or later, so that the atmosphere starts to get a bit tense or even fraught. That is when at least some of those involved need to go away for a while and get a view of the whole picture again. You do need to be rather careful when you get back from some time away; the refined energy level that you bring back from retreat is likely to be in danger of being dissipated as it comes into contact with coarser, more tense energies. You get irritated; those who have not been away get resentful. If it is feasible, the best thing is perhaps for half the people living or working together to go on retreat at a time.

As a general rule, we need to alternate between life in the country, where it is easier to establish contact with the greater mandala, and life in the city, where that attitude of appreciation can readily engage with a situation in which we are giving of ourselves. Both of these are absolutely necessary for the vast majority of people. Our activity requires the serenity of meditation, while our meditation needs to be vibrant and dynamic, not just a pleasant little relaxation session. If we get the balance right, we go on retreat with our energies aroused and return to the city with the perspective of the greater mandala to apply to whatever we do. The aim—which may take a long time to achieve—is to bring an attitude of pure aesthetic appreciation to whatever circumstances come our way.

YOU DON'T HAVE TO JUSTIFY YOUR EXISTENCE BY BEING USEFUL.
YOU YOURSELF ARE THE JUSTIFICATION FOR YOUR EXISTENCE

When I lived in Kalimpong I got to know a French Buddhist nun who was quite a scholar—she had been at the Sorbonne and was in fact a very high-powered lady, intellectually speaking. She had a terrible temper, she was very demanding and exacting, and she was always busy. Whenever I went to see her she would be washing and scrubbing, feeding her dogs and cats, cooking and studying (at the same time), writing letters, rushing off to see this person or that, meeting lamas, going to the bazaar, coming back from the bazaar, building things, knocking them down, chopping them up … she never stopped. One day she came to see me and said 'Bhante, I just can't seem to meditate.' I said 'Anīla (this is the polite way of addressing a nun), you're very good in many ways, but there's just one thing you've got to learn; then you'll be able to meditate.' 'What is it? What is it?' she asked excitedly, getting ready to rush out and do it. I said, 'You must learn to waste time.' At this she nearly jumped out of her robe. 'Waste time!' she shrieked. 'With so many things to be done, you're asking me to waste time? Is that your Buddhism?' 'Yes', I said, 'so far as you are concerned that is my Buddhism. Just learn to waste time. You'll get on much better.' Unfortunately she never did learn to waste time. It is just as difficult for someone like her to change as it is for people who need no encouragement whatsoever to waste time, but who on the contrary need to bring a little more focus into their lives.

The Bodhisattva does useful things, but he or she enjoys them. This is why it is said that the Bodhisattva *plays*. The idea of *līlā*, the 'play' or the 'game', plays quite a prominent role in modern Indian spiritual life. The spiritual life itself is thought of as a *līlā*, a purely spontaneous welling-up of spiritual energy that is, in a way, purposeless. In Tantric Buddhism this is termed the *sahaja* state—the state which is completely natural, innate, and spontaneous. In Mahāyāna Buddhism, however, it is called the *anubhogacarya*, the 'spontaneous life' of the Bodhisattva, which represents the culmination of the whole *carya* series. The first of these is the pre-Buddhistic *brahmacarya*, or 'Brahma-faring', taken up by early Buddhism; then *dharmacarya* is the Buddhistic, especially 'Hinayanist' term. *Sambodhicarya* is the general Mahayanist term, and *anubhogacarya* comes from the later Mahāyāna. The idea of *anubhogacarya* is even enshrined in the title of a rather late, legendary, and embellished life of the Buddha, the Lalita-vistara, or 'Extended Account of the Sports of the Buddha'. His life is described here in terms of 'sports' because, according to the Mahāyāna, his actions were spontaneous, free, and natural, just like the play of a child.

The difference between work and play is that play is not necessary. It is not harnessed to any goal; it serves no purpose. In Sanskrit the fine arts are called *lalitakala*, the 'playful arts', because they're of no earthly use. You can live without the arts: no one ever dropped dead from lack of art. It is quite superfluous—which is why it's so necessary. Likewise, the Bodhisattva's life—the life that is depicted in the *Prajñāpāramitā*—is behovely because it is the useless life. All that meditation and study and Right Livelihood culminates in the experience of being happy just being yourself, with nothing in particular to do. You might just be dancing around the room, aimlessly, unselfconsciously—not trying to be playful or spontaneous, but just being yourself. Some busybody will then turn up, of course, and say 'Come on, what are you wasting your time like that for? There's work to get on with.' But that's putting the cart before the horse (or rather, harnessing the horse to the cart).

Someone came to me once and said that he did not feel that he could be very useful because he had no particular talent. I told him, 'Think of yourself as an unspecialized human being.' People think that if they can't make themselves useful in some way—they can't type, they can't keep accounts, they can't cook, they can't write or give a talk or paint or play a musical instrument—there's something wrong with them. But consider: this apparently useless human being is the product of millions upon millions of years of evolution. You are the goal; you are what it has all been for. You don't have to justify your existence by being useful. You yourself are the justification for your existence. You haven't come into existence after all these millions of years of evolution just to sit down in front of a typewriter, or to keep accounts. *You* are the justification of that whole process. You are an end in yourself. All that you can really be said to be here for is to develop into some higher form of human life—to become a Bodhisattva, to become a Buddha. So don't be ashamed of sitting around and doing nothing. Glory in it. Do things spontaneously, out of a state of inner satisfaction and achievement. It is a virtue to be ornamental as well as useful.

If you take this seriously, you have to be watchful for people trying to work on your feelings of guilt. How can you be spontaneous if you're riddled with guilt? So don't let people get at you with any kind of emotional blackmail. If someone starts saying to you 'Look how hard I'm working for the Dharma! Don't you feel bad just sitting there doing nothing, letting me do it all?' you should just say 'No, I feel fine. I'm really enjoying watching you do it all.' It is important not to give in to this sort of emotional arm-twisting; it is highly unskilful, appealing to negative emotions in order to get things done instead of arousing an enthusiasm to work for the joy of it. Don't take your Buddhist activities too earnestly. I am not advocating irresponsible frivolity or a frittering away of energy in unmindful hilarity. But even while you are doing your best to succeed at whatever you are doing, remember that you are essentially at play—and you don't lose sleep over a game; it isn't worth it. Being serious doesn't mean being solemn, just as practising puja in front of a shrine does not call for long faces and a 'dim religious light'.

There is something further to take into account when we look at the spirit in which we approach Dharmic activities: the question of psychological types or temperaments. For example, there are people who are 'organized', and there are others who are 'non-organized'. Organized types tend to do the organizing, and non-organized types are the people the organized types organize, often whether the non-organized like it or not. But just because you don't function in that organized way, it doesn't necessarily mean that you are lazy or less committed, or even that you are doing less than those who *are* organized. It is possible to function positively and creatively and energetically in a way that is anathema to the organized type.

Unfortunately, any kind of collective Buddhist activity nearly always caters for those who like being organized—and those with the opposite sort of temperament tend to get roped in willy-nilly. But why not cater for the non-organized person occasionally? Why not a have a non-organized retreat, with no programme to it at all? Call it a 'Dharma holiday'—all the retreat facilities would be there, but it would be up to you how you went about benefiting from them. Some people might want to get together, elect a leader, and organize a programme, but others would go their own way and still have a very productive retreat. Some might even decide—in the most mindful, objective, responsible, and positive way—that the best thing to do with this Dharma holiday would be to get up late and sit in the garden doing nothing. For some people this could be quite a challenge; even on a retreat it is possible to fill up the day with useful activities in such a way as to lose sight of the greater mandala.

The Bodhisattva has resolved this opposition or antithesis between aesthetic contemplation on the one hand and practical activity on the other, and feels no conflict. But so long as we have to switch over from the one to the other, and so long as the presence or experience of the one implies the absence or non-experience of the other, there will always be some difficulty in the transition. All we can do is somehow try to carry the aesthetic experience into the practical activity—which is exactly what the Bodhisattva does, as represented in the Perfection of Wisdom—a very difficult process. We can make a start by adopting a more light-hearted attitude towards practical things. By all means be useful, but only within the much larger context of complete uselessness. Taoism is quite good on this whole theme. Taoists say that the man of Tao is like a great tree, which is so big that it is good for nothing—the branches are too thick for making axe-handles, and so on. One should try to be too big to be useful. However important the work a Bodhisattva does, he or she sees, in the Perfection of Wisdom, that it takes place in a tiny circle within the greater mandala of quite pointless appreciation.

This, then, is the vision of the Perfection of Wisdom. If, when we take up the *Ratnaguṇa-saṁcayagāthā*, we find that it resists our attempts to make sense of it, if it refuses to be contained by our intellectual expectations, this is because it is not supposed to be useful to us in any way that we can understand. It speaks to us in the common currency of all our intellectual transactions, but in such a way as to demonstrate that it is coming from somewhere altogether different. It comes—so to speak—from the greater mandala.

THE SUTRA

HOMAGE TO ALL THE BUDDHAS AND BODHISATTVAS!
Thereupon the Lord, in order to gladden the four assemblies, and to
further lighten up this perfection of wisdom, preached at that time the
following verses:

PRELIMINARY ADMONITION

Call forth as much as you can of love, of respect and of faith!
Remove the obstructing defilements, and clear away all your taints!
Listen to the Perfect Wisdom of the gentle Buddhas,
Taught for the weal of the world, for heroic spirits intended!

THE SOURCE OF SUBHUTI'S AUTHORITY

The rivers all in this Roseapple Island,
Which cause the flowers to grow, the fruits, the herbs and trees,
They all derive from the might of the king of the Nāgas,
From the Dragon residing in Lake Anopatapta, his magical power.

Just so, whatever Dharmas the Jina's disciples establish,
Whatever they teach, whatever adroitly explain—
Concerning the work of the holy which leads to the fullness of bliss,
And also the fruit of this work—it is the Tathāgata's doing.

For whatever the Jina has taught, the Guide to the Dharma,
His pupils, if genuine, have well been trained in it.

From direct experience, derived from their training, they teach it,
Their teaching stems from the might of the Buddhas, and not their
   own power.

THE BASIC TEACHINGS

No wisdom can we get hold of, no highest perfection,
No Bodhisattva, no thought of enlightenment either.
When told of this, if not bewildered and in no way anxious,
A Bodhisattva courses in the Well-Gone's wisdom.

In form, in feeling, will, perception and awareness
Nowhere in them they find a place to rest on.
Without a home they wander, dharmas never hold them,
Nor do they grasp at them—the Jina's Bodhi they are bound to gain.

The wanderer Srenika in his gnosis of the truth
Could find no basis, though the skandhas had not been undone.
Just so the Bodhisattva, when he comprehends the dharmas as he
   should
Does not retire into Blessed Rest. In wisdom then he dwells.

What is this wisdom, whose and whence, he queries,
And then he finds that all these dharmas are entirely empty.
Uncowed and fearless in the face of that discovery
Not far from Bodhi is that Bodhi-being then.

To course in the skandhas, in form, in feeling, in perception,
Will and so on, and fail to consider them wisely;
Or to imagine these skandhas as being empty;
Means to course in the sign, the track of non-production ignored.

But when he does not course in form, in feeling, or perception,
In will or consciousness, but wanders without home,
Remaining unaware of coursing firm in wisdom,
His thoughts on non-production—then the best of all the calming
   trances cleaves to him.

Through that the Bodhisattva now dwells tranquil in himself,
His future Buddhahood assured by antecedent Buddhas.

Whether absorbed in trance, or whether outside it, he minds not.
For of things as they are he knows the essential original nature.

Coursing thus he courses in the wisdom of the Sugatas,
And yet he does not apprehend the dharmas in which he courses.
This coursing he wisely knows as a no-coursing,
That is his practice of wisdom, the highest perfection.

What exists not, that non-existent the foolish imagine;
Non-existence as well as existence they fashion.
As dharmic facts existence and non-existence are both not real.
A Bodhisattva goes forth when wisely he knows this.

If he knows the five skandhas as like an illusion,
But makes not illusion one thing, and the skandhas another;
If, freed from the notion of multiple things, he courses in peace—
Then that is his practice of wisdom, the highest perfection.

Those with good teachers as well as deep insight,
Cannot be frightened on hearing the Mother's deep tenets.
But those with bad teachers, who can be misled by others,
Are ruined thereby, as an unbaked pot when in contact with moisture.

THREE KEY TERMS DEFINED

What is the reason why we speak of 'Bodhisattvas'?
Desirous to extinguish all attachment, and to cut it off,
True non-attachment, or the Bodhi of the Jinas is their future lot.
'Beings who strive for Bodhi' are they therefore called.

What is the reason why 'Great Beings' are so called?
They rise to the highest place above a great number of people;
And of a great number of people they cut off mistaken views.
That is why we come to speak of them as 'Great Beings.'

Great as a giver, as a thinker, as a power,
He mounts upon the vessel of the Supreme Jinas.
Armed with the great armour he'll subdue Māra the artful.
These are the reasons why 'Great Beings' are so called.

This gnosis shows him all beings as like an illusion,
Resembling a great crowd of people, conjured up at the crossroads,
By a magician, who then cuts off many thousands of heads;

He knows this whole living world as a mock show, and yet remains
    without fear.

Form, perception, feeling, will and awareness
Are ununited, never bound, cannot be freed.
Uncowed in his thought he marches onto his Bodhi,
That for the highest of men is the best of all armours.

What then again is 'the vessel that leads to the Bodhi'?
Mounted upon it one guides to Nirvāṇa all beings.
Great is that vessel, immense, vast like the vastness of space.
Those who travel upon it are carried to safety, delight and ease.

THE TRANSCENDENTAL NATURE OF BODHISATTVAS

Thus transcending the world, he eludes our apprehensions.
'He goes to Nirvāṇa,' but no one can say where he went to.
A fire's extinguished, but where, do we ask, has it gone to?
Likewise, how can we find him who has found the Rest of the Blessed?

The Bodhisattva's past, his future and his present must elude us,
Time's three dimensions nowhere touch him.
Quite pure he is, free from conditions, unimpeded.
That is his practice of wisdom, the highest perfection.

Wise Bodhisattvas, coursing thus, reflect on non-production,
And yet, while doing so, engender in themselves the great
    compassion,
Which is, however, free from any notion of a being.
Thereby they practise wisdom, the highest perfection.

But when the notion of suffering and beings leads him to think:
'Suffering I shall remove, the weal of the world I shall work!'
Beings are then imagined, a self is imagined,—
The practice of wisdom, the highest perfection, is lacking.

He wisely knows that all that lives is unproduced as he himself is;
He knows that all that is no more exists than he or any beings.
The unproduced and the produced are not distinguished,
That is the practice of wisdom, the highest perfection.

All words for things in use in this world must be left behind,
All things produced and made must be transcended—

The deathless, the supreme, incomparable gnosis is then won.
That is the sense in which we speak of perfect wisdom.

When free from doubts the Bodhisattva carries on his practice,
As skilled in wisdom he is known to dwell.
All dharmas are not really there, their essential original nature is
   empty,
To comprehend that is the practice of wisdom, perfection supreme.

Where Bodhisattvas Stand

He does not stand in form, perception or in feeling,
In will or consciousness, in any skandha whatsoever.
In Dharma's true nature alone he is standing.
Then that is his practice of wisdom, the highest perfection.

Change and no change, suffering and ease, the self and not-self,
The lovely and repulsive—just one Suchness in this Emptiness they are.
And so he takes not his stand on the fruit which he won, which is
   threefold—
That of an Arhat, a Single Buddha, a Buddha fully enlightened.

The Leader himself was not stationed in the realm which is free from
   conditions,
Nor in the things which are under conditions, but freely he wandered
   without a home:
Just so, without a support or a basis a Bodhisattva is standing.
A position devoid of a basis has that position been called by the Jina.

Wherein Bodhisattvas Train

Those who wish to become the Sugata's Disciples,
Or Pratyekabuddhas, or likewise, Kings of the Dharma—
Without resort to this Patience they cannot reach their respective goals.
They move across, but their eyes are not on the other shore.

Those who teach dharma, and those who listen when it is being taught;
Those who have won the fruit of an Arhat, a Single Buddha, or a
   world-saviour;
And the Nirvāṇa obtained by the wise and the learned—
Mere illusions, mere dreams—so has the Tathāgata taught us.

Four kinds of person are not alarmed by this teaching:
Sons of the Jina skilled in the truths; saints unable to turn back,
Arhats free from defilements and taints, and rid of their doubts;
Those whom good teachers mature are reckoned the fourth kind.

Coursing thus, the wise and learned Bodhisattva,
Trains not for Arhatship, nor on the level of Pratyekabuddhas.
In the Buddha-dharma alone he trains for the sake of all-knowledge.
No training is his training, and no one is trained in this training.

Increase or decrease of forms is not the aim of this training,
Nor does he set out to acquire various dharmas.
All-knowledge alone he can hope to acquire by this training.
To that he goes forth when he trains in this training, and delights in its
    virtues.

THE FACTS OF EXISTENCE

Forms are not wisdom, nor is wisdom found in form,
In consciousness, perceptions, feeling, or in will.
They are not wisdom, and no wisdom is in them.
Like space it is, without a break or crack.

Of all objective supports the essential original nature is boundless;
Of beings likewise the essential original nature is boundless.
As the essential original nature of space has no limits,
Just so the wisdom of the World-knowers is boundless.

'Perceptions'—mere words, so the Leaders have told us;
Perceptions forsaken and gone, and the door is open to the Beyond.
Those who succeed in ridding themselves of perceptions,
They, having reached the Beyond, fulfil the Teacher's commandments.

If for aeons countless as the sands of the Ganges
The Leader would himself continue to pronounce the word 'being':
Still, pure from the very start, no being could ever result from his
    speaking.
That is the practice of wisdom, the highest perfection.

CONCLUSION

And so the Jina concludes his preaching, and finally tells us:
'When all I said and did at last agreed with perfect wisdom,
Then this prediction I received from Him who went before me:
"Fully enlightened, at a future time thou shalt a Buddha be!"'[45]

Chapter One

FOR HEROIC SPIRITS INTENDED

Homage to all the Buddhas and Bodhisattvas!
Thereupon the Lord, in order to gladden the four assemblies, and to further
lighten up this Perfection of Wisdom, preached at that time the following
verses.

Already we know that we are in the presence of a Mahāyāna sūtra, if only because the Homage is addressed to 'Bodhisattvas' in the plural. The Theravādins revere only one Bodhisattva, Maitreya. There is, however, another fairly clear indication in this short prelude to the main text that this is not only a Mahāyāna sūtra, but quite an early one. This clue lies in the audience—the 'four assemblies', the *caturvarga*, the original sub-divisions within the *mahāsangha*: *bhikshus*, *bhikshunīs*, *upāsakas*, and *upāsikās*; that is, monks, nuns, male lay-followers, and female lay-followers. Whoever adopted this term *caturvarga* probably—though I do not know whether this has occurred to anyone else—intended a parallel with the Brahminical *caturvarna*, the four 'colours', or, as we would say, the four castes, of Brahminical society: the *brahmin*, the *kshatriya*, the *vaishya*, and the *śūdra*; that is, priests, aristocrats, merchants, and labourers. The parallel would be meant presumably to highlight the principle of division in each case, the *caturvarna* obviously dividing society according to inherited caste while the *caturvarga* divides the Sangha according to sex and life-style.

The audience here, then, is a very straightforward representation of the spiritual community. Later sūtras were at pains to exercise a more open 'admissions policy' to the *mahāsangha*, and the congregation became in these works altogether more colourful, including not only Bodhisattvas and Arhats, but also devas, nāgas, gandharvas, and even animals—representatives, in fact, of all the different classes of living beings. But in this sūtra one's imagination does not get stretched in this way, and this helps to identify it as an early Mahāyāna work.

Once it has established who is present, the sūtra wastes no time in setting out the Buddha's purpose in 'preaching' (an unfortunate translation) these verses. And his purpose is firstly to 'gladden' the four assemblies—to give them a special treat. Instead of *śīla* or *samādhi*, they are getting *prajñā*; they are getting, indeed, *prajñāpāramitā*—though not, it would seem, for the first time, because the Buddha is going to *further* illuminate the Perfection of Wisdom.

Preliminary Admonition:
Call forth as much as you can of love, of respect and of faith!
Remove the obstructing defilements, and clear away all your taints!
Listen to the Perfect Wisdom of the gentle Buddhas,
Taught for the weal of the world, for heroic spirits intended!

The translator's heading is apt: here is a cautionary word of advice. Reflect on the emotional attitude you are bringing to this sūtra. If the Buddha's first aim is to awaken a joyous emotional response, then we need to think again about our whole approach to the Perfection of Wisdom. It is not good enough, if we do not understand it, to assume that we are just not up to it intellectually. The first thing the Buddha asks is not 'I hope you have your wits about you,' or 'Do you have a degree in philosophy?' but 'Are you emotionally positive? Are you receptive to the Dharma? And are you allowing this positivity and receptivity to develop without limitation?'

The expression 'call forth', after all, suggests that we are to bring out something that is already there. The love, the respect, and the faith are all there, latent within us: they are natural human endowments. It is as though the Buddha is saying 'Let them express themselves, let them manifest themselves. They are there, and they are the appropriate emotions to bring to the Perfection of Wisdom. So don't place any limitation on them by imagining that you have to start laboriously manufacturing them. You are better than you think you are.'

This idea, fundamental to Buddhism, is one that goes against the grain for those of us who imagine that our socialized selves are sitting on a lot of unattractive, basic animal urges, and that if we become less inhibited, all sorts of unpleasant negative emotions are going to come pouring out. But that is a one-sided view of things; there is a lot that is good and positive that also gets repressed. In a largely secular society this is perhaps especially true of devotional feelings. If you no longer believe in the Blessed Virgin Mary, for example, you cannot offer even so much as a candle in a church, and in this way your love and reverence and faith remain unused and stifled. You may even come to the conclusion that you simply have no devotional feelings. I have known a lot of apparently quite intellectual people who, while they used to find the devotional demands of Christianity quite suffocating, nevertheless discovered, when they eventually took up Buddhist devotional practices, that they enjoyed being devotional. They found—rather to their surprise—that they really rather enjoyed offering flowers and lighting candles; that it was, in fact, quite a relief to feel able to do so at last. So call forth as much as you can of love, of respect, and of faith!

Remove the obstructing defilements, and clear away all your taints!

Yes, clear them away. But do so on the basis of developing positive emotions and removing whatever stops them arising. Remove whatever it is that obstructs the arising of insight and clarity of vision, the development of Perfect Wisdom. The ten *kleśas*, or defilements, and the three *āsravas*, or biases (towards sensuous experience, conditioned existence, and speculative opinions) must be removed because they obstruct energy—indeed they also misuse energy, they cause it to leak away, they squander it. They waste the energy you need if you are to adopt an attitude of perfect receptivity to the Perfection of Wisdom.

Listen to the Perfect Wisdom of the gentle Buddhas,

This may come as a bit of a surprise. Surely we are about to receive a very 'strong' teaching here—the ultimate teaching, in fact. Surely it should be trumpeted forth in a voice like thunder? Why the *gentle* Buddhas? Well, strangely enough, spiritual power bears no relation to anything we would recognize as potency. This is demonstrated in the Bible, in the well-known passage (in Kings I) in which God pays a visit to the prophet Elijah 'and a great and strong wind rent the mountains, and brake in pieces the rocks before the Lord; but the Lord was not in the wind: and after the wind an earthquake; but the Lord was not in the earthquake: and after the earthquake a fire; but the Lord was not in the fire: and after the fire a *still small voice...*' Elijah recognizes this as the voice of the Lord, and goes out to meet him.

THE PERFECTION OF WISDOM IS SUBTLE AND ELUSIVE. IT EVADES YOUR GRASP. YOU CAN'T QUITE GET HOLD OF IT.... THE ONLY REAL CHANCE YOU HAVE LIES WITH THE NON-RATIONAL, DEVOTIONAL APPROACH

The Perfection of Wisdom does not call for physical power; it does not express itself in a lot of psycho-physical energy; it has nothing to do even with intellectual power. It is something of an entirely different character. For a parallel to this, consider the way mantras are chanted. The Tārā mantra—*oṁ tāre tuttāre ture svāhā*—is recited softly, but that does not make it weaker than the Padmasambhava mantra—*oṁ āḥ hūṁ jetsun guru padma siddhi hūṁ*—which is usually recited more loudly (although it is really a mistake to think that you can express the spiritual vigour of the Padmasambhava mantra by shouting and roaring).

In the *Vajracchedikā-prajñāpāramitā Sūtra*, we are given the 'Perfection of Wisdom which *cuts like a diamond*'. Han Shan, the Zen master, called it the Diamond Cutter of Doubts, representing Perfect Wisdom in its function of cutting through all doubts, like a *vajra*. In the *Diamond Sūtra*, Perfect Wisdom is powerful, thrusting, and effective. Don't imagine, however, that you're going to get a great powerful blast from the *Ratnaguṇa-saṁcayagāthā*. Here, Perfect Wisdom comes softly, gently, un-obtrusively. It does not come by way of a great upheaval from the depths; nor does it descend cataclysmically from the heights. Rather, it seems to come sideways, obliquely, indirectly. You don't quite notice which direction it's come from at all—just that it's there.

It is little wonder that when the *Prajñāpāramitā* became embodied as a Bodhisattva, it should have appeared in female form. The Perfection of Wisdom is subtle and elusive. It evades your grasp. You can't quite get hold of it. Thinking about it rationally is as useless as it would be for a man to try and understand a woman (and this is to speak traditionally, even mythically) by taking a course in logic. The only real chance you have lies in the non-rational, devotional approach. Of course, the logical corollary of this idea would be to suggest that women should be more capable of grasping—or rather of not-grasping—the Perfection of

Wisdom than men. But this is the literal, 'masculine' mind at work again. Logic simply does not apply here.

To avoid further misunderstandings let us briefly unpack this whole parcel of male prejudice towards the female mind. Certainly women can be frustrated when their deep-rooted desires are not satisfied, but that has nothing to do with being irrational. Women only appear to men to be irrational when men ignore or fail to acknowledge these deep motivations. In fact, everybody is irrational; nobody is guided by objective, logical considerations. If anything, women are more practical and less irrational than men in that they are less likely to disguise their irrationality beneath a layer of rationalization. My own experience is that men tend to fly off at a tangent and react in a highly emotional way rather more than women do.

The 'elusiveness' of woman is, more simply, a symbol. It retains its symbolic value even when we look a little more deeply at this fabled feminine elusiveness; when we recognize that, from the point of view of the male psyche, the feminine is ungraspable because it isn't 'out there' to be grasped at all. In the same way, from the female angle, the masculine is not really 'out there'. You are attracted by a certain quality—which you call femininity (or masculinity), which you think is 'out there', and which you have to go in search of. But of course it is actually a quality—a potential quality—of your own, waiting to be developed. The same goes, up to a point, for the Perfection of Wisdom. It is not an intellectual object to be mastered. It is to be found and nourished, in a manner of speaking, within yourself. To go searching for it in any other way is like looking into a mirror and trying to catch hold of your own face. It is ungraspable because it isn't an object standing apart from a subject ready to be grasped by that subject. Intellectually, it has to be an object, because when you think at all you make something an object, but looked at psychologically, it is subject rather than object.

Ultimately we have to go beyond all this. Beyond the psychological, at the metaphysical level, there is neither object nor subject. Perfect Wisdom is beyond the subject–object distinction altogether. In fact, it is not something apart from the Buddha himself. It is not even something he has mastered. Perfect Wisdom *is* the Buddha; the Buddha *is* Perfect Wisdom (as well as all the other *pāramitās*). When a Buddha 'thinks', Perfect Wisdom comes into operation. If Prajñāpāramitā is said to be the *Jinamātā*, the 'mother of the Conquerors', it is in the sense that a Buddha comes into being through the arising of Perfect Wisdom. But by the same token, Perfect Wisdom comes into being through the Buddha's communication of the content of his Enlightenment. It is a circular relationship: Perfect Wisdom seeds a Buddha; a Buddha generates Perfect Wisdom.

Taught for the weal of the world, for heroic spirits intended!

When the Buddha sent out his first sixty disciples, he told them to go forth and teach the spiritual life as he had made it known to them to the common people (*bahujana*) for their welfare (*hitaya*) and their happiness (*sukhaya*). So the sublime teaching of the Perfection of Wisdom is taught for no other purpose than this simple and straightforward one: to make everybody happy.

Of course, you will only be happy if you are evolving, developing, moving forward—not if you are standing still and stagnating—and this means making demands on yourself. The demands made by the teaching of the Perfection of Wisdom are tremendous, and only to be met by a heroic spirit. This conquering spirit is that of the Bodhisattva, the ultimate practitioner of the Perfection of Wisdom, the hero of all the Mahāyāna sūtras: brave, enterprising, resolute; adventurous and pioneering; always taking initiative; always taking responsibility.

Chapter Two

THE VOICE OF THE BUDDHA

**THE IDEA THAT MATTER IS DEAD IS AN ENTIRELY MODERN CONCEPT,
AND REALLY RATHER A PERVERTED ONE**

The rivers all in this Roseapple Island,
Which cause the flowers to grow, the fruits, the herbs and trees,
They all derive from the might of the King of the Nāgas,
From the Dragon residing in Lake Anopatapta, his magical power.

Just so, whatever Dharmas the Jina's disciples establish,
Whatever they teach, whatever adroitly explain—
Concerning the work of the holy which leads to the fullness of bliss,
And also the fruit of this work—it is the Tathāgata's doing.

'This Roseapple Island' is Jambudvīpa, sometimes translated as the land, or island, or continent (because of course it refers to the Indian subcontinent) of purple fruit trees. To the ancient Indians, however, India was more than a continent; it was the whole world. This world was dominated by the Himalayas, and amongst those peaks is Mount Kailash, at the foot of which is the lake called by Hindus Manasarovar, and by Buddhists Anopatapta, which means 'not hot'—in other words 'cool'. Ancient Indian belief held this lake to be the source of all the rivers of Jambudvīpa. A glance at any map of India confirms that this is in fact so: the Brahmaputra rises from the eastern side and flows through Tibet and back into

India; the Indus rises from the north, the Sutlej from the west, and the Karnali from the south.

Given the great significance of Lake Anopatapta, it is no surprise that the nāga who resides there should be the greatest of all the nāgas or dragons that animate the waters of the world. What, though, are we to make of this nāga? Well, we can view it in 'primitive', animistic terms as a spirit of the waters, a spirit, if you like, of the depths—or, more suggestively, the *life* of the waters. In ancient Indian thought nothing is regarded as inanimate. The idea that matter is dead is an entirely modern concept, and really rather a perverted one. The Jains, for example, have always looked upon the elements as living beings—not, you notice, living *things*, but living *beings*. The earth is a *jīva*, a living being, and it must not be harmed. Nor must water be harmed, nor air, nor fire. Everything is alive, and that life is personified in what we call mythological creatures.[46]

'Magical power' is a translation of *ṛiddhi*, or, in Pāli, *iddhi*. This means power and potency in a very general sense—sometimes, for example, you read of the *ṛiddhi* of the king, the power or influence that he emanates—but it also means the power and influence that emanates from the fourth dhyāna, a highly concentrated state of mental absorption by virtue of which you may work what seem to be miracles. Here, though, the miracle which emanates from the *ṛiddhi* of the king of the nāgas is the fructifying power of the rivers of India, which causes the plants and trees to grow and blossom and bear fruit.

The comparison between this fructifying power and the *ṛiddhi* of the Tathāgata recalls the Parable of the Rain Cloud in the *Saddharma-puṇḍarīka Sūtra*. Both use the metaphor that through the power of the Buddha, beings blossom, grow, and bear fruit, each in accordance with their own nature. We have to imagine the Dharma like a great river flowing down from its fountainhead, the Buddha, through the channels of his disciples, and down through the centuries, through conduits of all scales of capacity, even through little pipes that have to be pumped really hard to get a trickle to come through.

The Buddha says here that 'whatever the Jina's disciples teach … it is the Tathāgata's doing.' In other words, when an Enlightened disciple speaks, it is really the Buddha speaking. So does this make the Buddha a ventriloquist, and the disciples his puppets? Well, obviously not. If you have recapitulated, as it were, the Buddha's experience within yourself it is not as though another individual or person were speaking through you. Your personality doesn't go into abeyance while the Buddha takes over; you don't suppress your own thoughts and ideas, and let the Buddha just use you. Much less still do you copy or imitate the Buddha. Just as the ideal of the Imitation of Christ has often been misunderstood in the West, so in the East people make the mistake of trying to imitate the Buddha by just reproducing the externals and repeating what the Buddha said. What we are aiming for is not to reproduce the Buddha's way of communicating the Enlightenment experience, but to have the experience itself (without, of course, thinking of it as a thing to be experienced). It is more as though we should be *functioning* in the way that the Buddha *functions*.

So why does the text imply that when an Enlightened disciple speaks it is 'the Tathāgata's doing'? It is because the egoistic part of that in-dividual has not just gone into abeyance, but has gone completely. When you give up your own will, then you really do have your own will; when you give up insisting on having your own way, then you really do get your own way. To the extent that you are Enlightened in the way that the Buddha was Enlightened, to the extent that you have any real insight, any real experience of reality, to that extent you will feel strongly that the words you are uttering are indeed the words of the Buddha. Of course, the corollary is also the case: when you speak from your deepest essence, it is in truth the Buddha who is speaking.

In this verse the Buddha stipulates that the 'adroit explanation' should be 'concerning the work of the holy which leads to the fullness of bliss'. It would be possible to give a very interesting series of talks, based entirely on the *Majjhima-Nikāya*, the 'Middle Length Sayings', about social and economic conditions in the Buddha's day. It would all come straight out of the Buddhist scriptures. But would you be communicating the Dharma? No—you would simply be looking at the wrappings of the Dharma, not the essentials. If you were setting out to teach the Dharma, you would speak of manners and customs in the time of the Buddha, to take that example, only so far as that might be helpful in providing a suitable framework for the Dharma, and as a point of departure for the teaching. You might bring in such details to make the whole thing come more alive, but not for their own sake.

> For whatever the Jina has taught, the Guide to the Dharma,
> His pupils, if genuine, have well been trained in it.
> From direct experience, derived from their training, they teach it,
> Their teaching stems from the might of the Buddhas, and not their own
> power.

The Buddha is a guide; he takes you along with him and shows you the Dharma so that you can see and experience it for yourself. The Dharma is not to be taken on trust. It is to be experienced. But notice that the Buddha *guides*. He doesn't lead. This point is established unequivocally in an episode in the Vinaya where Devadatta asks to be allowed to lead the Sangha, suggesting that it is time the Buddha retired.[47] The Buddha's reply exposes the false basis upon which Devadatta's request rests. He says 'Not even to Sāriputta and Moggallana would I entrust the leadership of the Sangha, not to speak of entrusting it to someone like you. The Tathāgata does not consider that he leads the Sangha. If anyone considers that he leads the Sangha, let him come forward.'

WITHIN THE SPIRITUAL COMMUNITY, WITHIN THE SANGHA, THERE SHOULD BE COMPLETE ANARCHY

Does a community of Enlightened beings need a leader? No—it's unthinkable. 'The Leader' occurs as an epithet for the Buddha later on in this text, but it must be understood—in the light of this unambiguous declaration from the Pāli Canon—as meaning simply the one who leads the way. A group may need a leader to function in an emergency, when decisions cannot be quickly or easily taken by all the members of the group, or even their representatives. But within the spiritual context, there is no circumstance under which you can hand over your responsibility to someone else. You may ask for advice from others; you may get inspiration, even instruction, from them; you may have a teacher, a guide—but not a leader.

By the same token, the sangha cannot be represented. You cannot have 'ambassadors' for the spiritual community. A political ambassador is invested with the whole power of the state he or she represents; this is why, according to diplomatic protocol, ambassadors take precedence over everybody except heads of state. In this way the members of the group surrender their power to one individual, and accept his or her actions and utterance as their own. This is politics. If someone asks for a 'Buddhist representative' at some ecumenical gathering, this is just ecclesiastical politics.

It is certainly not for your guru to represent you. If there were to be any question of representation, it would be the other way round—the spiritual community would represent the guru. A teacher or preceptor may express an opinion, may clarify the situation as he or she sees it, and may disagree with the decisions made by other individuals within the spiritual community; but an individual's freedom of choice has to include the possibility of making a mistake. In the degree to which Buddhists can be represented, in that degree they are not actually Buddhists.

Even if you are a member of a Buddhist order you do not represent it; you are not invested with any power to speak for it. What we *can* say is that this order is present in your person. You are complete in yourself, so you are a microcosm of the order, and wherever you happen to be, you are the presence of the order in that place. It is not that the order is in some other place, and you are representing it; it is more like the Cathar idea of the whole Cathar church being present in the body of the individual believer. But when someone meets you, it is you they meet, not the order—except inasmuch as you embody the order in miniature. The order is not responsible for what you say, and you are in no way a mouthpiece for the order. By definition you are a member of the order as an individual: you stand on your own two feet. If you are really a Buddhist, you cannot represent Buddhism.

This may be clear enough to you if you are a practising Buddhist, but it will not be so to other people, and sometimes it will seem to you that you are afloat on an endless ocean of wrong views, paddling desperately for dry land. If members of an order are recognized by some distinguishing feature of dress (in the case of the Western Buddhist Order this is a simple *kesa*[48]), it will almost certainly be mistaken for a badge of group membership, rather than being taken for what it is, 'an outward and visible sign of an inward and spiritual grace'[49]—in other words, another form of communication.

If you say 'I am speaking for myself, not as the representative of any particular group of Buddhists', you are still likely to be seen as a member of a group, but as one who has rather gone astray—an idiosyncratic, eccentric Buddhist perhaps, or a black sheep, or even an unfrocked Buddhist, drummed out of the Sangha. If you present yourself as an individual Buddhist, this is how people will see you. They want to know what Buddhists *generally* think, not what you yourself think. They want the party line—so that they can compare it with their own party line, and work out what common ground there is between the two.

You make yourself a channel for the Dharma to the extent that you have realized it; but to the extent that you have not realized it, you can only be a 'representative'—and this can be quite a false and uncomfortable position to be in. It is like the situation you can find yourself in when you are abroad. If you come from a democracy, people often feel justified in holding you personally responsible for the actions of your own government, which you are supposed to have had a hand—albeit nominal—in appointing. When I had been living in India for ten years, people would come and ask me 'Why have you done this?' I would say 'Done what?' And they would say 'Invaded Suez, of course—why have you invaded Suez?' Similarly, as a Buddhist, one is strangely held accountable for all the sins of omission and commission of all Buddhists everywhere.

A Buddhist is not even answerable for a 'Buddhist state'; in fact, a 'Buddhist state' is really a contradiction in terms. A state might well decide to act to, say, repel an invader by force, or alternatively to offer no resistance and take the option of unequivocal non-violence; but, either way, it would not be acting as a *Buddhist* state. As a Buddhist you make your own individual decisions. If someone else were to make them for you, they wouldn't be a Buddhist; and if you accepted their decisions on your behalf, you wouldn't be a Buddhist either. The notion of government has no place within the spiritual community. It is ideally an anarchy. Anarchy doesn't mean not having any government; it means not needing any government because you are governing yourself. Inasmuch as we are all governing ourselves according to the same spiritual principles, we don't need any external government. Within the spiritual community, within the Sangha, there should be complete anarchy—a smoothly functioning, harmonious anarchy.

In this respect, the modern political development towards regionalism and devolution—the principle of 'subsidiarity'—is altogether healthy. What our rulers are afraid of is not that anarchy doesn't work; they're afraid that it does. They'll say 'If Great Britain splits up into smaller and smaller independent, self-governing units, there will be complete anarchy.' Well, yes, there will be. That's the whole idea. No doubt there would be confusion at first. No doubt a certain amount of co-ordination between these units would need to go on, and various international agencies would have to be developed to sort out differences. But people should be able to sort out their own affairs—they don't need some higher authority doing it all for them.

The Buddha may say of his disciples 'From direct experience, derived from their training, they teach ... the Dharma', but we may find ourselves in the position of speaking *about* the Dharma when we are still short of realization, when we do not yet *speak* Dharma. In these circumstances we must make it clear, both to ourselves and to others, that we are handing something on which is not our own. The key is at all times to remain true to our own experience, to connect the teaching with our own experience whenever and wherever we possibly can—even if our own experience reflects back only a glimmer of the Dharma—and always to bring general principles down to concrete applications.

There's really no point in going into a lengthy exposition of all the different kinds of karma as though one had personally observed their operation, and had looked into every heaven and every hell oneself and seen people being reborn there. It is enough to give an outline summary of the doctrine, or to indicate the general principle, and say 'This is what I have understood of the Buddha's teaching.' If one has indeed been able to deepen one's understanding and experience of the Dharma, on retreat say, one may well want to find an opportunity to communicate some of it, if only because expressing it will establish and strengthen it within oneself. But if the Buddha's voice is coming from one's mouth, and one has not acknowledged that it is not really oneself speaking, it will feel quite inappropriate.

The second mistake to avoid when teaching Buddhism is the assumption that one is standing up as the representative of Buddhism *in its entirety*. It is a delusion to think that we can present Buddhism as if it were a kind of monolithic block, as if the Abhidharma, the Yogācāra, the Mādhyamika—not to mention the outer edges of, say, modern Japanese Buddhism—fitted snugly together, because it isn't, and they don't. Does this mean that we cannot represent the teaching at all? Of course not. In the end it comes down to experience: we don't have to set ourselves up to represent doctrines and teachings which do not seem relevant to our own individual practice here and now.

If you have realized the teaching to some extent, to that extent the teaching can speak through you, and to that extent you can be said to represent the teaching. Even if you have not realized it at all, but you have a feeling for it—if you are not wholly cut off from the unrealized truth about which you speak—you can still be confident in communicating from that degree of connection. This is assuming, of course, that you aren't using the Dharma to 'sound off' on your own account, expressing your own thoughts and feelings in the guise of expressing the Dharma. When the Buddha expresses himself, he is expressing the Dharma, but *we* cannot assume so much.

Does all this mean that we should duck out of speaking on a subject that we haven't properly understood, or had time to prepare for properly? Well, not necessarily. It is not ideal to consciously allow the Buddha to use your *nāma-rūpa* (psycho-physical organism) in a kind of ventriloquism of the spirit, but it is certainly not out of order. It is just that it would not be you doing the teaching. The verbal formulation of the Enlightened point of view can actually create an impression on the hearer that is more profound than the impression it makes on the person speaking. Even in the context of a poor lecture the teaching can mean more to the listener than it does to the speaker. In other words, a teacher can allow for some kind of inherent power not just in the Dharma, but in the Dharma as formulated, and also for the possibility of particular receptivity in an audience.

Chapter Three

NO WISDOM CAN WE GET HOLD OF

**THE TRANSCENDENTAL LIFE IS THE BODHISATTVA'S NATURAL ELEMENT.
THIS IS WHY THE BODHISATTVA DOES NOT THINK 'HERE I AM, A BODHISATTVA',
OR 'HERE I AM COURSING IN PERFECT WISDOM'**

No wisdom can we get hold of, no highest perfection,
No Bodhisattva, no thought of enlightenment either.
When told of this, if not bewildered and in no way anxious,
A Bodhisattva courses in the Well-Gone's wisdom.

This is the crux of the whole of the Perfection of Wisdom. The Bodhicitta, the 'thought of Enlightenment', is one of the fundamental concepts with which we could, if we wished, sum up the whole of the Mahāyāna (the others would be *bodhi*, Buddha, and Bodhisattva). Because it is such a crucial concept it must be very clearly understood. For a start, *thought* of Enlightenment—in the sense of a mere concept devoid of experiential content—is not actually quite right. The Bodhicitta is more like the *will* or *aspiration* to Enlightenment—Enlightenment, of course, for the sake of all sentient beings. As for the Bodhisattva, he or she is supposed, in the Mahāyāna, to be the living embodiment of that aspiration.

Even these definitions are not scrupulous enough. As soon as we speak of 'wisdom', or 'highest perfection', or the 'Bodhisattva', or 'bodhicitta', we have named an object 'out there', but all these terms pertain to ultimate reality, which by definition transcends the subject–object duality. We need to keep reminding ourselves that if we indicate that which transcends the subject–object duality by naming an object, we have not really indicated it—in fact, we have falsified it. 'Wisdom', 'highest perfection', 'Bodhisattva', and 'bodhicitta' are, by their very nature as concepts, objects of thought; but what they mean, what they refer to, the reality they denote, is not an object of thought at all. As long as we are dealing with concepts, we are not dealing with ultimate reality.

So a Bodhisattva is not actually a being—or, if you like, an ego—in search of the highest perfection. One who was, or who thought they were, would be in search of something that wasn't there—'No wisdom can we get hold of, no highest perfection.' But what then, you may ask, am I supposed to be doing? Surely the whole spiritual life consists in trying to get hold of wisdom? If I'm not supposed to be trying to get hold of wisdom, if I'm not supposed to be trying to live like a Bodhisattva, like a good Buddhist, what am I supposed to be doing?

The fact is, of course, that we need these supports to begin with. We cannot help thinking in these terms; they provide our frame of reference. If that framework is taken away we won't know what to do—we will feel spiritually insecure and bewildered. Sooner or later, however, it will *have* to be taken away if we are to continue functioning, spiritually speaking, if we are going to be able to grow. What happens in the end—when we have reached a stage when we no longer feel anxious and bewildered as our props, our intellectual frames of reference, are taken away—is that our spiritual functioning just becomes spontaneous.

As a Buddhist, your actions conform to three successive levels of understanding. You start off with the common sense approach to ethical behaviour based on a perception of yourself and others as distinct and palpable egos. Next you refine your view of things so that you see them all as mere composites of *dharmas*, the ultimate psycho-physical elements that are identified in the Abhidharma's analysis of existence. But finally this 'scientific' approach to ethics gives way to a mode of behaving and functioning skilfully that is quite spontaneous, based on no conceptual rationale whatever. You are not behaving in a particular way for any particular reason that you have worked out—getting to heaven, becoming Enlightened, or whatever. You just do it—only don't imagine that this actually means what we think of when we say 'You just do it.' This 'doing' is on a completely different level; it is a coursing in the Perfection of Wisdom which may manifest as *śīla*, but all the time you see only *śūnyatā*.

'Coursing' is the rather awkward English translation for *carya*, which can also be translated as 'faring' or 'walking', as in *brahmacarya* for instance—the 'Brahma-faring'. The Bodhisattva fares, or courses, in the wisdom of the *sugata*, the 'well-gone', the one who has happily gone, or gone to a happy state. The suggestion is that Enlightenment—or the Buddha's *prajñā*—is like a great ocean, and that the Bodhisattva, having reached that ocean and plunged into it, disports in it, courses in it, experiences it, lives and moves in it. The transcendental life is the Bodhisattva's natural element. This is why the Bodhisattva does not think 'Here I am, a Bodhisattva' or 'Here I am, coursing in Perfect Wisdom.' In the same way, a great artist at work is not thinking 'Here I am, the great artist, painting a masterpiece.' As soon as you have that sort of thought, the work, the creation, stops. But the Bodhisattva is absorbed to self-forgetfulness in this way all the time, without ever stopping and turning away, so to speak, from the easel.

In form, in feeling, will, perception and awareness
Nowhere in them they find a place to rest on.
Without a home they wander, dharmas never hold them,
Nor do they grasp at them—the Jina's Bodhi they are bound to gain.

The five classes of phenomena that make up the psycho-physical being of the individual—the five *skandhas*—offer a provisional, practical model that is not ultimately valid. There is not actually such a thing—or even process—as 'form' or 'feeling' or 'will' or 'perception' or 'awareness', any more than there is an unchanging 'self' behind them.

Nor is this idea so very inaccessible. You only have to look at the way physicists describe the atom, as a sort of minute planetary system, with the proton and the electron revolving around the neutron, when in fact these components are more like different forms of energy—negative, positive, and neutral. Building a model of an atom out of billiard balls may be a helpful way of elucidating its structure, but it must not be taken literally. Similarly with the *skandhas*—if anything, they represent temporary condensations of energy: they are *śūnyatā*.

This is not to say that we have to reject intellectual models and structures; only that we should not put our spiritual security (let alone our psychological security) into a provisional intellectual structure in such a way that if the structure is disturbed, our security is disturbed. In this way we can avoid the danger inherent in embracing any system of belief, religious, political, or whatever, of getting bewildered and anxious when people try to rock that particular doctrinal structure. In this way too, by not 'resting on' anything, we keep moving and growing. Again and again in the Mahāyāna, in the Perfection of Wisdom literature, as well as in the Pāli texts, the Buddha exhorts his disciples not to settle down in views.

'Without a home they wander' suggests the traditional image of the bhikkhu, and we are likely to take it literally at first. But 'dharmas never hold them' makes it clear that wandering without a home is not to be taken just in the material sense, but also psychologically. The Bodhisattvas have no psychological home. Indeed, they have no spiritual home—there is no home of any kind to be found in the spiritual community. In this way the ideal of homelessness is given a much more profound interpretation—as, indeed, it is in the more archaic of the Pāli texts like the *Sutta-nipāta*. Resting nowhere, being quite free, and not being bound by such provisional concepts as *skandhas* and *dharmas*—using them but not being enslaved by them—*that* is the ideal of homelessness.

We do not even have to drop the concept of 'self', so long as we are clear that it is an *operational* concept. Many years ago, when I was a comparatively young Buddhist, I was very careful to avoid the word 'self', and always—indeed religiously—put 'non-self' instead; but after a few years I began to wonder what I was so afraid of. If you start getting too scrupulous about these terms, it means you are taking them too literally, in which case even your non-self will become a self. As for trying to avoid using personal pronouns, this is at best pseudo-impersonal vagueness—as in 'it has been decided that'—and at worst completely alienating. We can safely use these locutions if we do so in a colloquial, poetic sort of way, rather than taking them literally.

Intelligence is sometimes defined as the creative use of concepts—and the intelligent Buddhist makes a creative use of Buddhist concepts. They are not to be taken literally, as matters of dogma or blind belief. The Dharma is probably closer to poetry than to science, and *really* communicating it is more like putting across the beauty of a work of art that you have experienced than trying to convey a set of scientific laws that you have understood.

To commit yourself to 'the known is a contradiction in terms

The wanderer Srenika in his gnosis of the truth
Could find no basis, though the skandhas had not been undone.
Just so the Bodhisattva, when he comprehends the dharmas as he should
Does not retire into Blessed Rest. In wisdom then he dwells.

The wanderer Srenika is a figure from the Sanskrit tradition—appearing in a Sarvāstivādin text—who approaches the Buddha with a theory of his own. This is that the Tathāgata is to be identified with the 'true self'—or rather, that the 'true self' is to be identified with the Tathāgata. To this the Buddha replies that Srenika is mistaken; the Tathāgata is not to be considered as identical with the *skandhas*, nor as different from them, nor to be found in their absence. In other words, the Tathāgata cannot be comprehended in terms of the five *skandhas* at all. He is ineffable, inexplicable. Nonetheless, in a supreme act of faith (Conze's expression) Srenika goes for Refuge to the Buddha—even though he has no intellectual grasp of what the Buddha actually is.

Srenika goes for Refuge from a basis of emotion. Even though he has no *reason* to go forth, he is carried forward by a momentum that he has generated and can't stop. This is what is meant by faith. Does this mean that faith is irrational? By no means. After all, do we necessarily have to be able to work things out intellectually before we act? Do we ever, in fact, determine the pros and cons of a situation fully and exhaustively, without possibility of error, before taking any action? Of course not. It is simply impossible to know what all the different factors involved in a particular situation might be. We can never act with complete knowledge. We really do live by faith. This is not to say that faith is the *only* thing to live by—but having found out as much as we reasonably can, we always have to take a chance. We can have a reasonable number of facts at our disposal before we make a decision, but we can't have *all* of them.

In certain situations, like that in which Srenika finds himself, we cannot have any facts at all. Then we really do have to take the plunge, we really do have to commit ourselves, because of course we cannot commit ourselves to something we know. To commit yourself to the known is a contradiction in terms. You always commit yourself to the unknown—or at least, there is always an unknown element in whatever you commit yourself to. It's like getting to know another person—can you ever say you know them completely? Committing yourself to a friendship has to be an act of trust, an act of faith. Indeed, the deeper and more creatively a friendship runs, the more there is within it that is unknown. The more deeply you can rely on someone, the less predictable they become. Conversely, if you really are sure of what someone is going to do next— what they're going to say, or how they're going to respond to a particular situation—you can also be pretty sure that they are essentially reactive rather than creative in how they behave, that they move along deep ruts of unconscious habit, and that in the end they are going to be deeply unreliable.

Srenika 'could find no basis' in which to settle down with an idea that the Buddha was this or that, or was not this or that, even though the Buddha's 'skandhas had not been undone'—even though, that is, the Buddha's psycho-physical personality had not yet finally ceased with the attainment of *parinirvāṇa*. There were the Buddha's *skandhas* in front of him, but he could not decide whether the Buddha was to be found in them, or outside them, or in their absence.

There is an alternative way of reading this line, however, which is to say that Srenika 'could find no basis' because, although the *skandhas*— whether the Buddha's or his own—'had not been undone', he saw that they were like a magical illusion: he did not take them as ultimate realities.

ACTUALLY, WHAT IS BEING TURNED DOWN IS NOT NIRVANA AS A PERSONAL POSSESSION, BUT THE IDEA OF NIRVANA AS A PERSONAL POSSESSION

The verse tells us that just as Srenika 'could find no basis ... the Bodhisattva, when he comprehends the dharmas as he should, does not retire into Blessed Rest.' The Bodhisattva, seeing all *dharmas*, including even the idea of nirvāṇa, as void, as 'operational concepts' (Guenther's expression)—no longer taking all this talk about attaining or not attaining nirvāṇa literally—has no notion of retiring into 'Blessed Rest'.

The Bodhisattva rejects nirvāṇa not in the ultimate sense, but in the pejorative sense given to the word by the Mahāyāna—as something attainable for the individual alone. This conception is not, however, to be taken literally. In the Pāli Canon 'nirvāṇa' is a term for the ultimate realization. But how can you conceive of possessing nirvāṇa for yourself to the exclusion of others? It is a contradiction in terms, because in nirvāṇa there is no question of self in contradistinction to others.

In fact, pejorative as the Mahāyāna may be, this way of thinking is just as typical of the Pāli Canon as of the Mahāyāna. There is a Pāli sutta, for example, in which Ānanda notices that his friend Sāriputta is looking very fresh and bright, and remarks on it, saying 'You look like you've had a good meditation.' By way of explanation, Sāriputta replies that he has spent the whole afternoon meditating in the forest, abiding all that time in the second dhyāna. He goes on to say 'Although I spent the day abiding in second dhyāna, there never came to me the thought that I was abiding in second dhyāna.'[50] If the archetypal Hīnayāna Arhat, Sāriputta, does not perceive even an attainment as basic as the second dhyāna to be his own experience, can it be remotely possible for anyone to say 'Well, here I am attaining nirvāṇa'? Is it even possible to *reject* nirvāṇa as a personal attainment? If there's a question of your rejecting it, this means that you are still thinking of the possibility of attaining it for yourself. If 'Blessed Rest' could be retired into, it wouldn't be Blessed Rest—it would not be nirvāṇa.

The confusing thing about the Mahāyāna is that it uses terms derived from the earlier traditions in a debased sense. No doubt by the time the Mahāyāna developed there had been some decline in the ideals of the Hīnayāna so far as actual practice was concerned. It may even be that some of those who considered themselves Arhats, or who were regarded as such, had started looking at nirvāṇa in a limited and false way, as consisting in no more than an experience of the four dhyānas. If they *had* started thinking of nirvāṇa in that way, they could hardly have been expected to look up from these blissful states and concern themselves with the fate of other beings. This might explain why the Mahayanists were saying 'You have to go beyond nirvāṇa': they meant, perhaps, that you have to go beyond the four dhyānas.

It is possible that the terms the Mahāyāna took in a debased sense, like 'Arhat' and 'nirvāṇa', were actually being used in that debased sense at the time of the rise of the Mahāyāna. They certainly weren't, however, in the Buddha's day. Nowhere in the Pāli Canon is there anyone called an Arhat who begins to live up to—or rather down to—the caricature of the Arhat drawn by the Mahāyāna. Nor does the spurious nirvāṇa peddled by these caricatures get any kind of airing in the Pāli scriptures.[51]

If you attempt to sort out all the different approaches to nirvāṇa taken by all the different schools of Buddhism, you come down to four main modes of 'definition'.[52] There is the positive approach—nirvāṇa as Enlightenment, supreme bliss, etc.—emphasized by the Mahāyāna. There is the symbolic approach, through images—nirvāṇa as 'the cool cave' etc.—which tends nowadays to be ignored, except perhaps by the Pure Land schools. Then there is the paradoxical approach, which asserts that all conceptual determinations of nirvāṇa are inapplicable; this is stressed by the Perfection of Wisdom and popularized by Zen. Finally there is the negative approach of the Hīnayāna: nirvāṇa as the annihilation of ignorance, of the passions, of the *saṃskāras*, of the conditioned. Because it is so easy to misunderstand these approaches, it is wrong to give undue weight to any single one of them.

The symbolic approach to nirvāṇa, through imagery and poetry, seems to be attended by few misinterpretations, and these are relatively innocuous. One of the services performed by Carl Jung has been to assert the definite value and function of such archetypal symbols as that of the Pure Land, even while we do not take them literally. As for the paradoxical approach, however, the dangers here, as should by now be clear, are very real. Firstly there is the danger of exalting irrationalism; secondly there is the danger of the rational mind misunderstanding these paradoxes to the extent of thinking that it can live with them; thirdly there is the danger of imagining that the *ultimate* emptiness of all spiritual practice means that one can dispense with spiritual practice even on the *relative* level.

The drawback with the negative approach is that so little is said about nirvāṇa, and you can, as a result, think of it as a sort of blank, featureless state into which you merely disappear and cease to exist. Nirvāṇa does literally mean extinction. It is most likely to have been a Buddhist coinage from the verb *nibbuta*, which refers to the extinction of a flame. But the extinction of flame had a particular significance in ancient Indian thought. When a physical flame was extinguished it was supposed to revert, as it were, to a sort of archetypal fire. When one spoke of the extinction of a flame it was understood not as annihilation but as transformation, a passing of the flame into a higher or more subtle state. So it would seem that originally the word 'nirvāṇa' was simply not open to a nihilistic misreading.

The Hīnayāna, we might say, takes a more reticent, even respectful attitude towards nirvāṇa than does the Mahāyāna. It is quite happy to get you there, but after that it leaves you to it. Nirvāṇa will let you know what it is when you get there. Certainly you have in the Hīnayāna an indestructible transcendental principle—only it is not said to be, say, 'all pervading', or 'the ground of being', not because it is *not* all-pervading and so on, necessarily, but because to say that it was would constitute a metaphysical statement, and the Hīnayāna steers clear of metaphysical statements. The Hīnayāna says that once you are Enlightened there is no more involuntary rebirth, in the sense of rebirth motivated by craving and ignorance. It does not presume to speculate on whether or not there is any further *voluntary* rebirth out of compassion. The Mahāyāna does go in for this kind of speculation, and one can see at once the sort of problems that the Hīnayāna refuses to get involved in.

The 'positive' approach to nirvāṇa offers a richer perspective on the goal of the spiritual life, but at the same time it is also wide open to misinterpretation. A 'voluntary' rebirth suggests an individual consciousness somehow picking and choosing; but if you try to avoid saying this and say instead that the Enlightened consciousness *must* manifest in a particular way out of compassion, you are trying to put limitations on that which by its nature is completely free. To say that it expresses itself at all presupposes a distinction—between what is to be expressed and the expression itself—that is inapplicable. The Enlightened consciousness is infinite: it is already 'in' all things; it is already ubiquitously expressed and expressing and expressible. It is not to be conceived as something static, a 'Blessed Rest' into which you 'retire' once and for all. There is activity, and that activity is called compassion—though it is not an activity that is distinct from rest, or that starts up from a state of quiescence. In a state of consciousness that is inconceivable, quiescence and activity are not incompatible.

You could say that the Bodhisattva, on the attainment of complete Enlightenment, participates in the universal compassionate activity of the *dharmakāya*—not that from the Absolute point of view there was any deficiency before that Enlightenment, nor that there has been any annihilation of individual Bodhisattvahood. Perhaps from our point of view there is one more Enlightened being, one more Bodhisattva—but not from (as it were) the point of view of the *dharmakāya*.

Despite the Mahāyāna's emphasis on compassionate activity, it has to be said that until very recently Theravāda missionaries far outnumbered Mahāyāna ones. Tibetans did not think of propagating Buddhism outside Tibet until they were thrown out by the Communists. The Chinese and Japanese Buddhists also arrived in the West well behind the Theravādins. The most one can say for the Mahāyāna really is that it stresses the altruistic implications of the spiritual life more than the Hīnayāna, and aims more deliberately at making the spiritual life in its fullest expression available to as many people as possible through the Bodhisattva Ideal.

The Bodhisattva Ideal, in its popular version, is commonly misunderstood. According to this 'exoteric' version you selflessly postpone your attainment of nirvāṇa until *all* beings are Enlightened. But you cannot literally postpone nirvāṇa. It is more that as you progress you are less and less able to make any distinction between helping yourself and helping others. You see more and more that they are different aspects of the same process. You gradually find that you cannot help yourself without helping others; you cannot help others without helping yourself. So there are not really two distinct spiritual ideals, the Arhat Ideal and the Bodhisattva Ideal, each of which may be followed separately through to the end. The further you progress on either so-called path, the more you see that the two ideals coalesce. The historical distinction, which is in fact a threefold one, between the Way of the Arhat, the Way of the Pratyekabuddha, and the Way of the Bodhisattva, is an unfortunate one, really. It took the *White Lotus Sūtra* to stress as its main teaching that the three ways are, in fact, one way—*ekayāna*.

What then is going on when we are told that the Bodhisattva deliberately turns down an exclusive nirvāṇa in favour of Enlightenment for the sake of all sentient beings? Actually, what is being turned down is not nirvāṇa as a personal possession, but the *idea* of nirvāṇa as a personal possession. On the earlier stages of the path you cannot but speak in terms of 'attaining nirvāṇa', 'gaining Enlightenment', but as you begin to approach the goal it becomes quite clear that these expressions just do not square with reality. The Mahāyāna presents this perception in rather a crude, popular way by saying that the Bodhisattva rejects an individual nirvāṇa, but what is in fact being rejected is that particular way of thinking about it. So the Mahāyāna picture is not actually different from that of the Hīnayāna. What the Mahāyāna did, to some extent at least, was simply to restore the original spirit of the Buddha's teaching and bring it out even more fully.

Having said all this, my own experience is that, perhaps because the compassion aspect is more explicit, there is something in the Mahāyāna teaching and practice which is not there in the Theravāda. The kindliness and friendliness of Theravādins is very welcome, but with Tibetan Buddhism particularly you get the impression of a much more definitely spiritual and even transcendental kindliness and compassion. It is the difference between mettā, which is wonderful, and the Bodhicitta, which is even more wonderful.

The Theravādins are quite willing to teach you, but only on their own rather rigid terms. True Mahayanists will try to help you where they find you, without standing on tradition. Of course, one can make all sorts of generalizations: Burmese monks, who go in for the Abhidharma, and Mongolian monks, who are often very good *geshes* and pursue the Mahāyāna equivalent of the Abhidharma, tend to be hot-tempered; Thais, who specialize in the Vinaya, are known for their discipline and mindfulness, while as for the Sinhalese, well, they are always good company—jolly good fellows, you might say. Chinese and Japanese monks, on the other hand, are often very cold; they just don't want to know you. And yet a story I was told by a friend I had in India, Sister

Palden, illustrates how individuals slip out of any such categorizations as these.

She had been staying in a Japanese temple near Rajgir, and when she left, the Japanese monk who was head of the monastery went with her to the station. Her suitcase was rather heavy and he was carrying it for her (a Theravāda bhikkhu could never have allowed himself to compromise his dignity in this way) when they saw the train pull in. They were still a little way from the station, and the head monk saw that there was only one thing for it if she was to catch her train. Without more ado he hoisted the big suitcase on his head like a coolie and *ran*. So she caught her train. The point of the story is that he was able to drop his dignity without a moment's hesitation when it was helpful to do so. This is the Mahāyāna spirit.

No one is more emotional or less reasonable than an intellectual

So we learn of the Bodhisattva that 'comprehending the dharmas as he should … in wisdom then he dwells'. The life of wisdom is the spontaneous life. It is not dependent upon intellectual supports; it goes beyond the evidence. If we look at the way we function, we can say that the senses supply our raw materials, and then the mind gets to work on them, and then we come to various conclusions. But we cannot take this level of functioning as our basis. There is more to us than our senses, and thus more to us than the reasoning faculty, based as it is on sense data. If we allow ourselves to be limited by sensory input, we restrict our whole being.

So, as an experiment, why not try doing something without finding a reason for it first? Listen to the voice of reason—it is useful as a starting point—but don't be guided by it all along the way. You are bigger than your reason; hence the need for faith. If you have faith, you go beyond the current situation, you get along with the minimum of rational, intellectual, support. To give to a situation less thought than it requires is stupid, but to give it *more* thought than it requires is neurotic, and leads to anxiety. Faith and worry are incompatible: if you've got faith, you can't be neurotic.

The integrated person acts as a total person, acting with reason—in the sense of an aware recognition of certain objective facts and circumstances and possibilities—but also with emotionality. You are more likely to be able to be truly rational and to take into account the objective facts of a situation if you are also more freely emotional. There is, in fact, far less genuinely rational thinking going on than we like to think. In most cases, so-called rational people are those with the greatest capacity for rationalization and the most deeply buried emotions. Take scholars, for example. When I first started coming into contact with scholars of Buddhism in the early fifties, it surprised me how very irrational they all were. As soon as one of them had an article published, another specialist in the same field would have a violent emotional reaction and then do some 'objective' research in order to refute and utterly demolish the conclusions of their rival. Nor were they averse to academic intrigue, to arranging for unfavourable reviews to be sent out, or pulling strings to get rivals dismissed from their posts. In my innocence I had imagined that scholars were objective, impartial, rational beings—but not a bit of it. No one is more emotional or less reasonable than an intellectual.

Since then I've come to see that most people are like this. There are those, of course, who don't make any attempt to disguise their emotions, and quite openly act from them. Others, however, have a greater capacity to dress up their emotions as reasons. We may find reasons for doing things, but really it is our emotions that are pulling the strings. Not that there is anything wrong with being emotionally motivated—the problems arise when that emotional motivation goes unacknowledged. It's what you might call the X factor: the factor which does not get mentioned when people are explaining their actions. The X factor is not exactly unconscious, but people get into an absolute and thus practically unconscious habit of not acknowledging it, so that it finds a sub-terranean, indirect, and therefore negative expression. It is better to clarify the emotions, have them out in the open, and—if not make them more positive—at least act from them more directly. If we allow the emotions a more free and open play, they will be more amenable to reason where reason is called for. We can see them for what they are and take steps either to bring them under control—with awareness—or to purify them and make them more translucent and refined.

If you can't reason things out, you have little chance of finding any direction for your energies. At the same time, you are unlikely to get much done if your heart isn't in it. But when you are totally integrated—when your reason is your emotion, and your emotion is your reason—it is then quite difficult to say whether you are doing something for a particular reason, or simply because you feel like it. At your best, you are unable to say whether you are reasoning or emoting. You are aware of why you are doing whatever you are doing, and you are emotionally engaged in what you are doing—but they seem to come to the same thing. This is intelligence. When the intelligence splits off from the rest of the personality and functions autonomously, however, it becomes what we call the intellect, and starts rationalizing.

The word 'intellect' has, of course, a highly respectable record in European thought. 'Reason' or 'intellect' originally meant the supra-individual higher faculty for the apprehension of truth, and Kant was able to initiate a distinction between this and what he called 'the understanding'. However, these terms 'reason', 'intellect', and 'understanding' no longer express any such distinction for us; indeed, our vocabulary no longer has any term at all for intellect as that higher faculty. At best we have the altogether too ambiguous word 'intuition', which can usefully refer to the direct apprehension of something that does not require demonstration—i.e. 'intuitive understanding'—but not to that higher intellectual level.

The decline of this sort of language must be associated with the decline of Christianity; the word 'intellect' in its traditional sense is in use nowadays only amongst Catholic theologians. Traditional Platonic, Neoplatonic, and Christian Catholic thought operated within a threefold classification of man into 'body', 'soul', and 'spirit'. Then 'spirit' became equated with 'soul'; and now even 'soul' has rather petered out, leaving us with 'body' virtually on its own, and a terminology which reflects that narrowing of perspective.

As Buddhists, we won't want to restore the old status of words if this also means restoring their Christian connotations. We should be careful, therefore, to make a clear distinction between such terms as *prajñā* and *vijñāna*. *Vijñāna*, which is of course one of the five *skandhas*, is not so much 'consciousness' as this whole rational, conceptual level of knowledge, in contrast with the altogether higher faculty of intellect represented by *prajñā*.

A healthy person has neither an intellect in our modern, debased sense, nor free-floating emotions. In the healthy, integrated person head and heart work together. As for the Bodhisattva's wisdom, or 'intellect', this has no more connection with the head than it does with the heart. It is rooted in both, it grows out of both, and it transcends both. Transcendental wisdom, for all its intellectual connotations, is equally accessible—and equally inaccessible—to both head and heart. So 'In wisdom then he dwells': he dwells as a completely integrated person.

Chapter Four

A LEAP OF FAITH

What is this wisdom, whose and whence, he queries,
And then he finds that all these dharmas are entirely empty.
Uncowed and fearless in the face of that discovery
Not far from Bodhi is that Bodhi-being then.

Our doubts and questions are resolved when we realize that no objects of thought denote existing entities or realities, which are empty, or indefinable, and thus not completely amenable to logical treatment. The discovery of the emptiness of all dharmas is a non-rational one; but going beyond the limits of reason, the Bodhisattva remains uncowed and fearless.

Offering the term 'indefinable' for *śūnya* is not to suggest that we translate *śūnyatā* as '*the* Indefinable'—like *the* Unconditioned or *the* Absolute. The teaching of *śūnyatā* tries to communicate to us the fact that reality, experience, life, cannot be adequately and fully represented by thought. Thought is not equal to or commensurate with experience. Experience transcends thought. To speak of *śūnyatā* as 'the open-ended dimension of being', as Dr Guenther does, perhaps comes too close to being a definition. Is life literally open-ended? If we use an expression like this it is only as a pointer, a warning not to try to superimpose our conceptual categories too rigidly upon life.

According to the *Prajñāpāramitā* there are twenty kinds of *śūnyatā*. We can say, for example, that something is *śūnya* in the sense of being completely non-existent: that which is illusory can be described as void in the sense that it isn't there at all. When we talk about the *relatively* real as being *śūnya*, however, *śūnya* cannot in this context be translated as 'non-existent'. The 'relatively real' arises in dependence upon causes and conditions, and ceases when those causes and conditions disappear; so in this case *śūnya* means 'relative', 'empirically existent', 'conditioned'— not 'non-existent'. As for when we say that nirvāṇa is *śūnya*, this means that nirvāṇa is empty of the whole cause–effect process, that there is nothing in it of conditioned existence. It does not mean that nirvāṇa is completely non-existent. Then in the highest sense we can speak of the *śūnyatā* of the *dharmakāya*. This means that the *dharmakāya* is empty of all discriminations. We cannot say that it is existent or non-existent, *śūnya* or *aśūnya*, void or not-void—it transcends all these terms. It is completely empty—but not, again, simply non-existent.

If one says 'Oh, in Buddhism everything is void' one lets oneself in for endless misunderstandings. One should never use the term voidness (or emptiness) at all without carefully relating it to its appropriate context. It is not a thing to be described, but more like a mode of being. If your experience is an experience of *śūnyatā* then you will see whatever you come into contact with as *śūnyatā*. It is like the experience of mettā: any person—indeed any sentient being—that comes within the range of your mettā will become an object of that mettā. The person hasn't changed, but at the same time—for you—they have changed. People who seemed pretty dreadful or despicable before now seem lovable, attractive, and appealing. In the same way, when insight has arisen, you see and experience as *śūnyatā* anything that happens to come within your spiritual vision, to the extent that you perceive and experience it at all.

> To course in the skandhas, in form, in feeling, in perception,
> Will and so on, and fail to consider them wisely;
> Or to imagine these skandhas as being empty;
> Means to course in the sign, the track of non-production ignored.

Don't imagine the *skandhas* as being empty if this means positing an actual entity, or something that the skandhas really are, which is qualified and thus substantiated by something called emptiness. To say that the *skandhas* are empty is just a way of saying that they are not to be taken literally, or at their face value. To imagine the *skandhas* as being really and truly empty 'means to course in the sign'—that is, it means to take something which has only a provisional and relative existence as being ultimately real. It means we have not realized the 'non-production' of things.

'Non-production' is an important concept (or rather non-concept) of the Mahāyāna, traditionally illustrated by the conjuror's magical show. If a conjuror conjures up horses and elephants so that you see what appear to be horses and elephants, have these horses and elephants really come into existence? Have they actually been produced? No—they may appear to have been produced, but in reality nothing has been produced at all. Likewise, the Bodhisattva sees all phenomena—which appear to be produced—as like a mirage or a magical show. They are perceived—and they exist in the sense that they are perceived—but they are not ultimately real. There is therefore no question of their being produced, as such. The Bodhisattva sees *dharmas*—all phenomenal things—as just appearing like a mirage in the desert. The mirage is seen, but it does not really exist.

The non-arisen—*anutpanna*—nature of all *dharmas* is connected with the practice of *kshānti*, patience, which is the third *pāramitā*. Strictly speaking, this *pāramitā* is called the *anutpattika-dharma-kshānti*, the patient acceptance of the non-origination of all *dharmas*[53]. This is patience in the deepest sense, as practised by the Bodhisattva in the eighth *bhūmi*—the eighth of the ten stages in the progress of the Bodhisattva. It is the patient acceptance of the fact that in their essential nature all *dharmas* are non-produced. They do not actually come into existence. Everything abides in a state of quiescence, calm, *śūnyatā*, with only an appearance of things being produced, like a mirage or the magic of a conjuror. The Bodhisattva's patient acceptance of the non-origination of all *dharmas* is the seeing and accepting of the fact that all things are like this. This is the track, or path, of non-production.

If the Bodhisattva were to take the absolute quiescence of all *dharmas* as an invitation to sit about doing nothing, however, this would imply a difference between attainment and non-attainment, when in fact, of course, they are both empty. Thus the compassionate activity of the Bodhisattva is based not on any mundane and thus essentially self-centred 'humanitarian' ideal, but on the realization of emptiness.

When we 'course in the sign' we are taking all the subjectively conditioned ideas and concepts with which we invest a particular sense perception in order to make it an 'object' of our perception—pre-eminently the concepts of 'being' and 'non-being'—as constituting the true nature of that sense perception.

> *But when he does not course in form, in feeling, or perception,*
> *In will or consciousness, but wanders without home,*
> *Remaining unaware of coursing firm in wisdom,*
> *His thoughts on non-production—then the best of all the calming trances*
>   *cleaves to him.*

When a Bodhisattva does not settle down in any particular set of ideas like the five *skandhas*, and does not take those ideas as representing absolute realities, but remains concentrated in the patient acceptance of the non-origination of all *dharmas*, so that there is no self-consciousness in the firm treading of the path of wisdom, then that Bodhisattva will naturally come to dwell in the dhyānas, the blissful states of higher consciousness.

THERE IS NOTHING INNATE IN THE DHYANA STATE THAT LEADS TO WISDOM;

BUT THERE IS SOMETHING INNATE IN YOU THAT IS NOT SATISFIED BY THAT EXPERIENCE

> *Through that the Bodhisattva now dwells tranquil in himself,*
> *His future Buddhahood assured by antecedent Buddhas.*
> *Whether absorbed in trance, or whether outside it, he minds not.*
> *For of things as they are he knows the essential original nature.*

The attainment of precedent Buddhas guarantees the Bodhisattva future Buddhahood, *provided that* he or she makes the same effort that the previous Buddhas made before their Enlightenment.

The Bodhisattva understands the fundamental nature of all things, including the dhyānas (or 'trances', as Conze unfortunately translates the term), as being essentially non-arisen, non-originated, and is not, therefore, attached to them. Enjoyment there may be, but the Bodhisattva is not misled by that enjoyment into taking the dhyānas as existing, so to speak, in their own right. It should be said, though, that looked at even from the relative point of view, the dhyānas are part of the phenomenal world, and as such should not be objects of attachment.

Although from a Buddhist perspective these experiences are limited, they are of course very powerful, and Hindu theism is firmly based on them. To give them their due, Hindus are comparatively familiar with higher states of dhyāna; it is only too easy if we don't have much experience of these states ourselves to criticize the Hindus for getting stuck in them. But it is also easy to get stuck in them, because they are very seductive, intoxicating states. Overflowing with bliss, you feel uplifted and joyful and carried away by a kind of divine wind. When you speak to people they say 'Oh, you're so different from anyone I've ever met before.' On the strength of that, you might start giving discourses and expounding the *Bhagavad Gītā*. The crowds of people who flocked to hear you would pretty soon be wanting to build you an ashram, saying 'You must have realized God; you're a God-realized soul'—and you would no doubt start thinking 'Well, perhaps I am.' In the end you would get a few Western disciples, and then you would really be made. You would do a world tour, collect a lot of money, and build an enormous ashram.

This is the story of dozens upon dozens of gurus nowadays. They are certainly not fakes—they are often sincere, helpful, likeable people, full of emotional positivity, and it's very good that there are such people around—but you can see what the Buddha was up against, and why he adopted the attitude that he did. In India people are all too ready to claim God-realization, and others are all too ready to credit them with it. Ordinary religious or spiritually-minded people in India tend to think only in terms of dhyāna or *samādhi*, and reckon that if you reach such a state you are Enlightened: you have 'realized God'. They use this sort of language very easily and loosely. You can set yourself up as a guru on this sort of basis with no trouble at all, especially if you have an exuberant, lively, communicative temperament. Your exuberance is said to be the overflow of the Divine Bliss that you've realized.

Dhyāna prepares you for wisdom, but it does not take you there, because there is no dhyāna apart from the person experiencing dhyāna. There is nothing innate in the dhyāna state that leads to wisdom; but there *is* something innate in *you* that is not satisfied by that experience, despite the egoistic tendency to settle down in it. It is the positive concentrated energies that come from the practice of dhyāna, indeed from the practice of all the *pāramitās*—giving, morality, patience, vigour, meditation, and wisdom—that transform your purely intellectual understanding into an actual experience. But penetration into the truth comes from you, as an integrated, powerful individual—possibly with the help of certain intellectual supports (as it were) derived from the tradition. This penetration into the truth brings about first insight, in the sense of *vipaśyanā*, or intermittent flashes of insight, and then, gradually, wisdom, *prajñā*,

which has more the nature of a permanent faculty, although the terms
vipaśyanā and *prajñā* are sometimes roughly equated.

Within Hinduism there is of course a tradition of *jñāna* as well as of
samādhi, and the position of Advaita Vedanta is that it is indeed *jñāna* or
gnosis which gives ultimate realization. From my own contact with
followers of the Vedanta, however, I would say that their knowledge is
almost always intellectual, and rarely backed up with dhyāna. There
seems to be a rather strange division between the two traditions; it is
extremely rare for someone to develop both *jñāna* and dhyāna. Indeed,
according to a non-dualist Vedantin I met in India, spiritual practice was
completely unnecessary since the world was nothing but an illusion.
Even his evident ill-humour was an illusion, apparently.[54]

Quite the opposite, though also in the end one-sided, was the rather
more distinguished example of Ramana Maharshi. From him I got the
quite distinct impression that he had had experience of the *arūpa dhyānas*,
the formless dhyānas, and that he was perhaps even established in that
experience, but that he did not have wisdom in the full Buddhist sense.
The absence of compassion in his ashram was noticeable, in that the caste
divisions were still maintained, and allowed to be maintained. A Buddhist would say that this is simply incompatible with compassion, and that
without compassion there is no real wisdom. Buddhism is much more
aware in this sort of way—much more critical, and self-critical—than
Hinduism.

> *Coursing thus he courses in the wisdom of the Sugatas,*
> *And yet he does not apprehend the dharmas in which he courses.*
> *This coursing he wisely knows as a no-coursing,*
> *That is his practice of wisdom, the highest perfection.*

> *What exists not, that non-existent the foolish imagine;*
> *Non-existence as well as existence they fashion.*
> *As dharmic facts existence and non-existence are both not real.*
> *A Bodhisattva goes forth when wisely he knows this.*

> *If he knows the five skandhas as like an illusion,*
> *But makes not illusion one thing, and the skandhas another;*
> *If, freed from the notion of multiple things, he courses in peace—*
> *Then that is his practice of wisdom, the highest perfection.*

It is crucial to realize that all intellectual structures, even Buddhist ones, are provisional. Their function is essentially practical—to stimulate the corresponding feelings. Ideas and concepts rest upon you; you don't rest upon them. If you get this the wrong way round, you can get into quite unnecessary semantic confusion. For example, there is apparently a semantics experiment in which you take one word from a simple concrete sentence and define it. You then take one word from that definition and define that, and so on—until after five or six sentences you find that you are having to use words from the first sentence in order to define the new word. The process of defining meaning is totally circular and, in its own terms, meaningless: it does not rest on anything.

But actually you would know exactly what I meant if I said 'go through that door', because if you wanted to, and if it were possible, you could carry out the instruction. Meaning would have been communicated. The statement carries meaning because you can understand it for practical purposes. It is only if you try to go into the abstract meaning of words apart from the concrete situation in which they are used that you set yourself to go round in circles. The meaning of a word rests on the person using it, not the other way round. If you insisted on 'understanding' the meaning of a sentence before you did anything about it you would never get round to doing anything. It would be like demanding proof that the door is a real door, that it will actually open when you turn the handle, and that there isn't a deep ditch on the other side for you to fall into. Why not just go through the door? In the end it comes down to faith on the one hand and fear of the unknown on the other. We know nothing in advance. You can't know what it is like to go through the door until you have gone through it.

The same goes for signs and symbols. The Bodhisattva reads signs and symbols in the same way that we read road signs, simply registering what each sign conveys about the destination and the condition of the road ahead. There is no question of stopping and wondering what each square sheet of painted tin really means—Why is it blue?—Why square? The Bodhisattva just sees the sign and drives on—assuming it's the right road, of course.

Those with good teachers as well as deep insight,
Cannot be frightened on hearing the Mother's deep tenets.
But those with bad teachers, who can be misled by others,
Are ruined thereby, as an unbaked pot when in contact with moisture.

'The Mother' is of course Prajñāpāramitā, the 'Mother of all the Buddhas'. This verse concludes what Conze entitles 'The Basic Teachings' with a severe warning to handle them with extreme care. Those who do not have the sense to be able to discriminate between a good teacher and a bad one, and who do not properly exercise their own judgement, will misunderstand the Perfection of Wisdom, and will not get the requisite guidance in its practice. To try to go beyond the intellectual categories of Buddhism before one has grasped and worked with those categories is ruinous. The Perfection of Wisdom needs to be approached with a sense of awe and reverence, because without a good teacher it is very easy to get it wrong.

YOU BEST IMITATE YOUR TEACHER BY BEING YOURSELF. IF YOU DELIBERATELY TRY TO COPY THE EXTERNALS IT MEANS THAT YOU ARE UNSURE OF YOURSELF, AND UNSURE, IN THE END, OF YOUR ESSENTIAL NATURE WHICH, LIKE YOUR TEACHER'S, IS SUNYATA

But how can we recognize a good teacher? If there is a tendency in the teaching of Buddhism towards one particular weakness it is a tendency towards becoming institutionalized and conformist. A useful rule of thumb that one can use to ascertain whether there is any real communication of wisdom going between teacher and disciple is to observe how faithfully the disciples *appear* to follow the example of the teacher, and how like-minded they are. The more closely the disciples emulate the life-style, temperament, and expression of the teacher, the more superficial the communication is likely to be. If the disciples are carbon copies of the teacher, this is highly suspect. It's like looking at some modern Thai paintings of scenes from the life of the Buddha, in which the Buddha is surrounded by twenty or thirty so-called disciples, all spitting images of himself. The Buddha may be distinguished by a few black curls, but otherwise they could all have popped out of one mould.

If you have a very devotional guru surrounded by a lot of devotional disciples, for example, you have to be on your guard. They could just be getting together on the basis of a common temperament, an intense kind of gregariousness, which would make it unlikely that insight is being passed on. (This is not to say that a certain level of spiritual experience is not being attained, for the dhyāna levels can be very powerful, quite apart from any question of insight.) If you have anything of wisdom to communicate to a disciple it is something that goes beyond temperament. You have to be careful that you are communicating the truth *through* your own temperament, and appealing to that which transcends temperament in someone else, rather than merely communicating an *expression* of your temperament. If you put the teaching in a certain way that appeals to someone of a certain temperament, all well and good—but this is only to get the teaching accepted so that it can go right through the temperament into the person.

It is quite reassuring when a teacher who is a strict monk, leading a disciplined life in a monastery, has a faithful disciple who is laid-back and anarchic, and doesn't bother with robes and so on—or vice versa. Disciples might seem to teach in a completely different way from their teacher, they might even appear to be giving completely different teachings, but this may be because they are communicating the teaching to people of quite different temperaments from either their own or their teacher's. No one experiences the same thing in the same way, and you have to allow for that. The medium is important, but it is not the message; we must not be misled by externals. Think of Marpa and his disciple Milarepa—differences of temperament were transcended, and something was really passed on. You best imitate your teacher by being yourself. If you deliberately try to copy the externals it means that you are unsure of yourself, and unsure, in the end, of your essential nature, which, like your teacher's, is *śūnyatā*. You are equally suchness, equally unique.

Chapter Five

THE NATURE OF THE BODHISATTVA

What is the reason why we speak of 'Bodhisattvas'?
Desirous to extinguish all attachment, and to cut it off,
True non-attachment, or the Bodhi of the Jinas is their future lot.
'Beings who strive for Bodhi' are they therefore called.

In the *Ariya-pariyesana Sutta* the Buddha refers to himself before he attained Enlightenment as the *bodhisatta*—this is the Pāli word, the Sanskrit form apparently having come later. In the context of the *Ariya-pariyesana Sutta* the term clearly refers to the Buddha himself when he was bent upon Enlightenment, but in Pāli *satta* can mean either 'being' or 'striving', so that we can take *bodhisatta* as meaning either a 'Bodhi-being' or 'one who strives for *bodhi*'. The Sanskrit equivalent, *sattva*, however, means just 'being', so strictly speaking *bodhisattva* can only mean 'Bodhi-being'. If you take *bodhisatta* as meaning 'one who strives for Bodhi'—and it is likely that this is the original meaning—the Sanskrit equivalent becomes, strictly speaking, *bodhiśakta*, but for some reason it was taken to be *bodhisattva*.

We could even render *bodhisattva*—in the sense of *bodhiśakta*—as 'one who is capable of Enlightenment'. In modern Hindi for instance, *śakta* means 'can'—if you want to say 'I can do it' you say *me śakta hun*—so *śakta* signifies capacity, energy, or power. Probably the best translation of *bodhisattva*, then, is 'one who is bent upon Enlightenment' or even 'one who is oriented in the direction of Enlightenment'. In the Mahāyāna, all Buddhists—all Mahāyāna Buddhists anyway—are regarded as Bodhisattvas, inasmuch as they all accept the Bodhisattva Ideal, at least in principle. One could take the term *bodhisattva*, again in the sense of *bodhiśakta*, but without restricting it to the specifically Mahāyāna ideal, and apply it to anyone who has *bodhi*, Enlightenment, for their ultimate goal. It could then be used in a non-sectarian sense in place of the term 'Buddhist'—because a Buddhist is simply one whose Going for Refuge is a striving to become Enlightened.

The definition of *bodhi* not as 'supreme knowledge' or 'supreme bliss', but as 'true non-attachment', is telling. The force of 'true non-attachment' lies in its application not just to worldly things, pleasures, and knowledge, but, in a more profound sense, to ideas, to the teaching as doctrinally formulated. There is, however, a simpler and more practical way of looking at it. Given that attachment is what we immediately come up against when we start trying to lead the spiritual life, it is only natural that we should project the goal of Enlightenment as a state of non-attachment.

What is the reason why 'Great Beings' are so called?
They rise to the highest place above a great number of people;
And of a great number of people they cut off mistaken views.
That is why we come to speak of them as 'Great Beings.'

When the Buddha sent out the first sixty disciples, he said 'I, O Monks, am free from all bonds, human and divine; you, too, O Monks, are free from all bonds, human and divine. Go forth then therefore, O Monks, for the weal and the happiness of many people.'[55] Clearly in passages like this no distinction is made between the Enlightenment gained by the Buddha and that gained by the disciples who came to be called Arhats. 'Arhat' is actually a pre-Buddhistic term, meaning literally 'one who is worthy, or worshipful', and it seems to have been used originally as a mode of address, just as we say 'his worship, the Mayor'. In the early days of Buddhism it came to mean someone who was spiritually worthy, but it was not used in a very precise sense. Later on, though perhaps still within the lifetime of the Buddha, it came to have the technical meaning of a disciple who had gained Enlightenment, although the Buddha himself continued to be titled Arhat.[56] As time went on, however, there was an increasing tendency to glorify the Buddha, and his Enlightenment was seen as a special—a sort of superrogatory—Enlightenment, by comparison with which that of the Arhat came to be regarded as something less. The distinction crystallized in the term *anubodhi*, or 'subsequent *bodhi*', which was applied to the realization of one who has attained the same *bodhi* as the Buddha, but only by following in his footsteps.

Eventually, this slight distinction (in the mode of attainment rather than in the attainment itself) between Buddha and Arhat widened to such an extent that the Mahāyāna was able to say 'Don't aim at the lesser Enlightenment of the Arhat; aim at the superior Enlightenment of the Buddha.' Clearly, this exhortation rests upon a false antithesis. Enlightenment was the same for the Arhats as for the Buddha; *anubodhi* is exactly the same in content as the Buddha's *bodhi*. Nevertheless, the Mahāyāna does get us back to the original Buddhist position that there is just one goal for all. It offers its own hierarchy (in contradistinction to the 'Hīnayāna' hierarchy of the *arya-pudgalas*—the Stream Entrant and so on) based upon the ten *bhūmis*—with the difference that on accomplishing the tenth *bhūmi* you become not 'just' an Arhat, but a Buddha.

'Great Being', *Mahāsattva*, is a synonym for 'Bodhisattva' in Sanskrit; in the Perfect Wisdom texts Bodhisattvas are frequently referred to as *Bodhisattva-Mahāsattvas*. Late Mahāyāna thought defined a 'Great Being', a *Bodhisattva-Mahāsattva*, as a Bodhisattva who had attained at least the eighth *bhūmi*. At this early stage, however, such a distinction does not seem to have been made.

Of course, the prefix *mahā-* appears in other compound words, like *mahāprajñā* and *mahākaruṇā*. According to a friend and teacher I had in Kalimpong called Mr Chen, who was a master of Ch'an Buddhism, *mahā* in these contexts signified *śūnyatā*: it wasn't to be taken in the sense of spatial extension, but as emptiness. From this point of view the Mahāyāna is the *yāna*, the vehicle, of emptiness; the *Mahāsattva* is the being who has realized emptiness; *mahāprajñā*, the Great Wisdom, is the wisdom that consists in the realization of emptiness; and *mahākaruṇā* is not just the ordinary compassion that one person might feel for another, but the compassion that issues from a realization of the voidness of the subject–object distinction. Whatever follows the prefix *mahā-* is to be understood as having been transformed by the experience of *śūnyatā*, or, as Mr Chen used to put it, 'as having passed through the purifying flames of *śūnyatā*'. Looked at in this way, a *Mahāsattva* is a being who has passed through the fires of *śūnyatā* and been purified thereby. That was Mr Chen's way of putting it, although the general principle is a traditional one. In the next verse the 'great armour' is another way of representing *śūnyatā*—the armour of *śūnyatā* as the true protection, the source of true fearlessness.

'Great Beings ... rise to the highest place above a great number of people' because they are very few and far between. The suggestion is that the Bodhisattva is a real individual—well, you have to be an individual to make up your mind to set out for Enlightenment—'the highest place'.

Mistaken Views are Only Cut Off by Reaching their Emotional Basis

Although cutting 'mistaken views' off a great number of people is a special function of the Bodhisattva—indeed, it is one of the things that make him or her a Bodhisattva—this is in no way to suggest some sort of intellectual guillotine in operation. It seems clear from various statements by the Buddha in the Pāli Canon that a *micchā-diṭṭhi*, a false view, is essentially a rationalization for a basic wrong attitude that is as much emotional as cognitive. The wrong view is like a symptom from which you can infer the presence of the deep-seated disease which is the wrong attitude. For example, the Buddha clearly associated *vibhava-taṇhā*, craving for non-existence, with the *micchā-diṭṭhi* of *ucchedavāda*, literally 'cutting off-ism', or nihilism—the belief that when you die you are 'cut off', that death is absolutely the end. Likewise, the basic attitude of *bhava-taṇhā*, thirst for existence, finds a conceptual expression in the *micchā-diṭṭhi* of *sassatavāda*, eternalism, the belief that something unchanging and immortal, like the 'soul', survives death. In other words, we *believe* that we are in some way eternal because we *want* to be eternal, or alternatively we *believe* that death is an absolute full stop for us because that is how, at some level, it suits us to think of it.[57]

So a wrong view is not simply an intellectual proposition that someone has arrived at by quite disinterested and objective intellectual means which just happen to be wrong. It may be given a purely conceptual expression, but as a *micchā-diṭṭhi* it is pseudo-rational, because it is held in accordance with an unacknowledged emotional basis. A *micchā-diṭṭhi* is said traditionally to be an 'extreme view', and the truth is said to reside in 'the middle way'. If you have a temperamental inclination to compromise, to paper over differences, however, and you call that the middle way, then your middle way itself becomes a *micchā-diṭṭhi*. Just how far you can get it wrong when you really *want* to is nicely illustrated by a question I was once asked by a rather clever caste Hindu at a public meeting. He said 'Buddhism teaches the Middle Way, doesn't it?' I agreed. 'In that case,' he went on, 'we should steer a middle way between truth and falsehood. And yet Buddhism also prompts us to speak the truth, in which respect it is surely not being faithful to its own principle of the Middle Way, is it?' The answer to this, of course, is that truth is the Middle Way between the two extremes of exaggerating and minimizing.

Unless one is schizophrenic, it is hardly possible to think without emotion. Even the most bloodless intellects have some tenuous threads connecting them with a set of emotions, however repressed and stunted. Mistaken views can therefore only be cut off by reaching their emotional basis. When someone has no real contact with their emotions, there is of course no hope of changing the wrong view until the emotions are freed, and there are various ways to do this. Inasmuch as people who are not in contact with their feelings may also not have much bodily awareness, then massage or even sport may help; music or art provide very positive ways for people to contact their emotions; and for quick results a little alcohol may be the lesser of two evils. I confess that there was a time in the early seventies when if someone visiting me seemed altogether too excruciatingly tongue-tied, I used to send out for a bottle of something to loosen their inhibitions—it never failed.

It does seem, however, as though one very often has to get back to negative emotions before one can experience positive ones—and stronger emotions are usually bound up with other people. If one is really deeply blocked emotionally, it is because there is something quite deeply wrong in one's relationships with other people, and in one's whole attitude to them. This is where the damage has been done, and this is where it has got to be undone. If one has violent feelings of resentment, they are not towards trees and flowers, or against nature in general; they are towards individuals one has encountered and known, maybe when one was very young, and an expression of that resentment has to be experienced in connection with another person. This is where simple communication exercises—or just straightforward interactions with open and sensitive individuals—are especially useful. More serious cases of course call for counselling or psychoanalysis; and some kind of therapy may be quite liberating in the short term.

Then, however, we need to orientate ourselves towards a positive goal. It is not necessary to explore our negativity exhaustively. We don't need to experience our anger, say, week after week. In fact, a therapeutic group situation can be quite unhelpful inasmuch as it tends naturally to create the feelings it is supposed to be exorcizing. If people get together and start thinking and talking about their negative emotions, after a time a very odd sort of atmosphere develops—quite sick and strained. There is a line to be drawn between the purging of old emotion that has lain like a poison in the system all our lives, and the creation of brand new negative emotion under this cathartic guise; and that line just does not get drawn when there doesn't seem to be anything to move on to, when there's no concept of a further step—in a word, no ideal. Nowadays a lot of people have their very livelihood invested in therapies of one kind or another, and perhaps they overvalue them at times and don't look beyond them. The 'Growth Movement' may work well as a sort of adjustment therapy, but we should look carefully at what, if anything, it is being proposed that we grow into.

If we really want to root out *micchā-diṭṭhis*, we have to work with our most deep-rooted conditionings in a way that challenges the most radical of conventional values. So as soon as possible we want to leave our negativity behind and turn round and start exploring something completely different. We want to start releasing not just the anger and the pain, but the love and the delight and the appreciation that we have also perhaps repressed for too long. The positive, once we get to it, is the great dissolver of the negative. With a strong meditation practice, if we are not seriously blocked, negative emotions may be dissolved without being consciously experienced at all, and we can start to relate to people powerfully and positively without going through that negative phase.

> *Great as a giver, as a thinker, as a power,*
> *He mounts upon the vessel of the Supreme Jinas.*
> *Armed with the great armour he'll subdue Māra the artful.*
> *These are the reasons why 'Great Beings' are so called.*

Giving, or generosity, is the first of the *pāramitās*. Sometimes it is said 'If you can do nothing else, at least practise *dāna*.' Even if you cannot honour the precepts, or meditate, or make sense of Buddhist philosophy, or feel any devotion or reverence at all—well, never mind. If at least you are generous there is hope for you yet—in fact, considerable hope. This is a subject that gets treated at tireless length in Mahāyāna texts.

The highest form of giving is, of course, the gift of the Dharma, and to be able to put the Dharma across effectively you do need some skill in the handling of concepts. The Bodhisattva, then, is great as a thinker—all this is clear enough. But 'great as a power' does not seem quite so straightforward. What is meant by power is the bodhicitta, the 'will to Enlightenment'. This power is not a property of the individual Bodhisattva in the sense that someone might be designated 'a powerful person'. The bodhicitta is a force or energy, which is not exactly impersonal—that makes it sound like electricity—but more like 'suprapersonal'. According to some of the texts the bodhicitta is not to be included in the five *skandhas*—this is to say that it is not among the constituents of the ordinary personality; it is not a function of the egoistic will. This makes the bodhicitta something transcendental, and its arising is not therefore anybody's individual thought or act of volition. The bodhicitta is best described as a supra-personal transcendental energy that manifests through the individual, although it is at the same time that individual's truest and deepest nature. It is in this sense that the bodhicitta is a 'power'—and in this sense, too, that the Bodhisattva in whom the bodhicitta has arisen is also a 'power'.

The word 'vessel' appears here in place of the customary 'vehicle', and it suggests the raft of the Dharma that carries us across the ocean—or the great river—of saṁsāra. The 'great armour' is usually understood to represent fearlessness.

ONE OF THE BODHISATTVA PRECEPTS IS TO REFRAIN FROM PREACHING THE DOCTRINE OF SUNYATA TO THOSE WHO ARE SPIRITUALLY UNPREPARED— BECAUSE THEY CANNOT BUT INTERPRET IT NIHILISTICALLY

This gnosis shows him all beings as like an illusion,
Resembling a great crowd of people, conjured up at the crossroads,
By a magician, who then cuts off many thousands of heads;
He knows this whole living world as a mock show, and yet remains without
*   fear.*

Illusion must be understood very precisely, otherwise you can come away from this verse with a completely mistaken idea of what gnosis consists in. It is the kind of misapprehension that the Emperor of China must have derived from Bodhidharma's answer to the question 'What is the highest truth of the holy doctrine?' Bodhidharma is not one to beat about the bush: he replies 'Vast emptiness and nothing holy.' Obviously bewildered by the idea of emptiness, the emperor's second question gropes for something upon which Bodhidharma must establish some kind of reality: 'Who is he then who stands before me? Are you not a holy man?' Bodhidharma is not to be toppled from his lofty viewpoint, however, and replies 'I don't know.'

We must assume that Bodhidharma was very clear about what he was doing—and as a kōan the whole exchange is to be investigated in the context of meditation. But it is a very big mistake indeed to try to communicate the Perfection of Wisdom and śūnyatā in this enigmatic way unless this absolute perspective is actually your perspective. Even then, you must remember that one of the Bodhisattva precepts is to refrain from preaching the doctrine of *śūnyatā* to those who are spiritually un-prepared—because they cannot but interpret it nihilistically. It is not enough to announce the absolute truth. You must also announce the relative truth on the basis of which that absolute truth is to be realized; and you must point out *how* it is to be made the basis for the realization of absolute truth.

If we regard the relatively existent as illusory we have no basis for the realization of absolute truth. We cut the ground from under our own feet. It is most important to distinguish between that which is really illusory (*parikalpita*) and that which is relatively real (*paratantra*).[58] If we confound the two and regard the relatively real as illusory, then the whole of our spiritual life (as well as our worldly life) just falls to the ground. If we do not exist, relatively speaking, who is saying that we do not exist? In this respect, much of the popular literature on Zen is disastrous in its effect on probably the large majority of those who read it without a Zen master around to beat them over the head when they think they've experienced *kensho*. Those with the spiritual maturity to benefit from it are, one would imagine, few and far between. And the same goes, unfortunately, for the writings of Krishnamurti, perhaps even more so.

However, when the profound import of these teachings is absorbed from the proper perspective, fearlessness is the quality required in order to sustain insight into reality. The Bodhisattva knows and perceives this whole living world as a mock show without being plunged into fear and madness.

> *Form, perception, feeling, will and awareness*
> *Are ununited, never bound, cannot be freed.*
> *Uncowed in his thought he marches onto his Bodhi,*
> *That for the highest of men is the best of all armours.*

According to the Abhidharma, the five *skandhas* are brought together by the force of *karma*, but the Buddha is here saying that in reality they are never united and never bound, so they cannot be freed. Furthermore, they *cannot* be united or bound. One cannot think in that sort of way at all, because the *skandhas* are unoriginated—they do not really come into existence. They too are like a magical show.

> *What then again is 'the vessel that leads to the Bodhi'?*
> *Mounted upon it one guides to Nirvāṇa all beings.*

Great is that vessel, immense, vast like the vastness of space.
Those who travel upon it are carried to safety, delight and ease.

Unfortunately we are just going to have to disagree with the text at this point. The impression you get is of the Bodhisattva as a sort of ship's captain, or navigator, steering the vessel that is ferrying a lot of passengers over the ocean of birth and death to 'safety, delight, and ease'. This impression is simply misleading, and the misunderstanding of the Bodhisattva's role which results from it in the Mahāyāna countries is the feeling that it is only for the monks to be exercised over becoming Bodhisattvas, while the lay people happily make do with the role of passengers, and just sit back in their deck-chairs and take it easy. Strictly speaking, there are no passengers in the spiritual life. The admirable Mahāyāna emphasis on the dedication of the Bodhisattva to helping others can leave you with the idea that those who are being helped are quite passive—that they are hitching a ride in someone else's vehicle, or vessel. In fact, all the Bodhisattva can do is help people to help themselves. If the Bodhisattva leads the way, they have to follow on their own two feet.

This comes down to recognizing that there's a limit to what you can do for other people. Even people who may not seem really to have a mind of their own do have at least a will of their own. You can inspire people, encourage them, exhort them, show concern for them and interest in them. You can provide the right conditions and the best facilities—you can take a horse to water but you can't make him drink. You cannot practise ethics for other people, you cannot meditate for them, you cannot develop insight for them—and there is no point in getting frustrated if they don't want to make the effort to do it for themselves.

The Bodhisattva never pits his or her will against the will of others. You have to leave people free to make their own mistakes. If they refuse to heed your good advice and follow the path that you have pointed out, there is nothing that you can do about it. You just have to accept the situation. It is not even that you have to accept defeat or failure, because there has never been any question of overcoming them in any way. You are not responsible for other people—you can do something for them, but you are not responsible for their decisions. You are responsible for what you can do to help them, but in the last analysis they are responsible for their own lives, even as you are responsible for your own life.

The true individual—taking the term in the sense of a person who is self-aware and emotionally positive, who can accept and exercise responsibility, and whose energies are liberated—does not put pressure on people. At the same time, of course, the true individual cannot be pressurized. If someone speaks his mind to me and I feel pressurized or manipulated or bullied by him, I am not an individual. Perhaps he isn't either, but that's another matter. It is actually impossible for one member of the spiritual community to pressurize or bully or manipulate another. An individual who is vigorously—even loudly—speaking their mind is not to be taken as trying to bend another individual to their will. Outside the spiritual community you may need to mitigate the impact of your individuality to avoid getting a response of submission or resistance from someone who is less secure, but within the spiritual community one individual should be able to stand up to another and sort out the differences between them freely and openly. You should be able to speak freely in the confidence that you are speaking to an integrated individual who is incapable of being pressurized, rather than to an untidy bundle of opinions loosely attached to a bundle of emotions, sounding off and reacting from various split-off, unintegrated attitudes. The spiritual principle that underpins this way of treating each other is that we all have to 'work our passage'. And to do this we have to be individuals.

The whole sentimental idea of the Bodhisattva ladling out Enlightenment to the humble masses is totally un-Buddhistic. Putting people in a passive role and imposing one's compassion on them is completely counterproductive as far as spiritual help and support goes, because it does not respect their individuality. If they are healthy they will react against this role and even experience quite a lot of resentment. Spiritual development is achieved by the individual—and this development may well include a refusal of patronizing help. In fact there is very little that we can do for others, even though that very little is important and should be done.

Chapter Six

THE UNFATHOMABLE INDIVIDUAL

THE ONLY WAY OF KNOWING ANOTHER INDIVIDUAL IS THROUGH APPRECIATIVE ATTENTION. IN THIS WAY A BUDDHA CAN KNOW ANOTHER BUDDHA, A BODHISATTVA CAN KNOW ANOTHER BODHISATTVA, AND AN INDIVIDUAL CAN KNOW ANOTHER INDIVIDUAL. IF ONE IS NOT AN INDIVIDUAL ONE WILL FAIL ESSENTIALLY TO SEE SOMEONE WHO IS

Thus transcending the world, he eludes our apprehensions.
'He goes to Nirvāṇa,' but no-one can say where he went to.
A fire's extinguished, but where, do we ask, has it gone to?
Likewise, how can we find him who has found the Rest of the Blessed?

The Bodhisattva's past, his future and his present must elude us,
Time's three dimensions nowhere touch him.
Quite pure he is, free from conditions, unimpeded.
That is his practice of wisdom, the highest perfection.

We can bring this right down to earth straightaway. Not only is the Bodhisattva not apprehensible; the individual is not apprehensible either. To the extent that someone is an individual, to that extent—if you are not an individual yourself—you cannot understand them, or even recognize them. You cannot know them because you cannot see them as they really are. It is not possible for someone who is not an individual really to see another person who is more of an individual. So if you are not yet a Bodhisattva, you cannot know someone who *is* a Bodhisattva—the Bodhisattva being the individual *par excellence*.

Another way of looking at this is to ask 'What is knowledge?' If we say that we know something, we usually mean that we can categorize it. If you take a flower and identify its genus and its species, you are then said to know what that flower is, botanically speaking. Something which can be classed with a number of other similar things may be known; knowing it means knowing which class, sub-class, and so on it belongs to. But an individual is unique, unrepeatable, and you cannot have a class consisting of only one thing—that is what is called in logic the 'infima species'. So the individual is unclassifiable; we can only classify someone to the extent that they are not an individual. Their individuality eludes us. They are unknowable in the ordinary, scientific meaning of the word 'knowledge'.

It takes an individual to know another individual—and even then that knowledge will not be classifiable, being more of the nature of an *experience* of that individual than a knowledge of them. It means being aware of that individual, not through a cold, scientific looking, but through a participatory awareness, a warm, empathizing regard, full of mettā and delight. In such a way one individual may apprehend another. This does not mean you have to become an individual yourself before you can get to know another individual—the two can go on together, one individuality sharpening itself on the other. It is like two mirrors facing each other. The other person's seeing of you not only helps you to see them as an individual more clearly; it also helps you to experience yourself more intensely.

This experiencing of yourself is not, of course, the same as self-consciousness in the sense of a division of consciousness. Experiencing yourself fully is a very different thing from being intensely aware of yourself in an alienated way, often with an anxiety about what other people are thinking of you. The adolescent phase of being very aware of your awkwardness, clumsiness, and inability to do things spontaneously seems to be a necessary transitional stage between the unselfconscious spontaneity of the child and the mature, integrated self-consciousness of the true individual. This sort of rudimentary self-consciousness is actually quite healthy and positive as a transitional phase. What may fix it in an unhealthy and neurotic form is guilt, under the influence of which, for example, you feel that 'the eyes of the Lord are in every place, beholding the evil and the good.'

True self-awareness, on the other hand, reconciles self-consciousness with the spontaneity of the child—and it is difficult to achieve. If you are spontaneous you are necessarily unconscious of what you are doing; if you are aware of what you are doing, how can you be spontaneous? But this is what you try to achieve, for instance, within the context of a meditation retreat. You may arrive feeling stiff and inhibited, so that you need to start off by relaxing and letting go, releasing your animal spirits to some extent. Then the retreat leader may feel the need to tighten up a little and introduce a bit more mindfulness, with extra sessions of meditation and periods of silence. And then he or she may need to inject a touch more liveliness again, to free up a bit more energy.

If one does not follow this sort of middle way one ends up being either unmindful but full of crude animal vitality, or else quite mindful but inhibited and unspontaneous. As one gets to a more refined vitality and a more creative mindfulness, however, these two qualities may be brought together, especially by means of positive emotions, to produce an integrated experience of awareness and spontaneity such as is commonly experienced only by the creative artist at work—aware of what he or she is doing, watchful, but at the same time unguarded and engaged.

It is this kind of self-awareness that we need to bring to our communication with others. The starting point is just looking, just being aware of the other person. How can we communicate with someone if we don't even see them, if we don't get a sense of them? But in whatever way we make contact, there must be the appreciative awareness that we are coming into contact with another *individual*—and this appreciation excludes flirtatious interest. The only way of knowing another individual is through appreciative attention. In this way a Buddha can know another Buddha, a Bodhisattva can know another Bodhisattva, and an individual can know another individual. If one is not an individual one will fail essentially to see someone who is. And if one doesn't really see them, how can one understand what they are doing, or why? They are just completely beyond one's ken.

But even a true individual is going to be at a loss when looking for any trace of the Bodhisattva, the transcendent individual. We may say 'He goes to nirvāṇa', but no one can say where he went to. 'A fire's extinguished, but where, do we ask, has it gone to?' Likewise, how can the ordinary individual 'find him who has found the Rest of the Blessed'? The Pāli texts similarly establish that the Buddha, the Tathāgata, cannot be known, fathomed, or classified. He is not a *deva*, nor a *gandharva*, nor a *yaksha*—he is not even a human being. He is just the Buddha—to call him *a* Buddha is strictly inaccurate as well, because it relegates him to a class, whereas the Buddha is unique. When we speak of a plurality of Buddhas, that plurality is metaphysical, not numerical. It is like the Neoplatonic idea that the 'One' which is designated the 'Absolute' is not a numerical 'one'—that is, it is not 'one' as distinguished from 'two' or any other number. We cannot entertain any idea that reality is one or many, or that there are one or many Bodhisattvas, or one or many Buddhas; our ideas of number in no way apply to the Absolute.

This is why the Buddha says to Anurādha that it is inept to say of the Tathāgata that after death he either exists or does not exist, or that he both exists and does not exist, or that he neither exists nor does not exist.[59] Just as during his lifetime it cannot be predicated of the Buddha that he exists or does not exist, or both, or neither, so in death. The Buddha is saying that he is as unfathomable in death as he is in life; as the complete individual, he cannot be categorized in any way whatever. It is in this way that the transcendental nature of the Bodhisattvas is to be understood, rather than through any metaphysical reading of these verses that one might be tempted to adopt.

WHAT THIS PARADOX IS TELLING US IS THAT IF WE THINK WE UNDERSTAND WHAT IS BEING SAID, WE HAVE NOT EVEN BEGUN TO UNDERSTAND IT

Wise Bodhisattvas, coursing thus, reflect on non-production,
And yet, while doing so, engender in themselves the great compassion,
Which is, however, free from any notion of a being.
Thereby they practise wisdom, the highest perfection.

So, coursing thus, wise Bodhisattvas reflect on non-production, do they? Who says they reflect on non-production? How do we know? What does it mean to reflect on non-production? Really, the words mean nothing to us at all. Well, luckily the text goes on to contradict itself. Wise Bodhisattvas, it says, reflect on non-production, and at the same time they produce great compassion—without having any notion of a being as an object of that compassion. Right, it's a paradox. That seems clear enough. 'Thereby they practise wisdom, the highest perfection'—and we think we've got an idea of what the Bodhisattva is about. But let's be frank, we haven't—not an inkling. We haven't the least idea of it at all. This is the danger of the Perfection of Wisdom texts and their conceptual way of putting things; we think we've understood because we understand the words. We even understand the ideas. Although they are quite abstruse we can work them out, or we can get Dr Conze, or Dr Suzuki, or Dr Guenther to do it for us. But what this paradox is telling us is that if we think we understand what is being said, we have not even begun to understand it. Actually, we have not understood anything at all. When we have understood *that* … well, then we are getting somewhere—but not before.

> But when the notion of suffering and beings leads him to think:
> 'Suffering I shall remove, the weal of the world I shall work!'
> Beings are then imagined, a self is imagined,—
> The practice of wisdom, the highest perfection, is lacking.

Now there's no problem here, is there? This is what the Bodhisattva shouldn't be thinking, and if it is what he or she is thinking then it's a sure sign that he or she isn't practising the Perfection of Wisdom. And it's easy enough to see from this how the Bodhisattva *should* think. If this is how we respond to this verse we are doing exactly what the Bodhisattva is not supposed to be doing. By thinking what the Bodhisattva is supposed not to be thinking we think that we have understood what the Bodhisattva is not supposed to be thinking. In this way we make complete fools of ourselves.

It is like the old Zen illustration of the finger pointing at the moon. The finger is the teaching, which points towards the moon of Enlightenment, and (at the risk of defeating the object of this image by expressing it in words) we may say that taking the teaching too literally is like mistaking the finger for the moon. So another finger is needed to point this out, and this often takes the form of a negation of any literal understanding of the original pointing out. But we remain engrossed in the finger, even though it is pointing more subtly, so yet another finger points *this* out … and so the history of Buddhist thought goes on, and we have to struggle through a whole series of progressively more subtle pointing fingers. But is it all really necessary? The Buddha just pointed at the moon (so to speak). It is the subtle medieval mind that came after him which we have to thank for all this intellectual juggling. Maybe *we* are much more simple-minded and practical—like the Chinese. They brought everything down to earth with a bump, especially in the form of Ch'an Buddhism.

> He wisely knows that all that lives is unproduced as he himself is;
> He knows that all that is no more exists than he or any beings.
> The unproduced and the produced are not distinguished,
> That is the practice of wisdom, the highest perfection.
>
> All words for things in use in this world must be left behind,
> All things produced and made must be transcended—

> *The deathless, the supreme, incomparable gnosis is then won.*
> *That is the sense in which we speak of perfect wisdom.*

This second verse probably sums up the whole matter. All human language is derived from sense experience, from reasoning upon sense experience, and from generalizations from such reasonings. But the transcendental is by definition something completely beyond, so no words can apply to it, and to approach it you have to leave all words behind. The words we apply to it—words like wisdom, Bodhisattva, and transcendental—don't apply. They are just pointing fingers, and sooner or later they have to be left behind. We may well sometimes have the experience that words don't mean anything at all in the ultimate sense. It is not that they are just inapplicable; they are totally irrelevant. All the time that we are talking about Buddhas and Bodhisattvas and coursing in Perfect Wisdom, and the 'Unproduced', et cetera, et cetera, we are preoccupied with words, or at least with thoughts, and so long as we are pondering on these words and ideas we are nowhere near what they purport to indicate. It's not that there's still a long way to go: we are nowhere near it at all. There are no degrees, no gradations between Perfect Wisdom and our words and thoughts, however profound. They all just have to be dropped.

> *When free from doubts the Bodhisattva carries on his practice,*
> *As skilled in wisdom he is known to dwell.*
> *All dharmas are not really there, their essential original nature is empty,*
> *To comprehend that is the practice of wisdom, perfection supreme.*

The Bodhisattva carries on his or her practice because he or she is free from those particular doubts to which Bodhisattvas are prone—doubts about non-production and so on. On our own level too, we carry on our practice only to the extent that we are free from the kind of energy-sapping doubt that expresses emotional resistance. To get that energy going we need to cultivate faith; and as faith is a form of emotion, to cultivate it we have to be in touch with our emotions. Then we must direct those emotions, indeed, the whole of our emotional nature, towards the objects of faith—towards things that are higher, nobler, and more sublime. In the Buddhist tradition this means contemplating the Three Jewels—dwelling on the positive qualities of the Buddha, the Dharma, and the Sangha, and admiring those qualities, delighting in them, yearning for them. That is faith.

Chapter Seven

TOPSY-TURVY VIEWS

IN METAPHOR LANGUAGE BEGINS TO TRANSCEND ITSELF.
METAPHOR OFFERS US A CLUE TO THE NATURE OF REALITY

He does not stand in form, perception or in feeling,
In will or consciousness, in any skandha whatsoever.
In Dharma's true nature alone he is standing.
Then that is his practice of wisdom, the highest perfection.

We have met with the idea already, but not in quite these terms. Instead of 'coursing', the Bodhisattva now 'stands'. The word suggests a confidence in one's position: standing in the *skandhas* you're actually standing on thin ice, and it's melting all the time, yet you're standing your ground, standing firm. So is this the extent of the imagery we can take from this verse? Well, no, because the expression is, in fact, not 'standing on' but 'standing *in*'. It is about roots.

We should be familiar—from the *Dhammapada*—with the image of a tree with shallow or weak roots that can easily be blown down by the wind.[60] If we are not rooted in the spiritual life, we are rooted in shallow, stony, loose, and shifting soil, maybe even in sand. We are rooted in phenomenal reality, and we can be blown over by Māra. So if we are not Bodhisattvas we stand very precariously. But if we are rooted in reality, our roots go much deeper, we draw our sustenance from a much deeper level, and we therefore stand much more firmly and grow much more vigorously. The Bodhisattva stands in the true nature of Dharma in the sense of being rooted in it, with roots that go very deep down—as deep as existence itself, you could say, and beyond.

The last line—'Then that is his practice of wisdom, the highest perfection'—now becomes more intelligible. If you are rooted in reality you don't have to think about practising anything. Sure, there is effort in the sense of *vīrya*, but it's not a question of will, it's not the ego-based effort that we usually make. Just as the sap flows up through the tree quite spontaneously and naturally, so the power needed for the practice of wisdom flows spontaneously from the Bodhisattva's being, rooted as it is in ultimate reality. By sending roots ever deeper into the Dharma the Bodhisattva enables the energy to flow ever more freely and abundantly. But just as the tree is only artificially separate from the sap that flows through it, so there is no distinguishing between the Bodhisattva and the energy that springs from the source of ultimate reality. When you are totally absorbed in something creative, you and the energy are one. Thus the Bodhisattva's acting from ultimate reality is his 'practice of wisdom, the highest perfection'.

When you live from the deepest level of reality, that is your practice of wisdom. Your practice is the way you live. Your whole life is the expression of what you are rooted in, just as all the leaves and flowers on the tree are the expression of the sap which rises from the earth. This verse is saying 'Don't draw your nourishment from any aspect of your conditioned being. Go deeper. Draw it from the depths of the Unconditioned, draw it from the true nature of Dharma, which is also, in a sense, your own true nature.' If you do that, everything you say, everything you do, and everything you think will be your 'practice of wisdom, the highest perfection'.

This way of thinking of the Bodhisattva—as a deeply rooted tree— gives us a more correct idea of the nature of the Bodhisattva and the Bodhisattva's life than can any generalized or abstract account. Abstract ideas are useful for conveying information and issuing instructions, but they can give us no idea of reality as such (and in saying this I am using abstractions, and thus conveying no notion of reality). If we imagine otherwise we are making a very big mistake indeed. We have to get back to the particular, to the concrete, to the unique, to the individual.

An abstraction is a general idea which does not correspond to anything you actually encounter and experience, whether a sense experience or a spiritual experience. Thus 'truth' is an abstraction; 'reality' is an abstraction. When do you ever encounter a thing you can label 'reality'? It's a concept; it is something you think. Do you ever see the universal quality of blueness apart from actual blue objects? You can form a concept of circularity, but does circularity exist apart from things that are circular?

Plato would have said that reality does indeed reside in such universals, rather than in particulars, and it might well seem that abstractions are large and embracing and whole, while particulars are bitty little separate things. But Plato seems to have experienced these universals not as abstract concepts but more as archetypes, so his experience of reality is not necessarily to be set in contradistinction to that of people who, like William Blake, experience reality as 'minute particulars'. When William Blake speaks of the experience of reality as being that of 'minute particulars', he is speaking about the operation of the Imagination, and for Blake the Imagination is not a faculty, but the operation of the whole man or woman, with reason and emotion fully integrated. And it is through imagery, symbols, myths, and metaphors that the Imagination, *the whole man or woman*, is able to apprehend or respond to or experience reality as minute particulars in their *totality*. If you do this, you are not just experiencing reality in one aspect, which leaves you sliding on the surface, nor are you just sliding from one aspect to another; rather, you are seeing all aspects of reality, not just on the surface, but in their depths.

When dealing with Perfect Wisdom, it is important to get away from the conceptual expression in which it is couched, which is so inappropriate and foreign to the meaning it articulates. We need to translate it, just as the Chinese did, into more concrete terms. But if the Chinese translated it largely into what we call Ch'an, or, in its Japanese form, Zen, we, on the other hand, will probably be on safer ground—not that as a Buddhist one is ever on safe ground—if we translate it into images, myths, symbols, and metaphors. There is then the possibility of the teaching coming alive. In metaphor language begins to transcend itself. Metaphor offers us a clue to the nature of reality. It communicates a sort of fusion—not, perhaps, of subject and object, but at least of one object with another. And it *is* a communication. If there were an absolute barrier between subject and object, or between one person and another, no communication would be possible at all.

Images are all the more potent if we can also take into account the fact that people are of different temperaments, that they see and appreciate things in different ways, and even do things in different ways. The idea of being rooted in reality suggests a reality that is tangible, solid, sticky, even smelly, and it will appeal to, or even inspire, someone of a certain kind of temperament, perhaps someone rather flighty and volatile. Someone a bit more stolid and earthy might want to turn the tree upside-down.

In the *Bhagavad Gītā* there is the image of the great banyan tree with its roots in the sky—higher consciousness growing downwards rather than upwards. Have your roots in the sky, it is saying—don't have them in the earth—and hang head downwards from reality. Turning yourself upside-down is a good Buddhist way of looking at things. Maybe this is a more refined image; it is certainly a bit more paradoxical. Of course, it may well be that neither of these images sparks you off. Perhaps instead the Bodhisattva needs to be set alight, to be *incandescent* with reality: you can be on fire with reality just as well as being rooted in it. Alternatively, of course, you could say that the Bodhisattva *breathes* reality, or that reality *flows* through the Bodhisattva's veins. These are just a few angles—based on the four elements—for the imagination to get to work on. There are many other approaches; it is for the individual to enrich them with his or her own experience.

THERE CAN BE NO ABSOLUTE DUALITY BETWEEN DUALISM AND NON-DUALISM. THE ABSOLUTE TRUTH IS THE ABSOLUTE TRUTH OF THE RELATIVE TRUTH. THEY ARE INSEPARABLE. ABSOLUTE TRUTH CANNOT BE REALIZED EXCEPT BY TAKING ONE'S STAND ON RELATIVE TRUTH

Change and no change, suffering and ease, the self and not-self,
The lovely and repulsive—just one Suchness in this Emptiness they are.
And so he takes not his stand on the fruit which he won, which is
    threefold—
That of an Arhat, a Single Buddha, a Buddha fully enlightened.

The pairs of opposites are the four *viparyāsas*, the four upside-down or topsy-turvy views. They are about seeing things the other way round, or the other way up, from how they really are. If you see that which is liable to change as unchanging, that's a topsy-turvy view. If you see that which is essentially painful as pleasant, that which is devoid of selfhood as possessing real selfhood, and that which is repulsive as being attractive and lovely, these are also topsy-turvy views. They are topsy-turvy because the characteristics of the Unconditioned are being falsely applied to the conditioned. The Unconditioned is indeed changeless and supremely blissful; it also possesses—at least according to the Mahāyāna—true selfhood; and it is truly beautiful. But we don't see the Unconditioned in this way; instead, this is how we view conditioned existence. You may think that this is ridiculous, and that we don't really regard things around us as changeless—but in practice we do. Our emotional attitude is that what we have is for keeps, and that what we are is for ever. In early Buddhism and in much of the Mahāyāna, great importance is attached to overcoming the *viparyāsas*.[61]

At the same time, however, this teaching rests on a dualistic basis, and the Mahāyāna does not regard dualism—the notion that we have the conditioned on the one hand and the Unconditioned on the other and that we simply have to go from the one to the other—as the last word, as ultimately valid. This is not to say, however, that the Mahāyāna rejects dualism as the necessary basis upon which to establish a spiritual practice strong enough to sustain any kind of non-dualistic realization. At the start we cannot afford to be non-dualistic.

In the *Ariya-pariyesana Sutta* from the *Majjhima-Nikāya* the Buddha says that when he was a Bodhisattva—that is to say, before his Enlightenment—being himself conditioned, he at first went in pursuit of conditioned things. But then it occurred to him to pursue not conditioned things, but the Unconditioned; whereupon he began his quest for Enlightenment, and eventually attained it.[62] So this duality is basic to Buddhism. For practical spiritual purposes we must think in terms of going from a lower state of consciousness to a higher state. Any kind of spiritual development has to be based upon dualistic assumptions; we posit two principles, one of which we move away from and the other of which we move towards. All spiritual systems have a practical working dualistic basis of this kind. Some, like Zoroastrianism, regard that basis as metaphysically ultimate, others, like the Mahāyāna, do not regard it as metaphysically ultimate, and still others, like Hīnayāna Buddhism, don't say anything one way or the other. The Hīnayāna is quite content to rest with practical dualism, saying nothing about the metaphysical or ontological status of that duality. Whether when you realize the Unconditioned, you realize a state which is a non-duality, or whether you then see that there is really no difference between the conditioned and the Unconditioned, is a question which the Pāli Canon leaves open.

The Mahāyāna, however, takes the bull by the horns. At the level of the Bodhisattva—and from our dualistic viewpoint it is a 'higher' level—the dualistic framework is seen to be insufficient, something to be dismantled or dissolved. This is achieved through realizing the third dimension of *śūnyatā*: *mahāśūnyatā*, the 'great *śūnyatā*', the emptiness or non-validity of the distinction between the conditioned and the Unconditioned. What this means from a practical point of view is that Enlightenment consists not in passing from saṃsāra to nirvāṇa—as though both were separate realities—but in realizing their essential non-difference. Thus in the highest sense the spiritual life is an illusion.

As this cannot be realized except through the spiritual life, it must be said that non-dualism has no meaning for us at all. It is only words, or at best an abstract idea. If a non-dualistic perspective discloses itself to us as we work our way up the spiritual ladder, that's fine. But we realize that there was never any ladder in the first place, or that there is no difference between the 'top' and the 'bottom', only when we have worked our way to the 'top'. We cannot base our spiritual practice upon a purely intellectual understanding of non-duality.

Even on the philosophical level the idea of non-duality presents an insurmountable difficulty. Owing to the fact that thought itself is irreducibly dualistic, it is impossible to construct a statement of non-dualism that is not dualistic, at least in form. It's a double bind. If you say 'the conditioned and the Unconditioned are not two', they must be two in some sense for you to be able to make that statement. If you say 'the difference between the conditioned and the Unconditioned is illusory,' you still have an illusory *difference*—and you still have the duality between what is illusory and what is not.

Shankara, who gave systematic form to the Vedanta in the early ninth century CE, countered the view of some Vedantin schools that the universe and Brahman (the ultimate reality) are one in the sense that the universe is made out of and emanates from Brahman, with the view that the universe only *appears* to emanate from Brahman. This he asserted to be unmitigated non-duality in its purest form. However, even if you maintain in this way that the universe does not originate in reality but only in appearance, there is still a duality between appearance and reality. In stating your position as one of non-duality you inevitably imply a duality. Every philosophy is bound to be dualistic inasmuch as no statement is possible without at least two ultimate principles.

If there is a non-duality, it can only take the form of a purely spiritual or transcendental experience which cannot be formulated in any way. It can only be communicated by means of a kind of 'ultimate dualism'—as in the *Prajñāpāramitā*—in which dualistic thought becomes trapped in its own coils and releases a higher intuitive realization. That is as far as we can go. If we try to suggest what has so mysteriously been realized—e.g. 'the state or principle that lies beyond'—we are clearly bringing in a third principle. When we start thinking of that reality in which the subject–object distinction does not exist, we make that reality an object out there, which falsifies it. By thinking of non-duality we succeed only in digging ourselves deeper into duality. We cannot even say 'Well, then we shall see what we shall see.' However indeterminate the object may be, it remains an object. We cannot win—we are not meant to win. There is really not much we can usefully discuss at all. We must change the very structure of our consciousness—especially through meditation—so that it ceases to split everything up into subject and object.

The Hīnayāna approach is therefore in some ways the wisest, although this is not to dismiss the speculations of the Mahāyāna. Some people have very subtle minds, and need to go on refining their dualism in order to transcend it. However, whatever the spiritual experience of individuals may be—dualist or non-dualist—those Mahāyāna traditions which profess to be based upon non-dualist assumptions have to be mistaken. There are, for example, schools which suggest that there is no difference between you and Buddha: you *are* Buddha. It might seem that a duality is being negated here—but in negating duality you are in fact setting it up.

There is a Zen story which illustrates just how careful you have to be if you take the Mahāyāna approach. The story concerns a Zen master who finds himself haunted by a 'spirit-fox' (not so much an unusual ghost as a very unusual fox, though not uncommon in Japanese folklore). Falling into conversation with it, the Zen master learns that it has undergone five hundred rebirths as a spirit-fox, but that before this run of disagreeable rebirths it was a great Zen master. His fall from grace was the result of an answer he gave to the question 'When one realizes one's Buddha-nature, what happens to the law of karma?' The howler that precipitated this Zen master of old into five hundred rebirths as a spirit-fox was his pronouncement: 'Well, when one achieves nirvāṇa, one supersedes the law of karma. The law of karma is wiped out.' The spirit-fox goes on: 'Obviously I got it wrong. What should I have said?' And the Zen master tells him the correct answer: 'When you are Enlightened, the law of karma doesn't get in your way.'

The Mahāyāna consistently makes the point that ultimate truth does not supersede relative truth. It insists that the absolute is to be realized within the relative as being its inner or deeper dimension (so to speak). Relative truth is in a mysterious way contained within absolute truth. Even the very distinction between absolute and relative is part of—or pertains to—relative truth, not absolute truth, because there can be no absolute duality between dualism and non-dualism. The absolute truth is the absolute truth of the relative truth. They are inseparable. Absolute truth cannot be realized except by taking one's stand on relative truth.

There are two extreme views to stultify us and negate all possibility of spiritual development. The nihilist extreme is to transfer the attributes of the illusory to the relatively real, so that one argues that if everything is unreal, meditation is unreal, the spiritual life is unreal. The eternalist extreme is to transfer the attributes of the absolute to the relative; this extreme is represented by the *viparyāsas*, which are sometimes termed 'the error of misplaced absoluteness'.

However, the eternalist error can also be represented by loose interpretations of the doctrine of the *Tathāgata-garbha*, the 'womb of Buddhahood', which expresses the potential of Enlightenment in the unenlightened mind. If we take the idea that every being has the Buddha-nature literally, if we reify the concept of *Tathāgata-garbha*, if we forget that it is empty, we can argue 'Well, if I already have the Buddhanature, it is useless for me to make any effort to attain it. If I try to attain it I am missing the point.' And we can perform the same sort of reifying trick with the bodhicitta, imagining that it is somehow within us, waiting in the wings, and that all we have to do is become aware of it. In a sense this might be true, but how do we put it? 'OK. I am mean, selfish, dirty, lazy, and ignorant, but beneath it all I am a Buddha.' This does not offer us any foothold. It is much more helpful really to say that along with those weaknesses are some *real* spiritual qualities, in however embryonic a form—moments of kindness and generosity and mindfulness—that are the real seeds of spiritual development, and that may, if they are nurtured, lead to actual Buddhahood. There *is* an Absolute, there *is* an Eternal, there *is* an Infinite—but it is *not* this empirical reality. The empirically, relatively real is not illusory, but nor is it absolutely real.

This verse tells us that the *viparyāsas* are 'just one Suchness in this Emptiness'. Although the spiritual content of the word *śūnyatā* ('Emptiness') is actually positive—or rather, neither positive nor negative—the word itself connotes the negative: an absence. *Tathatā*, which means 'thusness' or 'suchness', and indicates just the same reality, is, we may therefore say, its positive counterpart. *Tathatā* points to the inexpressibility of reality, which means, if you like, the inexpressibility of individual things, of Blake's 'minute particulars'. Whenever we try to describe something there always remains in our experience of it something which is incommunicable. In the end all we can do is point to the thing and say 'It is as it is'; 'It is thus'; 'Such is it'; 'Thus-so'. The 'thusness' of things is their unique, ineffable quality or essence. The reality of things cannot be described; it can only be experienced. Everything—whether saṁsāra or nirvāṇa, the conditioned or the Unconditioned, changing or changeless—is such as it is. Happiness is happiness; suffering is suffering. All things are equally indescribable. But when we describe everything as 'just one Suchness', let us be careful not to imply that *tathatā* is, in even the subtlest sense, some kind of 'stuff'. It is an operational concept—so it is only in a manner of speaking that we can reify it. When we point at things, we can only indicate their 'suchness', not their 'whatness'.

After all, what do we really communicate when we try to communicate our experience? Even on a much lower level than that of *tathatā*, much of our experience is incommunicable. Use an image and you may spark off an experience in the person you are talking to that is similar to that which gave rise to the image in your own mind—more directly at least than speaking in abstractions might—but the personal associations that come with that image are going to be different for different people. And never mind the impossibility of truly *communicating* our experience—it is in any case impossible for someone else to experience something as you experience it. Another person is not going to relate to an object exactly as you relate to it, because in a sense you modify the object by virtue of your very experience of it—you cannot take the object out of the context of your experiencing it.

'Experience' is another of these abstract terms that we tend to take literally as if we could experience an experience; but how can we lift the experience out of the context of 'having' the experience? You alone can have your experience; another person will have another experience which is their own. Give someone a book that you have enjoyed and they may also enjoy it, but their experience of it will be quite different from yours. Hold up a flower to someone, and their experience of that flower will be their own, not the same as yours. Same flower, different person. In this way on an ordinary, mundane, subject–object level we can develop an awareness of the uniqueness and inexpressibility in our experience of things.

This is not, however, going to be the same as the Bodhisattva's realization that 'Just one Suchness in this Emptiness they are.' And even if this is literally inconceivable to us the Bodhisattva does not stop there. 'He takes not his stand' on this or any other attainment—there is no resting content even with the fruits of full Enlightenment. Surely, though, there is nothing more to do at that point. Why this emphasis on not resting on one's laurels? One answer is to say that the Bodhisattva does not put his or her roots down in Enlightenment because even full Enlightenment is not the attainment of a fixed position, but rather the continuity and irreversibility of a process. Think of it perhaps—if provisionally—as a spiral, just going on and on, up and up, in ever expanding circles, to infinity.

> *The Leader himself was not stationed in the realm which is free from*
> *   conditions,*
> *Nor in the things which are under conditions, but freely he wandered*
> *   without a home:*
> *Just so, without a support or a basis a Bodhisattva is standing.*
> *A position devoid of a basis has that position been called by the Jina.*

'The Leader' is of course the Buddha, and he is not stationed in the Unconditioned as distinct from being stationed in the conditioned because he has transcended that duality. He freely wanders without a home in either the conditioned or even the Unconditioned. The Mahāyāna distinguishes two kinds of nirvāṇa: *pratishṭhita*, the nirvāṇa which is established; and *apratishṭhita*, the non-established nirvāṇa, the nirvāṇa which cannot be located in—you might say—any particular spot. So if the Buddha is stationed anywhere, he is stationed in the *mahāśūnyatā*, the Great Void. He is free from all concepts, all dualistic thinking. And his position is a non-position. His basis is no basis. His support is to have no support at all. What this verse suggests is an attitude of faith and trust towards life as a whole. Some people almost by nature have more of this than others: they're less anxious, less worried, less bothered, so that they can get along without plans and plots and structures.

TRANSCENDENTAL PATIENCE, THE PATIENT ACCEPTANCE OF THE ABSOLUTELY UNACCEPTABLE, IS LIKE—IT HAS TO BE SAID—ALLOWING REALITY TO HAVE ITS WAY WITH YOU

> *Those who wish to become the Sugata's Disciples,*
> *Or Pratyekabuddhas, or likewise, Kings of the Dharma—*
> *Without resort to this Patience they cannot reach their respective goals.*
> *They move across, but their eyes are not on the other shore.*

> *Those who teach dharma, and those who listen when it is being taught;*
> *Those who have won the fruit of an Arhat, a Single Buddha, or a*
> *   world-saviour;*
> *And the Nirvāṇa obtained by the wise and the learned—*
> *Mere illusions, mere dreams—so has the Tathāgata taught us.*

In very general terms 'this Patience' means being receptive to spiritual truths that go completely against the grain of your natural response to the world. You patiently accept the unacceptable. There is no patience called for in accepting what is acceptable—we can all put up with acceptable behaviour. It is only when we are confronted with the unacceptable that we can begin to try out our patience. So someone who tests your patience is—if inadvertently—doing their best to make you patient. Blaming someone for making you impatient is like blaming a beggar for making you mean.

So whereas the Bodhisattva is spoken of in the Perfect Wisdom texts as penetrating into wisdom—*prajñā* being feminine in gender—the practice of patience calls for a 'feminine' posture in the face of reality. One of the four functions of Buddhahood, according to the Tantra, is to seduce, to fascinate, and though it is an idea that is developed much more fully in Hinduism—with the figure of Krishna and the gopīs—it is not excluded from Buddhism. Indeed, the mettā bhāvanā practice involves seeing everything as *śubha*, as the purely beautiful. So why not be seduced by reality?—You can lay yourself open to the possibility of an experience coming upon you which you had never anticipated. Maybe reality fancies you. One must be open to all sorts of possibilities of expression—don't forget that the Bodhisattva is represented in Buddhist iconography with a hook of compassion to pull you in, or a lasso to haul you in like some reluctant steer. Transcendental Patience, the patient acceptance of the absolutely unacceptable, is like—it has to be said—allowing reality to have its way with you.

Here again is the *anutpattika-dharma-kshānti*,[63] the patient acceptance of the unnerving, indeed unacceptable fact that in reality nothing arises, because things have no objective existence which can arise; everything is unborn, unoriginated. It is also the patient acceptance of the fact that follows upon this, which is that even when you yourself have gained nirvāṇa, nothing has happened; nothing has arisen; you have not gained anything; you have not come into the possession of anything—it is as if your attainment is a dream. 'Mere illusions, mere dreams'.

If this is so, there is no need for us to take our own rather less distinguished accomplishments too seriously. If our spiritual practice is going well—our meditation is strong, our energies are flowing—all well and good. There is no need to ride too high, or to throw our weight around as if we had actually attained something. A sense of humour can help to bring out the incongruity of the ego claiming anything at all for itself.

> *Four kinds of persons are not alarmed by this teaching:*
> *Sons of the Jina skilled in the truths; saints unable to turn back,*
> *Arhats free from defilements and taints, and rid of their doubts;*
> *Those whom good teachers mature are reckoned the fourth kind.*

If one is not shaken by the teachings of Perfect Wisdom, that is probably because one hasn't understood them; one is just completely impervious to them. But if you are a bit more aware and intelligent, and if you are making a sincere effort to develop, then you cannot help but be shaken by them. They go against all your assumptions; they confound your whole conditioned being. You can sometimes read or hear something—whether a Perfection of Wisdom text or something completely different—that has this sort of existential effect on you, so that you are never the same again. An uncomfortable, even painful disturbance of one's whole outlook precedes the possibility of fully realizing these teachings deeply enough *not* to be alarmed and shaken by them.

> *Coursing thus, the wise and learned Bodhisattva,*
> *Trains not for Arhatship, nor on the level of Pratyekabuddhas.*
> *In the Buddha-dharma alone he trains for the sake of all-knowledge.*
> *No training is his training, and no-one is trained in this training.*

> *Increase or decrease of forms is not the aim of this training,*
> *Nor does he set out to acquire various dharmas.*
> *All-knowledge alone he can hope to acquire by this training.*
> *To that he goes forth when he trains in this training, and delights in its*
>   *virtues.*

The Bodhisattva has no goal to train for; does not set out to acquire various qualities or attributes; is not trying to get anywhere within the world of form; does not seek the increase or decrease of the conditioned. At that level you don't even think in that sort of way. You're not trying to make the Unconditioned more, or the conditioned less. For one thing, you don't distinguish between them; you transcend the very idea of increasing or decreasing, just as you transcend the idea of attainment or non-attainment, or both, or neither.

Now this is all very lofty, and it is a mistake to take it on prematurely. It is an important—and dangerous—transitional phase. The point to grasp is that even while the direction of one's commitment may become more certain and the momentum of one's practice may become more powerful, one's 'ideas' will change, one's way of looking at things will change—indeed, one's way of life will change. One's reasons for being a Buddhist—at least the reasons one formulates—may well change. Perhaps one was originally attracted by a view of Buddhism which one has subsequently found to have been misconceived, or even wrong. But in a sense it could not have been an entirely wrong view if it eventually led one to recognize it for a wrong view. These transitional phases need to be negotiated in a positive and creative spirit, although for a lot of people this is not easy. For example, at the very end of his life St Thomas Aquinas apparently realized that everything he had written was worth less than a load of straw, and was completely unable to come to terms with this sense of intellectual inadequacy in the face of reality.

Chapter Eight

THE FACTS OF EXISTENCE

Forms are not wisdom, nor is wisdom found in form,
In consciousness, perceptions, feeling, or in will.
They are not wisdom, and no wisdom is in them.
Like space it is, without a break or crack.

Of all objective supports the essential original nature is boundless;
Of beings likewise the essential original nature is boundless.
As the essential original nature of space has no limits,
Just so the wisdom of the World-knowers is boundless.

Wisdom is like space because the only thing you can conceive of that is without breaks or cracks is space. Space can only be conceived of negatively, through the things in it. It can't be divided or carved up; it doesn't consist of parts. It is omnipresent. These are the characteristics of wisdom in that cracks or breaks or divisions are only conceptual. You can't cut up space, and you can't cut up being—you can't cut up wisdom. Wisdom is wholly present everywhere. It can't be sliced into parts; you can't be partly Enlightened. Wisdom is absolutely continuous, without a break; it is boundless in the sense of being inconceivable. So with all things: in their essential original nature they are indefinable, inconceivable, and therefore boundless. 'Objective supports', the *skandhas*, are boundless—beings likewise, and space, and wisdom. In their essential original nature they cannot be grasped, analysed, or classified.

'Perceptions'—mere words, so the Leaders have told us;
Perceptions forsaken and gone, and the door is open to the Beyond.
Those who succeed in ridding themselves of perceptions,
They, having reached the Beyond, fulfil the Teacher's commandments.

If for aeons countless as the sands of the Ganges
The Leader would himself continue to pronounce the word 'being':
Still, pure from the very start, no being could ever result from his speaking.
That is the practice of wisdom, the highest perfection.

Perceptions require a subject and an object. When you transcend the duality of subject and object, therefore, perceptions are 'forsaken and gone'. There is nothing there that has really come into existence. You can realize this, but neither you nor anybody else can make it otherwise. Even if the Buddha himself were to say that beings existed—and as a Buddhist you can't put it more strongly than that—and even if he were to continue saying it for as many aeons as there are grains of sand in the Ganges, that would still not make it true, would still not alter the fact that in reality no beings exist. This means that there is absolutely no possibility of creation or a creator. In this way the Perfection of Wisdom brushes off the theistic viewpoint.

Theism does not seem to have been a prominent line of thought in the Buddha's day, and he referred to it only occasionally. It developed much more strongly later on, with the devotional theistic cults of what is called the Indian Middle Ages, and the qualified non-dualism—making space for a creator and creation—of various schools of Vedanta, from about the tenth century onwards.

Christian students of comparative religion in the past have tried to suggest that monotheism arrived on the scene after everything else and is thus the culmination of the religious quest. However, more recent research has established a persistent correlation of 'primitive' social structures with very definite and clear monotheistic ideas. Certainly monotheism is usually enough to satisfy the ordinary man or woman in the street: here's the world—someone must have made it, so whoever that was, he is God. You can't argue with that. People with that viewpoint would have to go outside their whole mental structure to see things differently, and that would probably be asking too much.

That aside, the whole question of the evolution of ideas begs one or two questions. Do you get an abstract development of ideas dissociated from the individuals who have them? Does the fact that you can arrange ideas in a historical sequence necessarily invite theories of evolution? You can say that one person's ideas have been inspired, either positively or negatively, by preceding ideas. But religion itself, or philosophy itself, doesn't develop—to say it does is just a manner of speaking. What we can say is that there are certain basic positions or attitudes which remain the same however much the degree of intellectual refinement that people bring to those attitudes varies. Simple people who are unable to articulate their views are not necessarily less 'developed', nor are the attitudes they adopt necessarily more primitive or less intelligent than those of intellectually sophisticated people. St Thomas Aquinas's monotheism is not necessarily more 'developed' than that of a 'primitive' tribesman.

THERE MAY WELL BE SOMETHING THAT CORRESPONDS TO SOME KIND OF 'LIFE-FORCE'
OPERATING THROUGHOUT THE UNIVERSE—IT IS QUITE A POSITIVE AND HEALTHY BELIEF.
IT MAY EVEN BE A SPIRITUAL FORCE.
BUT WHAT YOU CANNOT HAVE IS A TRANSCENDENTAL LIFE-FORCE

The business of building correlations between religions arises out of a fear that you might be missing out in some way if you were to commit yourself to one religion rather than another. Faith, on the other hand, involves a leap in the dark, a commitment to the unknown. When you become a Buddhist you cease to be a Christian—it's as simple as that. If you don't want to change your religion until you've made sure that the new religion is the same as the old one, what is the point of changing?

In trying to marry ideas together, there is a real danger of just getting into a muddle. Thus Mahāyāna Buddhism gets to be seen as a kind of theism. 'The Buddha watches over us and protects us—well, that's basically what God does....' This is the way the argument goes. But what do we mean here by Buddha? Is it Śākyamuni? Well, no. The Buddhahood which Śākyamuni fully realized is present everywhere, waiting to be realized, waiting to be contacted. It is limited neither by space nor by time, so it is accessible from any point in space and from any point in time, and therefore in a sense exerts an influence to which we can open ourselves. This is quite different from conceiving of the Buddha as a person watching over us, let alone a person who created the universe.

Let us be clear about the Buddhist position on theism. According to what the Buddha says in the Pāli Canon, theism arose from attempts to communicate the experience of another order, the experience of the brahmaloka, but not the experience of anything higher than that—certainly not the experience of śūnyatā. Characterizing Buddhism as 'non-theistic' of course defines it in theistic terms, which may not be very helpful beyond an elementary level because in Buddhism terms like 'theism', 'non-theism', and even 'pantheism' have no meaning. However, 'non-theistic' is preferable to 'atheistic', which has connotations that are militantly materialist, anti-religious, and anti-spiritual.

The *sarva-dharma-śūnyatā*, the 'emptiness of all dharmas', is sometimes interpreted as a form of pantheism. This might be fair enough—again at an elementary level—if you were to read the 'theos' element in the word as *śūnyatā*. But you would have to be clear that Theravāda Buddhism could not be seen as pantheism under any light whatsoever; and it would be a risky procedure even to apply that label to the Mahāyāna. There are two ways of looking at pantheism. You can see it as a materialistic monism, involving the idea that everything you perceive is a transformation, in one way or another, of one absolute *material* principle; or you can see it as the idea that everything is the transformation of one absolute *spiritual* principle. Either way, there is—and this is the Upanishadic doctrine—one basic 'substance', whether material or spiritual, which assumes different forms; everything in the universe is basically that. This is close in some respects to Spinoza's point of view that there is one absolute substance, 'God', with infinite attributes. What we know comes under the form of two of these attributes, space and time, but there are infinitely many more attributes of which we know nothing at all.

These are all forms of substantialism; but Buddhism is not substantialist. *Śūnyatā* is not to be interpreted as a metaphysical substance. It is not one transcendental thing or being which manifests as all the *dharmas*. We can say that there is a reality, represented by the word '*nirvāṇa*' or '*śūnyatā*' or '*tathatā*' or '*dharmakāya*', which transcends phenomenal or relative reality, and which we in the world can realize if we make the necessary effort. But it is not a sort of 'cosmological principle' present in the world.

Of these terms, *dharmakāya* is the one most vulnerable to quasi-theistic interpretations. In its original development by the Mahāyāna, the *dharmakāya* meant the ultimate reality of the human, historical Buddha and the archetypal Buddha, that aspect of his nature in which he is one with ultimate reality, as opposed to the aspect in which he appears on the human level (the *nirmāṇakāya*) and the aspect in which he appears on the archetypal level (the *sambhogakāya*). So the *dharmakāya* is not to be personified and thought of as a kind of cosmic force freely engaging in activities. The 'activity' of the *dharmakāya* manifests through Enlightened beings: because the Buddha is at one with reality, reality 'functions' directly and without impediment through the Buddha. The *dharmakāya* manifests to the extent that any individual is Buddha-like—and that partial manifestation is technically called the bodhicitta, which, you could say, progressively fills up the gap between unenlightenment and Enlightenment.

However, the concept of the *dharmakāya* was extended in China and Japan to mean the ultimate spiritual principle not just of the Buddha himself, but of the whole universe, which itself then became a manner of collective *nirmāṇakāya*. Obviously, when popularly expounded, this can all become a bit pantheistic. The point of difference is that in the earlier Indian version the Buddha is *consciously* at one with the *dharmakāya*, whereas in the case of the Far Eastern development of this idea the same can hardly be said for the entire cosmos.

We therefore need to be a little careful in our interpretation of this 'universal' *dharmakāya* not to see in it the 'one' as against the 'many'. For a start, we can perhaps see it quite simply as a kind of positive counterpart to the *anātman* doctrine, so that there is no question of regarding the ultimate spiritual principle as a state of annihilation. It tells us in which direction to look for reality. Then, without saying what it may be in itself, we can say that it is the inexhaustible source of spiritual meaning and activities which we personify in the form of Bodhisattvas. We may go on to say that the term *dharmakāya* is used to denote the transcendental principle as the principle through which everything else connects, which, in the ultimate analysis and within the widest possible perspective, enables all things—inasmuch as they *are*—to interrelate, to be woven into the great harmony that we call the *dharmadhātu*. It is in this way that we can see the *dharmakāya* as the principle of unity: not in the sense of the truth being one and duality being false, but in the sense of the principle of *harmony*. It is the pole or axis around which everything orients itself, the principle which enables everything, when seen rightly, to make up the great mandala which is the cosmos.

At the same time this image of the mandala is not to be taken literally. There is no periphery to it: you can find a periphery to something finite, but how can you be peripheral to reality? We should not allow the Mahāyāna's fondness for abstract speculation to steer us too far away from individual experience. All this speculation has to be understood in the light of the Perfection of Wisdom. If we take the structure of language as somehow reflecting the structure of reality, and start taking statements about transcendental reality literally rather than, say, poetically, we very quickly go off the rails. The extent to which Mahāyāna philosophy can be interpreted ontologically—indeed the extent to which Buddhism has an ontological standpoint at all—is really very questionable.

Once we admit the concept of a cosmological principle, it is easy to start thinking in terms of a 'life-force' and end up with a naïve sort of naturalistic pantheism. There may well be something that corresponds to some kind of life-force operating throughout the universe—it is quite a positive and healthy belief. It may even be a spiritual force. But what you cannot have is a *transcendental* life-force. No manner of life-force would correspond to the *dharmakāya*. And there is no question of phenomenal or relative reality 'emerging' in any sense from the transcendental.

WHAT IS MEANT BY 'EVERYTHING EXISTS ON ACCOUNT OF EMPTINESS'
IS THAT EMPTINESS, RIGHTLY UNDERSTOOD AS CONDITIONALITY,
MAKES EVERYTHING POSSIBLE—THE SPIRITUAL LIFE AS WELL AS THE WORLDLY LIFE

The cosmos, saṁsāra, consists of various levels and layers of being right up to the most refined and spiritual of all realms, the *brahmaloka*, and everything is said to emerge from that highest realm at the beginning of the aeon and to merge back into it at the end. This pulsation goes on indefinitely from an infinite past into an infinite future. So we could speak of a spiritual force of Brahmaic origin working through the cosmic process of evolution and involution. We could even call it 'God'. But if we wanted to make that equation we would have to be prepared to accept that 'God' was relative and phenomenal, because the transcendental is something different. At the same time it must be said that to confuse 'God' with the transcendental is understandable enough, because from our own perspective it is very difficult to distinguish the most highly evolved spiritual realms from the transcendental—as difficult as it might be to look up at the night sky and sort out nearby planets from remote galaxies.

When you look at the world process and try to trace it back to its origins, however far back you go you can never identify a point where it all begins. According to Buddhism, that is all you can say, and it is easy to see why. Time is itself part of our way of looking at things—it is, in a sense, subjective—so to ask the mind to go back to the beginning of time is self-contradictory. Where there is a mind—an ordinary consciousness—there will be a world perceived by that mind. The mind can never get back to a point where there is nothing to perceive, where everything begins and there is only the mind. It would be like trying to have just one side of a coin. The Buddha says simply 'When world ceases, mind ceases; when mind ceases, world ceases.' If you want to get to the end of the world you must stop the mind—stop, that is, the conditioned, empirical mind. That is the end of conditioned existence, and the start of the transcendental dimension, in which there is no space and time, no subject and object, no beginning and end. There is simply no perceivable causal nexus between the world process and the absolute. The finite mind cannot simultaneously perceive these two dimensions and they cannot therefore be embraced in any kind of intellectual synthesis. However far back we go we don't find a point at which the whole cosmic process issues out of—or is caused or created by—the absolute.

We want explanations, however, and so we find pseudo-explanations: e.g. 'Why does a flower grow? It is activated by a principle of growth.' An inflated re-statement like this is no explanation at all. 'Why are people good? Because they are activated by a principle of goodness.' 'How does the universe come into being? Well, it emerges out of a universal principle.' 'How do things evolve and develop? Through some kind of "life-force" or evolutionary energy.' These are all pseudo-explanations. Another plausible explanation for the world is to say that it is created by *avidyā*, ignorance—but in order to say this we have to reify an abstract concept, making the idea of ignorance into a 'principle of ignorance', and then into a sort of 'creative principle'. From there it is a short step to saying that the world has somehow 'lapsed' from the absolute, and then we can start talking about the 'Fall', and even the *lapsus felix*, the 'Happy Fall'.

Classical Buddhism, both Hīnayāna and Mahāyāna, refuses to take the first step down this path of reification, and the Perfection of Wisdom relentlessly hunts down all our attempts to reify concepts. It has to because we cannot help going on doing it. To someone who suggests that the doctrine of emptiness negates the whole possibility of the spiritual life we can say with Nāgārjuna: 'Everything exists on account of emptiness.' But then it is difficult not to think of 'emptiness' as a sort of cosmic principle that is somehow responsible for the existence of the world. In this way we reify an abstract concept expressing the fact that everything we experience arises in dependence upon causes and conditions. What is meant by 'everything exists on account of emptiness' is that emptiness, rightly understood as conditionality, makes everything possible—the spiritual life as well as the worldly life.

Sometimes it is said that according to Buddhism karma is the universal principle—but this is not so. Conditionality is the universal principle, and karma is only a particular application of that on the ethical plane.[64] To use a traditional analogy, if the *dharmakāya* is the ocean, conditionality is the waves. The waves may surge and froth, but the water is always just water. This rather crude image is not one to hang on to, of course, because it might encourage us to think of the *dharmakāya* as some kind of spiritual 'substance'.

It is important to distinguish clearly between this universal principle of conditionality and the notion of cause and effect. In Indian philosophy there are basically two schools of thought on cause and effect. One, that of the Satkāryavādins, says that cause and effect are identical. If you take a lump of gold and turn it into an ornament it is still the same gold. There is only a change of form; the substance remains the same. Therefore, according to the Vedanta, which is of the Satkāryavādin persuasion, the whole universe is a transformation of the *Brahman*—the Absolute, the First Principle—and inasmuch as cause and effect are identical, so God and the world, *Brahman* and the cosmos, are one. The opposing view, that of the Asatkāryavādins, represented by the Sarvāstivādin School of the Hīnayāna, maintains that, on the contrary, cause and effect are different, just as although curds are produced from milk, the one is sour, and the other sweet.

Nāgārjuna, however, points out that if cause and effect are identical, causation is impossible; and that if cause and effect are different, again, causation is impossible. The Buddhist idea of conditionality simply amounts to the observation that certain facts and events are sequentially connected: 'This being, that becomes; from the arising of this, that arises; this not becoming, that does not become; from the ceasing of this, that ceases.'[65] This teaching, the *pratītya-samutpāda*, 'conditioned co-production', is not a theory of causation. It is just saying that certain facts tend to accompany one another, without asserting a causal connection in the strict sense. In dependence upon hydrogen and oxygen coming together you get water. In dependence upon the residue of ignorance and craving left at the end of a life you get a 'new' consciousness in the 'next' life, which is neither the same nor different. Asking what actually passes over is just the mind reifying away.

According to Nāgārjuna, just as origination is inconceivable, so causation is unreal, a factitious construction of the mind, a dream. This of course means that *pratītya-samutpāda* itself is also unreal, empty, conditioned. It teaches not a real causal relation between somehow autonomous entities, but that things are mutually dependent and therefore lack independent 'selfhood'. It connects together not realities but appearances. It cannot be said to exist or not to exist or both or neither.

It is empty. In such fashion Buddhist doctrines contradict themselves when they are taken literally. Their validity is relative, not absolute. They are means to an end: Enlightenment.

And so the Jina concludes his preaching, and finally tells us:
'When all I said and did at last agreed with perfect wisdom,
Then this prediction I received from Him who went before me:
"Fully enlightened, at a future time thou shalt a Buddha be!"'

NOTES AND REFERENCES

*Notes followed by (S) are by Sangharakshita; the others have been compiled
by the editor.*

1 As regards the *yab-yum* symbolism of the Vajrayāna it would be true to say
that in a sense all female consorts are embodiments of Prajñāpāramitā—they
are even sometimes called *prajñās*. However it would be a gross
misunderstanding to take this symbolism literally, as though to suggest a sort
of sexual differentiation on the level of the transcendental.(S)

2 Buddhists and other non-Christians do not use the abbreviations AD—'Year
of our Lord'—and BC. They refer to years under this accepted dating
convention as either CE (Common Era) or BCE (Before Common Era).

3 A *śloka* consists of thirty-two syllables, and is quite common in Sanskrit, just
as the iambic pentameter is the standard line in English poetry. This does not
mean, however, that the text is written in verse. There are no metrically
redundant syllables in Sanskrit, so even prose can be reckoned by units of
thirty-two syllables. These 'lines' are therefore quite long, and there are a great
many of them, which makes this altogether a very considerable work
indeed.(S)

4 *The Middle Length Sayings (Majjhima-Nikāya) Vol.I*, trans. I.B. Horner, Pali Text
Society, London 1976, no. 23 (*Vammikasutta*), p.186. ('The cobra, monk, this is a
synonym for a monk whose cankers are destroyed.')

5 *Udāna: Verses of Uplift, The Minor Anthologies of the Pali Canon Part II*, trans.
F.L. Woodward, Oxford University Press, London 1948, V, v. p.67; *The Book of
the Discipline (Vinaya Piṭaka)* Part 5, trans. I.B. Horner, Pali Text Society, London
1952, *Cullavagga* IX, pp.332–6.

6 There is the same sort of thing, up to a certain point, in the *via negativa* of Western mysticism. The ever-present stumbling block for Western mystics is of course God, but the Perfection of Wisdom is quite clear about the need to negate even the concepts of 'Buddha' and 'Enlightenment'.(S)

7 The *saddhānusārin* (faith-follower) and the *dhammānusārin* (doctrine-follower) are two of the group of seven *ariya-puggalas* (noble disciples) enumerated in the Pāli Canon. See Nyanatiloka, *Buddhist Dictionary*, Buddhist Publication Society, Kandy 1980, pp.24–5; also Buddhaghosha, *The Path of Purity (Visuddhimagga)*, trans. Pe Maung Tin, Pali Text Society, London 1975, pp.806–7.

8 *The Middle Length Sayings (Majjhima-Nikāya) Vol.III*, trans. I.B. Horner, Pali Text Society, London 1976, *suttas* nos. 121 & 122 (*Culasunnatasutta* and *Mahasunnatasutta*).

9 See L. Gomez, 'Proto-Madhyamika in the Pali Canon' in *Philosophy East and West* 26 (2), pp.137–65.

10 This translation is taken from *Buddhist Wisdom Books containing the Diamond Sutra and the Heart Sutra*, translated and explained by Edward Conze, Unwin Hyman, London 1988, pp.99–129. For the purposes of the seminar Sangharakshita amended one sentence of the original translation. Conze's version of this sentence is: 'Therefore, O Śāriputra, it is because of his non-attainmentness that a Bodhisattva, through having relied on the perfection of wisdom, dwells without thought-coverings.' Sangharakshita's version is: 'Therefore, O Śāriputra, it is because of his indifference to any kind of personal attainment, and through his reliance on the Perfection of Wisdom, that a Bodhisattva dwells without thought- coverings.'

11 *Dharmakāya* literally means 'truth body'. The *trikāya* doctrine, a teaching of the Mahāyāna, differentiates three 'bodies' of the Buddha: the *nirmānakāya*, the human, historical Buddha; the *sambhogakāya* (literally the 'body of mutual enjoyment'), the archetypal Buddha; and the *dharmakāya*, the Buddha principle, which emanates the archetypal figures of the *sambhogakāya*. For extended discussion of the doctrine, see Sangharakshita, *The Three Jewels*, Windhorse, Glasgow 1991, pp.35–43; Sangharakshita, *A Survey of Buddhism*, Windhorse, Glasgow 1993, pp.277–292; Vessantara, *Meeting the Buddhas*, Windhorse, Glasgow 1993, pp.27–30.

12 These are two of the 'three levels of wisdom': *śruta-mayī-prajñā*, 'wisdom through hearing'; *cinta-mayī-prajñā*, 'wisdom through reflecting'; and *bhāvanā-mayī-prajñā*, 'wisdom through meditating'. See *The Three Levels of Wisdom*, Windhorse, Glasgow 1988.

13 'The Diamond Cutter of Doubts' and 'A Straight Talk on the Heart Sutra', trans. Lu K'uan Yu (Charles Luk) in *Ch'an and Zen Teaching (Series One)*, Rider, London 1960.

14 From *Buddhist Wisdom Books*, op.cit. pp.21–71.

15 The *Udāna*, op.cit. IV, v., p.49.

16 Conze's notes to chapter 1 call for some slight qualifications to avoid confusion:

(a) Ānanda did not recite *texts* he had heard; he recited *discourses* and other oral teachings. This is an inadvertent slip of the pen, of course, but symptomatic of a willingness to forget that the Buddhist canon consisted at one time not of a collection of texts, but of a collection of recollections.

(b) Śrāvastī is 'the City of Wonders' because there, according to one account, the Buddha performed the 'twin miracle'—the *yamaka-iddhi*—of walking up and down in the air and simultaneously emitting streams of water and streams of fire from his body.

(c) Kośala was the Buddha's homeland only inasmuch as the Śākyan territory was incorporated into the kingdom of Kośala. The idea that it once housed 900,000 families is probably an exaggeration on the part of the Theravāda tradition.

(d) Of the forty-five years of his ministry the Buddha passed twenty-five *rainy seasons* in Śrāvastī. The rest of the year he would have been on tour, walking from place to place.(S)

17 A Bodhisattva—a 'being striving for Enlightenment'—is one in whom the bodhicitta, the 'will to Enlightenment' has arisen. Upon the arising of the bodhicitta, the Bodhisattva's progress towards Enlightenment may be charted according to the stages of the 'Bodhisattva path'. The *Daśabhūmika Sūtra*, the most influential of the descriptions of this path, divides it into ten stages known as the ten *bhūmis*, literally 'grounds'. Once the Bodhisattva has arrived at the eighth stage (*acala*—immovable), there is no possibility of falling back—progress towards full Enlightenment is assured.

18 *Antarābhāva* is the Sanskrit equivalent of the more familiar Tibetan term *bardo*—literally 'between two', 'intermediate state', and so used to refer to the state between any two states of consciousness, but most frequently—as here—referring to the period between death and rebirth.

19 *Pāramitā*, although usually translated 'perfection', literally means 'that which goes beyond' (see page 12)—so the Six *Pāramitās* which the Bodhisattva practises are means of 'going beyond', transcending (oneself). The Perfections are: giving, ethics, patience, vigour, meditation, and wisdom—at least these are the closest English equivalents, not all of them entirely satisfactory. For more information, see Sangharakshita, *A Survey of Buddhism*, op.cit. pp.461–489; and

Sangharakshita, *The Drama of Cosmic Enlightenment*, Windhorse, Glasgow 1993, pp.11–15.

20 Quoted in Sangharakshita, *The Buddha's Victory*, Windhorse, Glasgow 1991, pp.62–64; also in *Some Sayings of the Buddha*, trans. F.L. Woodward, Pali Text Society, London 1975, p.103; and *The Book of the Discipline (Vinaya Piṭaka)* Part 4, trans. I.B. Horner, Pali Text Society, London 1982, *Mahāvagga* VIII, pp.431–2.

21 Going for Refuge to the Three Jewels (the Buddha, the Dharma, and the Sangha) is the act of committing oneself to gaining Enlightenment, and this is what the phrase Going for Refuge usually refers to. In fact, though, we go for refuge all the time, of course, whether to 'true refuges' which can really 'support' us, or to 'false refuges'—such as the sense objects mentioned here—which can offer us no real 'support'.

22 The six element practice is a vipaśyanā (insight) meditation practice which acts as an antidote to conceit, an emotion which arises out of a strong sense of self-identification. The practice is based on the fact that everything that we could possibly identify with as a self is included within the six elements—earth, water, fire, air, space, consciousness. There is no 'me' apart from these elements, and in reality they themselves are only 'borrowed', and must one day be returned to the universe. For a detailed description of the practice, see Kamalashila, *Meditation: The Buddhist Way of Tranquillity and Insight*, Windhorse, Glasgow 1992, pp.211–217.

23 See page 27 for a brief description of the five *skandhas*, the five 'heaps' of conditioned existence.

24 This is the third of the ten fetters which, according to the Hīnayāna tradition, must be broken before Enlightenment can be attained. Upon the breaking of the first three, transcendental insight arises, or—again to use Hīnayāna terminology—one becomes a 'Stream Entrant'. These first three fetters can be translated 'personality view, sceptical doubt, and grasping rules and rituals as ends in themselves'; in *The Taste of Freedom* (Windhorse, Glasgow 1990, pp.29–32), Sangharakshita terms them 'habit, superficiality, and vagueness', and recommends creativity, commitment, and clarity as their antidotes. See also Sangharakshita, *A Guide to the Buddhist Path*, Windhorse, Glasgow 1990, pp.105–107.

25 See Note 11.

26 See *The Book of the Discipline (Vinaya Piṭaka)* Part 1, trans. I.B. Horner, Pali Text Society, London 1949, pp.14–17.

27 See Herbert V. Guenther, *Philosophy and Psychology in the Abhidharma*, Shambhala, Boulder and London 1975, pp.231–2.

28 See Bhikkhu Ñāṇamoli, *The Life of the Buddha*, Buddhist Publication Society, Ceylon 1978, p.256; and *Middle Length Sayings (Majjhima-Nikāya) Vol.I*, op.cit. pp.173–4.

29 *The Book of the Gradual Sayings (Aṅguttara-Nikāya) Vol.I*, trans. F.L. Woodward, Pali Text Society, London 1932, pp.16–25.

30 In Candrakīrti's commentary on Nāgārjuna's *(Mūla-) Madhyamakakārikā*, xiii, 8.

31 *The Book of Kindred Sayings (Saṃyutta-Nikāya) Vol.III*, trans. C.A.F. Rhys Davids and F.L. Woodward, Pali Text Society, London. pp.281–2: see also Bhikkhu Ñāṇamoli, *The Life of the Buddha*, op.cit. pp.209–210.

32 *Dialogues of the Buddha (Dīgha-Nikāya) Vol.III*, trans. T.W. Rhys Davids, Sacred Books of the Buddhists, Pali Text Society, London 1977, chapter 16 *(Mahā Parinibbāna suttanta)*, pp.79–81; see also Bhikkhu Ñāṇamoli, *The Life of the Buddha*, op.cit. pp.289–292.

33 See page 164.

34 See Chih I, 'Dhyana for Beginners' in *A Buddhist Bible*, ed. Dwight Goddard, Beacon Press, Boston 1938, p.443.

35 See Sangharakshita, *The Thousand-Petalled Lotus*, Alan Sutton, Gloucester 1988, pp.208ff.

36 James Boswell, *The Life of Samuel Johnson*, account of 25 April, 1778.

37 'This being, that becomes, from the arising of this, that arises; this not becoming, that does not become; from the ceasing of this, that ceases.' See, for example, *The Middle Length Sayings (Majjhima-Nikāya) Vol.II*, trans. I.B. Horner, Pali Text Society, London 1976, pp.319–20.

38 Quoted in *Buddhist Texts through the Ages*, trans. Edward Conze, Shambhala, Boston 1990, p.103; and *Some Sayings of the Buddha*, trans. F.L. Woodward, The Buddhist Society, London 1975, pp.85–6.

39 See Note 17.

40 See Note 24.

41 This is not quite Conze's view. His understanding is that '[the Perfection of Wisdom] is illuminated, or explained, indirectly by stating the wise attitude to conditioned things, as in the stanza of four lines which follows'. This view is based on the premise that 'the *Prajñāpāramitā* concerns the unconditioned Absolute and Emptiness'—which, Conze says, cannot be revealed directly. See *Buddhist Wisdom Books*, op.cit. p.67.(S)

42 Conze offers a Hinayanist interpretation of this image: '...this world continues only while we have cravings. When craving ceases to supply the drive, the world will come to an end.' (See *Buddhist Wisdom Books*, op.cit. p.69). This is perhaps not completely true even from the Hīnayāna point of view. Inasmuch as on the cessation of craving, the world ceases to exist for *us*, by so much it continues to exist for others—given that other people exist as much as we do. You could say, to remove any suspicion of solipsism, that when craving ceases to supply the drive, the world will come to an end *to the extent that it is dependent on craving*.(S)

43 By 'message' I mean here the Dharma as Truth, Law, or Reality, and by 'medium', the Buddha's teaching, but outside this context one could of course just as well say that the Buddha himself was the message, and the Dharma the medium.(S)

44 T.S. Eliot, 'The Dry Salvages' part V, in 'Four Quartets'.

45 From *The Perfection of Wisdom in Eight Thousand Lines and its Verse Summary*, trans. Edward Conze, Four Seasons Foundation, San Francisco 1983, pp.9–14.

46 There is no observably direct connection to be made between the nāga and the 'serpent power' known in Buddhist Tantra as the *chandali*, the Fiery or Blazing One (*tumo* or *dumo* in Tibetan), even if an analogous mythology may be reflected in the two concepts. The symbolism is of fire rather than water, and represents a power latent in the microcosm of the human form, rather than free and flowing in the macrocosm of the world. As for what is known in Hinduism as *kuṇḍalinī*, this means literally 'that which is coiled up', conveying a sense of latent energy waiting to be released, and thus suggesting a coiled spring as much as a serpent.(S)

47 See Bhikkhu Ñāṇamoli, *The Life of the Buddha*, op.cit. p.259; also *The Book of the Discipline (Vinaya Piṭaka)* Part 5, trans. I.B. Horner, Luzac, London 1952, *Cullavagga* VII, p.264.

48 Originally a Japanese form of token robe, abbreviated to a strip of cloth, suitably embroidered, and worn loosely round the neck like a halter.

49 From *The Book of Common Prayer*: On the Sacraments.

50 See *The Book of Kindred Sayings (Saṁyutta-Nikāya) Vol.III*, trans. F.L. Woodward, Pali Text Society, Oxford 1992, pp.186–7.

51 There is a parallel in English history to this degradation of the term Arhat. In the seventeenth century those followers of Puritan sects who believed in their own salvation by predestination called themselves 'saints', and in the eighteenth century any morose and narrow-minded Puritan came to be mockingly dubbed 'a saint'.(S)

52 See Sangharakshita, *The Three Jewels*, op.cit. pp.130–145.

53 See page 171.

54 See Sangharakshita, *The Thousand-Petalled Lotus*, op.cit. p.234.

55 See Bhikkhu Ñāṇamoli, *The Life of the Buddha*, op.cit. p.52; also *The Book of the Discipline (Vinaya Piṭaka)* Part 4, trans. I.B. Horner, Pali Text Society, London 1982, *Mahāvagga I*, p.28.

56 See, for example, the *Diamond Sūtra*, chapter 2.

57 For more on the two extremes of nihilism and eternalism, see Sangharakshita, *A Guide to the Buddhist Path*, op.cit. pp.105–6.

58 See page 176.

59 See *The Book of Kindred Sayings (Saṁyutta-Nikāya) Vol.III*, trans. F.L. Woodward, Pali Text Society, London 1975, pp.100–101; also Bhikkhu Ñāṇamoli, *The Life of the Buddha*, op.cit. p.203.

60 See *Dhammapada*, chapter 1, verse 7.

61 For more on the *viparyāsas*, see Sangharakshita, *The Three Jewels*, op.cit. pp.82–3.

62 See *Ariya-pariyesana-sutta*, *The Middle Length Sayings (Majjhima-Nikāya) Vol.I*, op.cit. p.207; also Bhikkhu Ñāṇamoli, *The Life of the Buddha*, op.cit. p.10.

63 See pages 176 and 233.

64 The 'ethical plane'—*karma niyama*—is only one of the five *niyamas*, the five orders of cause–effect, or conditionality. For more on the five *niyamas*, see Sangharakshita, *The Three Jewels*, op.cit. p.69.

65 See Note 37.

Further Reading

Introductory Material

Sangharakshita, *A Survey of Buddhism*, Windhorse, Glasgow 1993, chapter 3,
part 4, 'The Scriptures of Perfect Wisdom'.
Sangharakshita, *The Eternal Legacy*, Tharpa, London 1985, chapter 10, 'The
Perfection of Wisdom Sutras'.
Paul Williams, *Mahayana Buddhism*, Routledge, London 1989, chapter 2, 'The
Perfection of Wisdom Sutras'.

Translations

The Perfection of Wisdom in Eight Thousand Lines & Its Verse Summary, trans.
Edward Conze, Four Seasons Foundation, San Francisco 1983.
Buddhist Wisdom Books: The Diamond Sutra and the Heart Sutra, translated and
explained by Edward Conze, Unwin Hyman, London 1988.
The Short Prajnaparamita Texts, trans. Edward Conze, Luzac, London 1973.
Selected Sayings from the Perfection of Wisdom, chosen, arranged, and translated
by Edward Conze, Buddhist Society, London 1968.
The Diamond Sutra and the Sutra of Hui-neng, trans. A.F. Price and Wong
Mou-lam, Shambhala, Boston 1990.

Commentaries and Studies

Thirty Years of Buddhist Studies: Selected Essays by Edward Conze, Bruno Cassirer,
1967.

Geshe Kelsang Gyatso, *Heart of Wisdom: a Commentary to the Heart Sutra,* Tharpa, London 1989.

Han Shan, 'The Diamond Cutter of Doubts' (a commentary on the Diamond Sūtra) and 'A Straight Talk on the Heart Sūtra' in *Ch'an and Zen Teachings,* First Series, trans. Charles Luk, Rider, London 1970, pp.153–206 and pp.211–220 respectively.

Prajnaparamita and Related Systems, Studies in honour of Edward Conze, ed. Lewis Lancaster, Berkeley 1977.

Donald S. Lopez Jr., *The Heart Sutra explained: Indian and Tibetan Commentaries,* State University of New York Press, New York 1988.

'The Manuscript of the Vajracchedika found at Gilgit', an annotated transcription and translation by Gregory Schopen, in *Studies in the Literature of the Great Vehicle,* ed. Luis O. Gomez and Jonathan A. Silk, University of Michigan, Ann Arbor 1989.

INDEX